HOW AIDS ACTIVISTS CHALLENGED AMERICA
(And Saved FDA from Itself)

A History and Memoir

BY JAMES DRISCOLL, PH.D.

**WHAT HAPPENED IN SAN FRANCISCO
IS REVEALED IN THESE PAGES**

HOW AIDS ACTIVISTS CHALLENGED AMERICA
(And Saved FDA from Itself)

A History and Memoir

BY JAMES DRISCOLL, PH.D.

WHAT HAPPENED IN SAN FRANCISCO IS REVEALED IN THESE PAGES

ACADEMICA PRESS
WASHINGTON~LONDON

Library of Congress Cataloging-in-Publication Data

Names: Driscoll, James P., 1946- author.
Title: How AIDS activists challenged America and saved FDA from itself /
James P. Driscoll.
Description: Washington : Academica Press, 2020
Includes bibliographical references and index.
Identifiers: LCCN 2020935347 | ISBN 9781680531404 (hardcover) |
ISBN 9781680531428 (paperback)
LC record available at https://lccn.loc.gov/2020935347

FOR DAVE, STEVE, JIM, DAVID, DUANE, AND
ALL THOSE WHO SUFFERED, FOUGHT,
AND DIED MUCH TOO SOON.

Contents

Prologue

Americans want to forget the terrifying details of the AIDS epidemic that raged through the country killing vast numbers over the dozen years between 1984 and 1996. President Reagan exhibited the reticence of many when he declined to speak the word AIDS while tens of thousands of his fellow citizens suffered and died from the disease.

We will have epidemics in the future, perhaps more lethal than AIDS. Will our leaders again turn a blind eye to the new mortal threat? If they do, will we be so lucky as to face a rather slow moving epidemic confined to sequestered segments of our population? Will our chaotic, overburdened healthcare systems delay adapting to the challenges of a novel disease, as they did with AIDS? Drug and biotechnology research, development, and approval still are beset with the regulatory featherbedding and wrong-headed priorities that almost stalled the life-saving AIDS multi- drug cocktails three additional years. Will FDA, NIH, NIAID, CDC again prioritize guarding their turf over bold action to save lives?

The "AIDS cocktails," were so named because, like mixed drinks, they combine two or more agents which, used together, prove more effective than single drugs, or monotherapies. The wily AIDS virus is extremely adaptive. HIV can develop resistance to a single drug in a short time, whereas multiple drugs retain their effectiveness much longer. FDA delayed approval of the earlier AIDS drugs and their use in combinations, and it tried to delay the cocktails by requiring time consuming efficacy trials before the new therapies could be approved for widespread use. Their delays triaged their fetish for pedantic accuracy above the patients' life and death needs for treatment.

To understand why FDA delays outraged AIDS activists and sparked protests one must bear in mind a crucial point: ***FDA delayed approval by demanding additional proof of the efficacy of AIDS drugs and combinations even after sufficient safety was established.*** The agency claimed to be protecting patients and sometimes intimated, disingenuously, that safety was at issue, when their real objective was always more extensive measurement of efficacy. Their regulatory over-reach is particularly shocking considering that high level FDA personnel who made life and death decisions on access to AIDS drugs included almost no one from the effected population which was more than 85% either gay or African American men.

To the patients, it made little sense to delay approval of new AIDS drugs just to get more exact measures of efficacy since there were no effective alternative drugs, none whatsoever. Given that we faced a deadly epidemic without effective long term treatments, the pragmatic and humane approach would have been to approve the drugs on an accelerated or conditional basis once their safety was known and we had evidence for efficacy, and then further test their degrees of efficacy clinically in the field. That is what the patients and their doctors wanted, but a rigid, paternalistic FDA bureaucracy blocked the way and that is why we needed clamorous, obstinate, and resourceful AIDS activists.

The efficacy standard was and remains key to FDA's power over the drug companies, researchers, and desperate patients. Testing efficacy gives FDA ascendency over a drug's market share and profitability by allowing the agency to assess the relative value of competing products. *Follow the money.* Drugs that come to market first enjoy a major competitive advantage. FDA decides the when and how as well as the if of drug approval, and it determines the conditions of use in the drug's labeling. FDA's delays of approving AIDS drugs were all about defending these powers.

The problem of efficacy testing overkill delaying approvals remains very much alive in FDA today. By driving up research and development costs and inducing gratuitous caution, it creates an impediment to medical innovation that poses a threat to patients in future epidemics as well as to patients currently afflicted with rare or untreatable diseases and conditions.

FDA's mistakes in AIDS are evident in the chronicles and documents from the 1988-96 period and remain in the memories of the dwindling number of survivors, but they have not been collated in comprehensive narratives with their lessons forthrightly drawn. That's a problem with all history, we like to bury painful memories. We want to forget the horrors of the AIDS epidemic, just as we want to forget the ugly strife and violence of the Vietnam war or the latest terrorist act. We even want to forget the last time we got food poisoning. Still we need to remember to avoid the source of contamination.

The following accounts describe actions, events, and the emotions behind them that many, sometimes including myself, want to forget. It was often painful dredging them out of my memory and from the documents of the time. Indeed, I did not want to write this book, yet I knew if it were not written an essential part of the AIDS and LGBT story might be lost. A precept from author Toni Morrison set forth my task: "If there is a book you want to read, but it hasn't been written yet, then you must write it." Doubting that any other surviving activists would tell the full story, I bit the bullet, pulled out my dusty files, and got to work.

The writing has often involved reliving the suffering, grief, injustice, and tragedy that so many, endured, myself among them. However, in 1988, I faced an even more painful and difficult task. While I did not have AIDS myself, I belonged to a community that was dying all around me. I chose to fight with the dying rather than abandon them, which many others did. Recalling decades later the heroic struggles and terrible suffering of friends who died, their lost brilliance, beauty, humor, and love, at times puts me in sadness bordering despair. How I long to see them again, in some cases to tell them in more ways than words what they meant to me. Yet time irreversible is a raven croaking nevermore, nevermore.

Like the rest of humanity, gay people are capable of awesome heroism, startling brilliance, great sacrifices, and of loving incandescently. Unlike the rest, our most passionate loves are toward members of our own sex. This is much easier for outsiders to comprehend on an intellectual level than it is to apprehend emotionally. The majority assume their shared views and experiences form the default setting of all humanity. Gays men and women partake in a difference that in important respects is as profound and consequential as race, religion, and culture. Gays often fail to appreciate the magnitude of their difference and how it affects what they think and feel, who they are, and who they are assumed to be. Gay consciousness has yet to emerge fully from the cocoon of a dominant society that in crucial aspects remains hostile and alien to us.

Surveying the literature on the AIDS epidemic, I was surprised at the paucity of accounts about its social, political, and psychological impact, and about the activists themselves, their backgrounds and ideas. Wars have general histories aplenty along with detailed accounts of the battles, heroes, and villains. The AIDS epidemic, like a major war, involved vast numbers, immense resources deployed, and it had major consequences for American society and many of its constituent cultures. Yet there are no serious general histories of the American epidemic or of AIDS activism. We do have memoirs aplenty, but these are mostly personal vignettes. Amazon lists only two books from the gay community that cover a broad swath of the epidemic, Sean Straub's *Body Counts* (2014), Randy Shilts *And the Band Played On*, whose account ended in 1986.*1* My efforts will focus on the crucial yet neglected struggle of activists to speed FDA approval of HIV drugs in the 1988-1996 period. Since I was a key figure in that struggle, my story will at times resemble a memoir, and will concentrate on people I worked with in activism centered in San Francisco, my home town at the time.

One advantage of living in the evening of life, as I do at 77, is being less concerned about the impact of what you write on your future career prospects. Freed of the distractions of youthful ambitions, the old know their journey must end soon at the great black wall of death. We can more easily afford to tell the unvarnished truth as we remember and understand it. We can afford to care more about its impact on the open ended future of others than on our own narrowing horizons. The young will be around to benefit from our wisdom and warnings, while we have left only that twilight zone of old age where passions and recriminations are usually muted. With that in mind, I tell my story willing to offend in the hope that those younger may learn from the past enough to help them avoid repeating its mistakes in a future they alone will possess.

The solar system has eight or nine planets, scores of moons and an unknown number of minor objects all held in thrall by the mighty gravity of our sun. My story is similar. Everything revolves around a single complex of events. The gravitational center is the 1995 decision by FDA, in response to intense, rising pressures, to suspend their sluggish drug efficacy testing procedures in order to approve the protease based anti-retroviral drug cocktails in record time several years earlier than they planned, or wanted. The planets and the moons all reflect the sunlight. In my story the lesser events gain meaning in the light of that 1995 decision. Histories are sometimes written this way. For example, the significance of the events prior to the Civil War is measured by how and whether they illumine decisions that led to and shaped the War itself. A shortcoming of nearly all accounts of the AIDS epidemic and AIDS activism is failure to show how the events leading up to the arrival of the antiretroviral cocktails illumine that game changing event itself. Consequently, the significance of the climacteric event, the veritable Gettysburg of the activist's struggle against AIDS, has largely been lost. Indeed, we have yet to recognize that dramatic turning point for the watershed that it was.

Prior to the cocktails, an AIDS diagnosis was a death sentence; the average life expectancy from diagnosis to death was eighteen months. In 1995 at the peak of the epidemic approximately 49,000 Americans died from AIDS. Just three years later in 1998 the death rate had fallen to 20,000, while the total reported cases increased by 175,000. By 2004 deaths from AIDS fell to about 7000 where they remain today. Yet the number of living US cases continues to rise at a rate of about 39,000 new cases reported by CDC each year. These statistics testify to the efficacy of the antiviral cocktails first approved in 1995-6, as well as to the shortfalls of our prevention efforts.

Before the cocktails, patients had only the highly toxic yet marginally effective nucleoside analogue drugs, AZT, ddI, ddC and d4T. Difficult for most patients to tolerate, the Nukes, as they were known, gave patients, including friends of mine, weeks or months of reprieve. A lucky few got extra years. The Nukes were more effective used in combinations, but here again FDA delayed approval of combination therapies always demanding more efficacy data, even after the drugs' safety profiles were established.

FDA Commissioner David Kessler, in his historically consequential but deceptively titled article "Faster Evaluation of Vital Drugs," in the March 1995 *Scientific American,* laid out his argument for seeking full rather than accelerated approval for the protease based cocktails. Full approval would require thoroughly testing their efficacy in large simple trials (LSTs) lasting three to four years.*2* That proposal was supported, indeed initially proposed and urged, by the Treatment Activist Group, or TAG, an influential New York based NGO whose thinking reflected that of FDA hardliners. Had FDA scrapped accelerated approval as its hard-liners wanted, tens of thousands of AIDS patients would have been denied access to the drugs that saved them. Moreover, the initial delay would have cascaded into further delays in initiating international HIV programs, and that likely would have cost hundreds of thousands of lives, or even more. For the first time in these pages is told the inside story of how opposing factions of AIDS activists put together a difficult and surprising alliance with leading clinicians, researchers, and political figures to thwart FDA's disastrous plans and thereby save countless lives.

The narrative incorporates extensive accounts and documents from the time letting them speak in their own voices rather than thru my summaries. My writings, published in newspaper opinion pieces and other accounts, document my positions, views, and roles. Reviewing them, I was pleasantly surprised by their pertinence and reliability. Herein, I have provided only a narrative outline, full documentation remains a task for future scholars and historians with time and resources not at my disposal. Throughout, I will stress critical points that have been largely ignored. I proceed this way primarily for two reasons.

First, as noted, no one enjoys recalling the horrifying details of that era, and we no more relish dwelling on its mistakes than we relish rehashing those of the Vietnam or Iraq wars. Yet we must take truth's bitter medicine and study accounts from the dark periods of history to know what really happened, how, and why. For it is the darkest periods that we above all want to avoid repeating.

Second, because of moral cowardice, and worse, indifference to truth and justice, no one has held the FDA bureaucracy accountable for their attempts to delay the life-saving HIV drug cocktails. Today these attempts and the activists often heroic struggles to defeat them are nearly forgotten. That means too few have learned the key lessons of that time. Indeed, no one has ever made FDA answerable for their actual delays during the early 1990s in approving ddI, ddC and d4T or AZT/ddC and AZT/ddI combination therapies, or for delaying the first protease drug Saquinivir in 1995, or their subsequent delays of the HIV rapid testing technology that is utterly crucial to effective prevention. All these delays unnecessarily cost or at least shortened lives.

Almost as bad, FDA was never held accountable for turning a blind eye to the burgeoning AIDS drug underground whose often defective and dangerous knockoffs of legitimate drugs bogged down in FDA efficacy trials endangered the precarious health of thousands of advanced AIDS patients. Although FDA knew the knockoff drugs were neither safe nor effective, and the underground sometimes ruthlessly violated the rights of community people who opposed it, FDA chose not to enforce laws against the promotion and sale of knockoff drugs in order to relieve mounting AIDS community pressure on the agency to approve expeditiously the safe, legal versions of those drugs.

Bureaucracies have a natural entropy moving toward regulatory feather bedding, dysfunction, and corruption. Those who try to hold them accountable are rarely rewarded or even recognized. Usually the whistleblowers are ostracized while the bootlickers garner the plaudits and rewards. In a worst case scenario, holding bureaucrats accountable requires a buildup of outrage ending in some form of revolution. That didn't happen because AIDS activists compelled FDA to wake up to the medical and political realities in time. The good news is that the activists and their allies saved countless lives; the bad news is that their full, highly instructive story, remains untold, its heroes, victims, and bad actors alike forgotten.

FDA was saved from making a truly catastrophic mistake, delaying the antiretroviral cocktails for several years, by the actions of an intrepid band of activists, the most essential of them being humble patient-activist foot soldiers who rebelled against being protected to death. They were never recognized by anyone in government, and are in danger of passing into oblivion today. I tell my story out of remembrance and admiration for deeds that saved so many, and in important ways moved our nation in a better direction, and to honor the suffering, resourcefulness, courage, and sacrifice that so far has either been ignored or too meagerly and begrudgingly recognized.

A word about the unusual organization of this work. It is a human story mixed in with and bolstered by essay analysis. You might view it as a literary version of mixed media. The main narrative recounts how resourceful, if contentious, activists and courageous patients fought the FDA to save themselves and the agency from catastrophic mistakes that would have swollen America's AIDS death toll by tens of thousands and severely damaged the agency's credibility. In contrast to standard histories, it digresses frequently into commentary to better illumine the regulatory, political, moral, and social contexts of the challenges facing the activists, and the obstacles to progress from within the culture of FDA and within American society itself. The material in the four appendices was too tangential to be integrated into the main story, but seemed, nonetheless, to significantly illumine that story. With all the explanatory material the reader must judge how successful my integration was, and I must beg her/his indulgence for its shortcomings.

AIDS:
A Tsunami of Death

US AIDS DEATHS DURING EACH YEAR, 1982-1999. (Figures compiled from AmfAR "Thirty Years of HIV AIDS," Kaiser Family Foundation, and CDC figures. Mortality totals often vary slightly among different sources.)

1982   618 deaths **Beginning of Epidemic**

1983   1,500 deaths

1984   3,578 deaths

1985   7,003 deaths

1986   12,030 deaths

1987   16,290 deaths AZT approved by FDA, March

1988   20,967 deaths

1989   27,257 deaths

1990   31,110 deaths

1991   35,690 deaths ddI approval, October

1992   38,333 deaths ddC approval, June

1993   39,779 deaths

1994   42,645 deaths d4T approval, June

1995   48,979 deaths--High point of Epidemic

1996   42,155 deaths -Drug cocktails in use.

Norvir & Crixivan approval, March

1997   28,688 deaths -Cocktails in wide use.

1998   19,892 deaths --Sustiva approval, September

1999   16,762 deaths --3 years after introduction of cocktails deaths decline by two thirds.

Today there are roughly 15,000 US deaths per year among our CDC estimated 1,150,000 people living with HIV. In around half, HIV is the principle cause of death.

Had FDA made the cocktails wait for full approval in 1999 under their large simple trials (LST) proposal, instead of giving accelerated approval in early 1996, during that three-year delay an additional 86,000 AIDS patients would have died unnecessarily.

The following tables show how that appalling figure was derived. The first number in the table below is the year, the second is the estimated number of deaths, and the third number is the estimated ratio of deaths in that year to deaths in the previous year.

1982 - 618
1983 - 1500 - 2.427
1984 - 3578 - 2.385
1985 - 7003 - 1.957
1986 - 12030 - 1.718
1987 - 16290 - 1.354
1988 - 20967 - 1.287
1989 - 27257 - 1.300
1990 - 31110 - 1.141
1991 - 35690 - 1.147
1992 - 38333 - 1.074
1993 - 39779 - 1.038
1994 - 42645 - 1.072
1995 - 48979 - 1.149
1996 - 42155 - 0.861
1997 - 28688 - 0.681
1998 - 19892 - 0.673
1999 - 16762 - 0.843.

The ratio does jump around a bit after a while. So a reasonable approach is to use the geometric mean for the last five years prior to the introduction of the cocktails, i.e., the product 1.147 times 1.074 times 1.038 times 1.072 times 1.149 raised to the (1/5)-th power = 1.095. In that case the projections for those who would have died waiting for the cocktails are:

1996 - 53632 = 48979 times 1.095
1997 - 58727 = 53632 times 1.095
1998 - 64306 = 58727 times 1.095
This assumes that the cocktails are introduced in 1999.
Then the estimated annual extra loss of lives is:
1996: 53632 - 42155 = 11477
1997: 58727 - 28688 = 30039
1998: 64306 - 19892 = 44414

This yields a total of 11477 + 30146 + 44414 = 85930, or approximately 86,000 additional deaths before the year 1999.*3*

However, if the startup for the cocktails was at the beginning of 1999, deaths would have been much higher in the years 1999 to 2001 making total avoidable deaths much more than 86000. The total avoidable deaths would likely have exceeded 170,000, or nearly three times the number of American deaths in the Vietnam war.*4*

The graph below shows deaths from HIV per year in Canada before and after the cocktail rollout. The Canadian figures are instructive because the drug cocktails were deployed more rapidly and effectively under their universal healthcare system than in the US. The Canadian graph gives an extremely clear picture of the effectiveness of the cocktails, and by inference the terrible mortality cost of delaying approval for marketing.

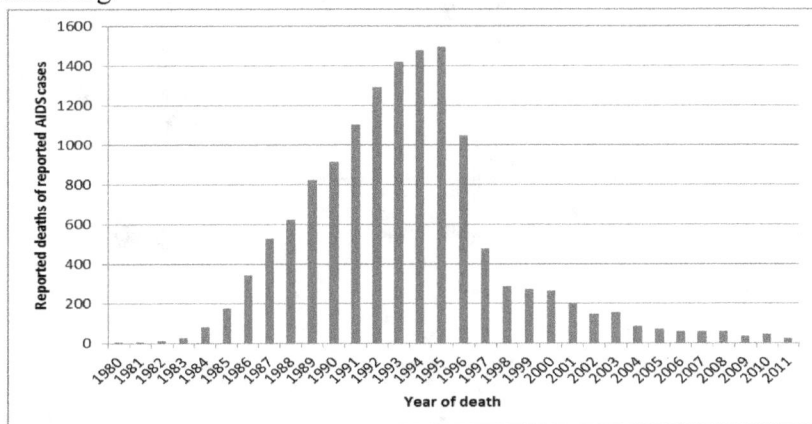

PART I: Plight

Chapter 1
Twice Aborted Lives

"Whoever aspiring, struggles on, for him there is salvation."
Goethe

More than 675,000 Americans with AIDS have died since the onset of the epidemic, at least 500,000 of that number died of AIDS related causes. The loss of life was greater than the 418,000 deaths in World War II. But AIDS more resembled the Civil War as it tore families apart and created division in every corner of our country. At the center of the Civil War and the AIDS epidemic were two profoundly oppressed peoples, enslaved African Americans and gay people cruelly stigmatized as incorrigible sinners and perverts who, on that basis, were denied equal protection of the laws as well as the compassion enjoined by the Judeo-Christian ethic.

Like the lives of soldiers lost in combat, these AIDS deaths represented aborted lives, the majority being under age 40. More than seventy percent of the deaths were among gay or bisexual men. Conservative estimates of the gay and bisexual portion of adult males vary between 4 and 6 %. AIDS decimated an entire generation of these men as no US war ever did with the general population. In San Francisco alone 15,554 died of AIDS prior to introduction of antiretroviral drug cocktails in 1996. That means, at a very rough estimate, 35% of San Francisco's adult gay males died of AIDS in the dozen years prior to 1996. The devastation was greatest among men under 40. In 1983 I turned 40, but most of my gay friends were a few years younger. I estimate that more than 70% of my friends and acquaintances died of AIDS. I reflected then that I was like an old person whose friends were all dying or dead. My father complained later about this, but he was in his 80s, not his 40s.

Profound psychological trauma was common among people who lived through this medical holocaust, particularly those who lost lovers, companions, close relatives, and dear friends. Many of the survivors suffered from some forms of post-traumatic stress disorder or PTSD. Either they still struggled with the disease themselves, although they were lucky enough to live for a reprieve from the life-saving cocktails, or were, like me, HIV negatives who had lost irreplaceable friends.

Few non-LGBT persons have ever said to me you've gone through a lot, how did you manage, how are you doing now? A common evasion among those outside our community was, you've chosen to be gay you're lucky worse didn't happen to you. Of course no one chooses to be gay in the way they choose to drive a Harley over a Volvo, or chew tobacco instead of carrots. The unspoken assumption too often was 'you deserved to die of AIDS because you chose to be gay, that's an abomination unto God.' The deadly stigma against LGBTs remains widespread in our culture today; it is still crassly purveyed for political gain by no less a figure than the current Vice President of the United States. Anti-LGBT stigma remains the greatest obstacle to fighting AIDS.

Of the gay men I was closest to during the 1970s and 80s, all but three had died by 1996. San Francisco became a city of the dead, spurring me to move to Portland in 1999. By then, my remaining friends in SF were mostly straight, and my surviving gay friends were scattered around the US, mostly in AIDS work. I was traumatized, but got scant sympathy from non-gay friends, nor did any of the gay survivors I knew report outpourings of sympathy or offers of help in re-adjusting and rehabilitating. More than once, people asked me why I bothered with AIDS since I myself did not have the disease.

As devastating as AIDS was, both actuarially and psychologically, it hit a population already ravaged by levels of discrimination during the 50s, 60s, and 70s, that are almost unimaginable today. Gay people routinely endured bias then that would be walloped by lawsuits, criminal prosecution, or active interventions today. The widespread abuse of and crippling stigma against gays inflicted psychological damage that left few victims unscathed. Many of us had post-traumatic stress already from discrimination we had suffered before AIDS raised its terrifying head.

In those decades, abuse in the family, both physical and emotional, was tolerated, all too common, and even expected. Tragically, it still is, though not so much as then. The gay child would often be the butt of scapegoating and bullying on the part of troubled or prejudiced parents or opportunistic siblings. Deleterious homophobia abetted or sanctioned as "morality" by atavistic churchly conventions, far from rare today, was par for the course then. The only refuge for too many was the deep closet. Few dared acknowledge openly who they were or who they loved.

The damage done to the spirit by society labeling as sinful and unnatural your most intimate feelings and deepest loves is insidious, and in the long term it can become incalculable. Suicide rates are a good index of suffering caused by emotional distress from social biases. LGBT youths today are still far more likely to attempt suicide than heterosexual youth. Since few dared to self-identify as gay in the 60s and 70s, we lack reliable suicide statistics for those years. Because discrimination and targeting were more frequent and severe then, the suicide rate was likely higher than today.5 I remember from my days as a college student in the 60s some professors worried quietly about this danger for their gay students. Even though no one acknowledged being gay, that was the first question people raised privately with a suicide.

In San Francisco in the 70s and 80s I met young gay men whose fathers beat them just for being gay, and they still bore the physical as well as emotional scars. There were men whose mothers guilt tripped and even disowned them or smother loved yet disdained them. One young friend dying of AIDS was devastated when his mother told him that she wished she'd been able to tell he was gay in the womb so she could have aborted him. Never did she blame his disease on the AIDS virus, the culprit was her son's sinful preference for whom he loved. Other gay men with HIV, and even without it, suffered verbal abuse and subtle body language contempt whenever they contacted family members. AIDS and the gay rights movement sharpened general awareness of homosexuality so that gay people became more likely to be identified and confronted.

African-American gay friends have often told me that the only thing worse than being gay was being African-American and gay. Stigma remains even more pervasive in the black community than in the white. Although one would hope that blacks' long history of suffering discrimination, both subtle and violently abusive, might tend to restrain their indulgence in bias. Nonetheless, even today fewer blacks feel comfortable coming out to their families and communities, which makes dealing with HIV lonelier and much harder for them. White gay men are the group most identified with HIV, yet the disease has been more pervasive and intractable in the African-American community and its effects often more tragic. In 2017 43% of new HIV cases were among blacks who are only 13% of the population; fewer HIV positive blacks are in care and their death rate is higher than among whites with HIV disease.

Let me disclose my story's personal background. Mine may seem a digression from AIDS, yet once finished the reader should better appreciate what gay people had to contend with in those times and better grasp their author's point of view. My parents were not religious and did not see being gay as a sin. My mother was generally tolerant, but always concerned about what "they think." However, my father saw my love of books and art along with distaste for sports and building things as signs of deficient masculinity, and resented this as a reflection on his own manhood. He strongly favored my younger brother, who was ever quick to exploit his bias. My father, the youngest son himself, deeply resented his own older brother for reasons that never really made sense, but he found an opportunity to even the score by focusing his anger on me and favoring my younger brother. That's how families sometimes operate.

Paternal outbursts of bad temper, threats of violence, and bullying were directed at me. As a father he was both a cruel bully and overly indulgent. My brother got all his indulgence, I got all his threats and bullying. My brother dropped out of Whitman College, and flunked out of the University of Oregon, yet got nary a word of reproof. I graduated with honors from Whitman and got an M.A. and Ph.D. from the University of Wisconsin without ever a word of praise. I wrote books and articles which he dismissed with a sneer. My brother was a pioneer in the Oregon "pot trade" which dad blamed on bad influences, including me; that was a stretch since I avoided that scene. My father managed to banish disturbing questions about how my brother collected bad debts in his business. At times life with father, seemed a reprise of *Mildred Pierce,* the old Joan Crawford movie, with father and sons replacing mother and daughters. But when it came to dad's inheritance, my brother jumped to a different narrative, Cain versus Abel.

As my father's mental grasp weakened in the months before his death at 85 in April 2001, my brother hauled him into his lawyer to arrange a major shift from my inheritance into his own. His rationale was that my parents had paid for my graduate education, whereby he, being a college drop-out, got short changed. The claim was prima facie spurious: my graduate school funds came from scholarships and from loans which I had to repay with interest. My brother's ventures had rewarded him with an upscale country estate atop a hill with sweeping views, various real estate investments, two or three boats, and a collection of valuable vehicles. He hardly needed the extra money. My own situation was far less comfortable. Snatching the bulk of my inheritance was his final affront to the brother he disrespected, exploited, and envied. Since my father's funeral, I've had no contact with my brother or my other relatives. My only family has been my leopard cat Ariel, and my loyal friends. Mine is a relatively common story within the gay community. Common also for those who suffer parental abuse as children, is a dark view of life and the world which I carried, to my detriment at times, into adulthood.

(Ariel on his throne)

As is frequent among gay men, I was my mother's favorite, but that never shielded me from paternal hostility, rather it sometimes intensified it. I suspect my father and brother were jealous of my mother's favoring me. It was a complicated family situation to be sure, but by no means unusual for gay men at that time. I suffered no physical beatings, which my mother would not have tolerated, although the psychological abuse and threats of violence from my father may have been no less damaging. At least it was never drummed into my head that my most intimate desires were offensive to God Almighty, and my mother was overall a good mother. Alone in my family, she was proud of my AIDS work; others considered it an embarrassment never to be discussed.

While I'm inclined to be a religious person, my family situation left me with a distrust of God the Father, church Christianity, and conventional authority. Einstein observed, "Unthinking respect for authority is the greatest enemy of truth," a wise maxim any serious thinker should heed. Jesus, an iconoclast who might have agreed with Einstein, remains a profoundly admirable figure to me. As a child my only religious artifact was a placard with his saying, "Ye shall know the truth, and the truth shall make you free."

Later, distrust of the Father drew me to Carl Jung and his analysis of the Old Testament Yahweh in *Answer to Job*. I saw in Jung's violent, irrational, unconscious, and morally obtuse Father-God my own psychologically abusive father. I also related personally to Jung's extensive writings on the Two Hostile Brothers archetype, one of the brothers being favored by the father and the other rejected. Like my father, Yahweh always favored the younger brother. I had spent much of the 1970's and 80s, studying Jung, reading widely in literature, philosophy and history, and writing two published academic books, the first on Jung and Shakespeare, the second on Jung and Milton._6_ A most unusual background for an AIDS activist, but it turned out to be a valuable preparation nonetheless.

My most damaging encounter with flagrant anti-gay discrimination was not within my family, as is most often the case, but in an unlikely place then, and an all but impossible place today---as a Ph.D. student in English at the University of Wisconsin in Madison. My dissertation advisor turned out to be a closeted homophobe who was deceptively civil to our faces but stabbed gays in the back when he got a chance. Little did I know that his malign bigotry would stymie my professional aspirations and blight much of my life. Open homophobia would not have been fully acceptable at UW Madison then, though it was a decade earlier in the 50s. Professors with his biases were common in otherwise liberal universities in the 1960s. It was perfectly safe to be homophobic or even racist then, though expressing those prejudices too openly was in bad taste. So the knife in the back was the weapon of choice for malefic homophobes. There were gay men and women on the department faculty, although all of them remained closeted. And none dared defend gay students who faced homophobic discrimination. Instead they shunned us, and sometimes voiced incidental support for the homophobes as a ploy to divert attention from their own vulnerability.

My adviser had inferred from my dissertation that I was not only gay, but likely to discuss homosexuality in literature and would become an advocate for changing attitudes on sex and gender once I joined the profession. He took it as an article of faith that Shakespeare and the other literary greats shared his own loathing for homosexuals. I later learned he compared homosexuals to coprophiliacs; he saw gays as equally repulsive but a greater danger to society. I was as clueless as Othello in the hands of Iago. My father for all his faults was not in Iago's league; though he behaved badly, he himself was not overall an evil man. My advisor, who wore his hair and moustache Hitler style, taught me that some people can be truly and deeply evil. That verity he taught by his example.

Any discussion of father-daughter incest or homosexuality in Shakespeare incurred his violent opposition. For that reason, he banned my dissertation chapter on *The Merchant of Venice* along with any mention of father-daughter incest in *King Lear* or elsewhere. I re-introduced the banned chapter and its once controversial subjects to my recent book, *Shakespeare's Identities*. Discussion of racial prejudice also infuriated my advisor, so he tried to ban my dissertation chapter on *Othello* which drew on Jean-Paul Sartre's *Anti-Semite and Jew* and Toni Morrison's *The Bluest Eye* to analyze Iago and Othello in terms of the psychology of racial hatred. My advisor's open animus against blacks wouldn't fly with the Department in 1971, so the *Othello* chapter remained. Two years later, I submitted an article based on that chapter to one of the major Shakespeare publications. The editor's rejection letter praised the paper, and urged me to submit it elsewhere. His letter ended with this revealing adjuration: "Please do not send this journal further submissions as long as our editorial board retains its current membership. I expect you know why." My advisor was on that board. I published the *Othello* material in my first book *Identity in Shakespearean Drama,* and have expanded on it in that book's successor, *Shakespeare's Identities.*

My advisor refused to leave the dissertation committee where he did his utmost to make my experience traumatic. He tried to prevent me from getting my Ph.D. The department balked, yet it did nothing to counter his destroying my chances for a career by sabotaging employment and publication opportunities: it's compromise was 'grant Driscoll the degree, otherwise do nothing to irritate professor X.' One of the big names in the profession, he was given very wide berth. I was not the first gay student he had damaged, and not the last. Gay men and women sometimes married each other for protection in those years. One such woman held my advisor responsible for her husband's suicide. The faculty knew this. It blamed the suicide victim and exonerated the alleged instigator. The victim was a weakling, they all whispered.

The bias in the UW-Madison English Department was not limited to a single homophobe targeting a few victims. At a meeting of candidates for jobs in the tight job market of 1971 they told us in no uncertain terms that candidates with wives and families to support would come first. Of 30 candidates, there were several gay or bi white males. So far as I know, none of them got jobs. One evidently committed suicide a few years later, at least one died of AIDS, and I became an AIDS activist.

The single thing in my life I wanted most was to teach Shakespeare. I loved the Bard, had published already, my dissertation had clear publication potential, and it was published later in articles and a book. I appeared to have an excellent chance for a tenure track position at a major Midwestern university, it depended upon my advisor. He killed it along with my professional future. I left the University of Wisconsin with a profound sense of violation; it felt like being raped, shoved into the gutter, and left to die.

Like too many other gay students, I had to find and build another life. That could not be done quickly or painlessly. For me it meant years of drift in near poverty in the underside of the Bay Area gay world, years of Jungian therapy and a troubled personal life, but also a wide sea of time to read and think, which for most part I used productively. Jung was my greatest, wisest teacher. Through studying Jung, I came to view the evil in my life and the world as a challenge and opportunity to create new good. That insight probably saved me from despair and perhaps worse. It has strengthened me across my life.

My experience at Wisconsin powerfully reinforced the distrust for paternalistic authority figures I first developed with my father. There too, Jung was a comfort and guide through the questions he struggled with in his own life and his breakthrough *Answer to Job*, which after the Gospels has most shaped my religious thought. Though I did not recognize it then, the wrongs I suffered at Wisconsin would give me a potent asset for activism, a readiness to challenge unjust authority.

With a profound sense of betrayal and abandonment, like so many other gay refugees who would become my friends, I sought sanctuary in San Francisco. Most of us were over-educated, over-qualified, burdened with educational debts, and facing a tight professional job market that had few places for anyone and none for out of the closet gay white males. Thus, in San Francisco as an unemployed 29-year-old openly gay man, I began my quest for a new identity. Most of the other gay men I met had suffered as I did, or worse, sometimes much worse. During my first decade there, all of the gay men I knew well came from various abusive family circumstances. Most were "overqualified" and working at low pay jobs far from the professions they had trained for. We were refugees from anti-gay persecution seeking the safety of the Castro district ghetto, a white working class district that in a few years became the first largely gay community in the nation. I surmise that the majority of gay men in San Francisco, who were not from the Bay Area itself, were refugees scarred by the homophobia rampant in the dark, intolerant places they had fled.

America and other advanced nations have only begun to come to grips with the systematic damage homophobic stigma inflicts and continues to inflict on LGBT people. What gay people endured during the transitional 1950-80 period was in some ways comparable to sufferings of Jews and blacks during 1910-1940. Granted that was less than slavery or Jim Crowe laws, and certainly far less than the holocaust. But remember that gay people have an ample share in the holocaust, as is impressively commemorated in the US Holocaust Museum.

For the Jews, and especially the Blacks, the decades prior to 1910 were a period where bias was seldom challenged or even questioned: it was accepted as normal. Similarly, before 1950 gay oppression had been par for the course for centuries, and nearly all gays were forced almost totally into the closet. But in the 1950 through 1980 period increasingly serious challenges began to erupt. At the same time the morality of stigmatizing gay men and women was being questioned by some religious leaders and more often in society. The challenges came into the open after Stonewall, and became boldly political with the barrier smashing career of Harvey Milk.

Guilt and lingering bias block honest recognition of the damage LGBT people have endured and still endure from stigma and because of discrimination enabled by our continued exclusion from fully equal protection under the 14th Amendment, not to mention routine bias sanctioned violations of the Judeo-Christian ethic. Our suffering is far from over, and protections still fall short of those granted Blacks and other minorities with a history of severe discrimination. Affirmative action is a form of reparation in recognition of the enduring damage from violating minority rights. Today America continues to disregard and deny the damage done by anti-gay bigotry. We have yet to start public discussion along the lines of what Nelson Mandela aptly styled Truth and Reconciliation.

Nonetheless, AIDS activism, which began with the epidemic in the 1980s, initiated a whole new era for LGBTs that greatly accelerated the movement for our rights. Indeed, it awakened and energized an entire people. Like many LGBT brothers and sisters, I realized that the strength, savvy, and self-respect gained from fighting AIDS could and should be used to further our rights as we struggle against discrimination.

In 1988 few believed that HIV could become a manageable illness, and even fewer thought anyone living would ever see gay marriage. Notwithstanding, AIDS became manageable 8 years later; 15 years more and the US Supreme Court legalized gay marriage. Much of the energy and public support that brought these changes had its origins in AIDS activism.

Yet there is scant understanding of the dynamics of AIDS activism: Why it worked, where it failed, what were its principle ideas, who were its true thought leaders, what did they believe, and why? And, crucially, what were the biggest obstacles and most serious threats to our rights and lives during the height of the epidemic? Was it greedy drug companies, unimaginative researchers, an ignorant and terrified public, anti-gay bigots like Jesse Helms, or just maybe the intractable bureaucratic culture of FDA? The truth has been blurred out in a fog of identity politics where individuals are but shadows, and groups are the real actors. The truth and the heroes, mostly ordinary people sacrificing for a very personal cause, all need to be brought out of the shadows to help us complete the work that began in the twin struggles to rid the world of AIDS and to give LGBT people our full human rights.

Pervasive systematic anti-gay discrimination meant that the war against AIDS started with most of the soldiers, the AIDS patients and their friends, already wounded. But sometimes a wound can be a source of strength. This, I found true for me and most of the activists I knew. That which does not kill you makes you stronger, as Nietzsche observed optimistically. In any event, it prepared the activists to fight back by endowing them with the fiery strength of anger. But it was not true for every gay person with AIDS, or even most. For too many, the abuse and stigma that did not kill them, made them fearful and hyper cautious, or crippled with psychological disorders. For others the stress made them stronger in part yet crippled in other ways. I met all the combinations and permutations in my activist years, and went through some of them myself.

Chapter 2
Refugees Become Activists
(1988: 20,967 AIDS deaths)

"Never back down to bullies. Just remember,
when you stand up for yourself, you stand up for everyone like you."
Harvey Milk

Dave Olson, another refugee, initiated my journey as an AIDS activist and was a prime influence shaping its direction. I was and am HIV negative, so was Martin Delaney the other key San Francisco activist thought leader in the 1988 to 1996 period. Like many, including the most famous of all early AIDS activists, Elizabeth Taylor, Delaney and I became involved on behalf of friends and lovers.

A bright farm boy from the great plains of Nebraska, Dave had won various 4H awards for his champion cows and earned a Master's Degree in Veterinary Science from the University of Nebraska where he first began to act on his identity as a gay man. After graduating he brought home a boyfriend to meet his conservative farmer parents. As was so often the case in those times, it was a mistake, a very big mistake. Mom and Dad didn't mince words in making it clear that the boyfriend was unwelcome, as was Dave himself if he ever brought any such boyfriend home again. Angered and distraught, Dave packed his pickup truck and headed west into Wyoming, then on to Oregon. He ended up in the Bay Area where he found professional employment with Syntex, a Palo Alto drug company.

Pursuing the gay life, he contracted the AIDS virus. He was not sure where or how, as he avoided high risk activities. Conservative and typically Midwestern in his personal habits, sometimes Dave could be a bit of a prude. He speculated that he must have been drugged and taken advantage of in a party that ran too late, though he was uncertain when or with whom. The majority of patients I knew then were unsure as to where or when they became infected. Many were infected before they had even heard of the disease.

We met at the gay gym we attended. In my mind's eye Dave possessed every attraction. Masculine with a gay flare, he was full of rural charm, exceptionally honest, surprisingly insightful, funny, and very handsome. He resembled a younger Paul Newman. I once took him to the Castro Theater to see the classic Newman movie, *Cat on a Hot Tin Roof,* so he could enjoy it and I could compare him to Newman. I decided that Dave was actually handsomer than Newman, in my eyes at least. I also took him to see a performance of Samuel Beckett's *Endgame* wondering how a bright farm boy might respond to that. Dave was mesmerized; we talked about the play for over an hour and he referred to it and its characters many times thereafter. Inquisitive by nature, he could converse intelligently on a range of subjects. In contrast to many he knew, I provided him with ample opportunities to exercise that aspect of himself. At forty-three, I thought myself too old to fall crazy in love again, but Dave proved me wrong.

In 1988 he was diagnosed with the fatal opportunistic illness toxoplasmosis and given at most 6 months to live. One of the most resourceful and determined patients I ever met, and many of the patients were notably so, Dave devised a dosing regimen that kept his toxoplasmosis at bay so that he died of other causes nearly four years later. Fortunately, he had excellent health insurance from Syntex which gave him access to the best available care and allowed him to try various experimental treatments, like plasmapheresis. Some of these helped a little, most proved useless beyond their initial placebo effects.

Dave was not able to tolerate for long AZT or the subsequent Nukes, ddI, ddC, and d4T. At first they made him a lot better, then their toxicities would set in. After a month or two he'd be suffering worse from drug toxicities than he'd been suffering from the disease itself. His doctor would then stop the drug. AZT made Dave vomit with little warning. We'd be driving on a busy freeway when he'd order me to pull onto the shoulder at once. Then he'd throw open the car door and vomit on the roadside. After failing AZT, his weight dropped to 130 pounds. He had been a muscular 175 before AIDS.

He seemed near death's door, but was not ready to give up. Never depressed for long, his voracious appetite for life kept him going. Facing death, he still yearned to complete the full repertory of life's joys, thrills, achievements, and hard work. His love of life, delight in its smallest pleasures, ability to bear its most terrible sufferings and hardest challenges, rubbed off on me pulling me out of my phlegmatic academic mindset with its characteristic angst induced spiritual ennui and moral paralysis. Without really noticing, I had leapt into the torrential floods of life and liked the experience if not its cause. Those who grew close to a dying AIDS patient frequently had similar stories. In the teeth of death, we live most intensely.

(Dave Olson 1988, several months after AIDS diagnosis)

A crucial reason Dave turned me into an activist and through me became a factor in activism himself was his passionate conviction that FDA drug approval procedures were prime obstacles to speeding research and development of new HIV medicines. His work with Syntex taught him firsthand all the troublesome dilemmas and unnecessary burdens FDA's hyper cautious regulation created for companies trying to develop new medicines. In delaying approvals, he explained to me, FDA increased the costs of drug development and thereby reduced the likelihood of new treatments coming to market while guaranteeing higher prices. Dave taught me how the drug development and approval processes work, and convinced me that FDA, whom he dubbed the Fascist Drug Agency, was the single Archimedean point where we could get leverage to move the process forward, and possibly save his life. Research depends on scientific discovery which is not predictable. Drug development, however, depends on regulation which can be adjusted to speed or delay the entire process.

Dave not only gave me my strategy and worked with me as his health permitted, he gave me his fierce encouragement. He had an unfailing "bullshit meter" to tell him, and me as well, if claims, theories, or people were genuine and reliable, suspect, or bogus and untrustworthy. As the saying goes, he could see right through people. Dave believed and repeatedly told me that he thought I was the most effective activist in the country, the one who could best find viable strategies and tactics, the one who best understood the complex relationships of FDA and the drug companies, the one who had the integrity and the good sense not be duped or co-opted by FDA. Of course I was his pupil doing what Dave wanted and taught me to do, and the strategies I developed were often ones he suggested. Since he was overall the most attractive man I knew personally, doing what he wanted, pleasing him, was a powerful motivation. We were usually of one mind on activist and political questions. He would criticize my ideas and wanted to read everything I wrote before I sent it out. But he was ever quick to defend me against criticism from others, and there was always plenty of that.

Let me interrupt Dave's story for a flashback to a paradigmatic lesson in activism from a decade earlier. In October 1978, I met the most famous of the San Francisco gay activist-refugees a few weeks before his assassination. A year prior, Robert Hillsborough, a gardener for the city, was brutally murdered in a wave of violence against gays sweeping the Bay Area. I lived in the Castro district then, and, like others, lived in fear. My downstairs neighbor had been savagely battered walking home at night a month before; no one felt safe from the marauders who came into our neighborhoods looking for gays to bait, rough up, shake down, or maybe worse.

One Saturday afternoon I stopped for a red light at the busy Castro and Market intersection then turned right onto 17th street. The old car behind followed honking and pulling up almost to rear end mine. I couldn't elude them, so I pulled over. Two big hombres jumped out to demand $100 claiming I had rolled back into their "antique" vehicle damaging it. There was no visible damage, and the car, no antique, would have barely been worth $100. With a firm no, I got into my car and left. They pursued me honking and again almost rear ended my car. Turning back into Castro Street, I spotted an open parking space in front of Harvey Milk's camera shop, pulled up, and ran in to Harvey. He had just been elected Supervisor, but had yet to take office.

Harvey advised me that there was no place in the Castro district for our people to take refuge when attacked by bullies, so the two of us would just have to face them alone. The bullies, large, heavy set guys in their late twenties, were menacing from the outset. A San Francisco cop drove by; Harvey tried to wave him over. He flipped Harvey an obscene gesture and bellowed "go to hell." "He doesn't know." I remarked to Harvey. "Oh yes he does!" Harvey shot back.

Jim Driscoll, 1980, San Francisco

Emboldened by the pig-headed cop, the two bullies pressed forward fists raised. In a flash I imagined Harvey and myself heavily bandaged in adjoining beds in the Davies Hospital ER down the road. But Harvey would not be bullied let alone out talked; they saw that after a while. "You know, you have a very big mouth," one of them yelled at Harvey, "Someday, someone is going to close that big mouth of yours for good. And the sooner the better!"

With that they turned and left, to my great relief. Harvey, however, took it in stride. This sort of flak, he noted, was commonplace in the Castro district, but if people stood up to the bullies that usually worked. We talked for half an hour. I never met Harvey again. His was the most totally satisfactory response I have ever received asking help from a public official. "Never back down to bullies," he shouted as I got into my car, "Just remember when you stand up for yourself, you stand up for everyone like you." That was my most important lesson as an activist, but I did not start putting it into practice until Dave Olson needed help ten years later.

Harvey's assassination a few weeks afterwards indelibly stamped his lesson and the memory of our encounter in my consciousness. His death was unspeakably painful for me and for tens of thousands of gay San Franciscans. For years I could not talk about our encounter without great difficulty, and it took fifteen years for me to recount it with full emotional control. It still can be difficult to recount. I have always believed that gay people lost our best, most sympathetic, and effective leader to an assassin's bullet. Had Harvey lived we might have moved faster and further with bolder, more creative strategies, more effective tactics, and less time and energy wasted struggling through the morass of identity politics. Imagine if Harvey had survived to become our preeminent AIDS voice, rather than the erratic Larry Kramer! Above all, Harvey would have led with unequaled charisma and sound judgment. With his death a potential for masterful leadership seemed irreparably lost.

Dave Olson was my prime motivator in becoming an AIDS activist, but he was not my only teacher. And I did need teachers because at that time my knowledge of the relevant medical science and the businesses of drug development and healthcare was minimal. Four other important teachers who became close friends were Jim Foster, Dr. Steven Wright, and fellow activists Barry Freehill and Jesse Dobson.

Jesse Dobson, an engineer by profession and by avocation a musician with a taste for great literature, grew up in South Carolina in the 70s. Not enamored of its culture, one of his favorite jokes was: "South Carolina and Las Vegas show the need for the two different types of nuclear weapons: South Carolina is a beautiful place with terrible people so you'd want to use a neutron bomb, with Vegas you'd use a regular H-bomb to blast away everything in the entire hideous place." Jesse's sense of humor was dark and sardonic. He was angry and bitter, but he was much more than just that. He was resourceful, talented, determined, and loyal after his fashion, I suppose.

His deterioration over the few short years I knew him was terrible and frightening, but that was true of everyone who died of AIDS. A picture of energetic, commanding manhood could descend into a helpless invalid so quickly he could lose the sense of who he was. For those around a friend succumbing to AIDS, denial was the ready and easiest escape from the unbearable briefness of their being, and the agonizing frustration over your own helplessness. Denial became a watchword for the entire epidemic. 'Denial is not a river in Egypt' was the joke of the era. The epidemic of denial transcended and dwarfed the disease itself infecting the general public and many public officials. Denial's evil twin was fear; whenever fear showed, denial clung to him like a demonic shadow.

The palpable fear and then almost metaphysical relief I felt upon first learning I was HIV negative remains as clear in my memory as if that day in 1985 were sometime last week. Like other HIV positives, Jesse and Dave had meticulously detailed stories of their "day of diagnosis." For most the diagnosis ended one kind of denial only to initiate other defenses in an ongoing struggle with fear. That was the case for their HIV negative friends and family too, including myself. An effective defense against fear and denial was to stand up and take the offensive. ACT UP, the AIDS Coalition to Unleash Power, provided a way for Jesse and me, along with hundreds of others across the nation, to turn the tables on frustration, fear, and denial by going on the offensive against unresponsive social and political institutions and their callous or somnolent officials.

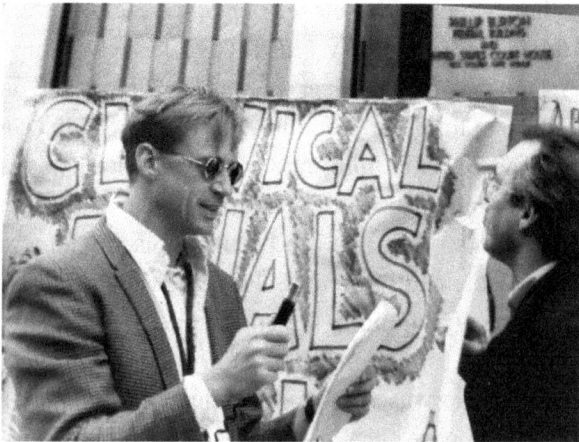

(Jesse Dobson with Microphone.)

Throughout 1989 Jesse and I were mainstays of ACT UP San Francisco. Early in 1990 the International AIDS Conference scheduled for that year in SF changed all that as attendance in ACT UP meetings exploded from a handful to scores of people. Jesse provided much of the backbone and brains of the organization in those early days, I also provided brains, imagination, and grit. Together we met with an array of different governmental, medical, and pharmaceutical people in a short space of two years. Jesse always had a list of things he wanted, and always said he wanted them all done yesterday. He was adept at instilling his own urgency into people accustomed to the deadening pace and facile excuses of bureaucracy. He frequently offended people, which given the circumstances usually worked to benefit the cause. An important lesson I learned from Jesse was the value of cool, relentless persistence. He believed that science could beat HIV, it was just a matter of time. He knew time was not on his side, but he was determined to make good use of the time he had.

Jesse and I pioneered what a *San Jose Mercury* reporter called an activist-lobbyist one-two punch. In an article on us published immediately prior to the 1990 San Francisco AIDS conference the reporter described our techniques:

> *A handful of skilled advocates, backed by growing numbers of militant troops are taking their life and death campaign directly to the companies developing AIDS drugs. Their goal is ambitious, to speed up the testing and release of promising AIDS treatments . . .Their weapons range from an exhaustive knowledge of the AIDS pharmacopeia to well-honed connections to federal regulators to profound moral pressure in the face of a devastating epidemic. And if those don't work there is always the threat of a noisy street protests . . .. That one two punch---quiet behind the scenes logrolling coupled with high-profile demonstrations has already enabled AIDS activists to make their presence felt in the research labs and boardrooms of America's drug companies. . .. "There's been a substantial impact by AIDS activists on the drug development process," said John Petricciani, medical and regulatory affairs director at the Pharmaceutical Manufacturers Association. (San Jose Mercury News, June 18, 1990)*

A year later in 1991 we had a bitter falling out over the AIDS drug underground, which Dave Olson and Steven Wright strongly opposed along with Barry Freehill who entered our activist scene the year before and soon became a close ally. Jesse supported Martin Delaney and his group Project Inform's alliance with Jim Corti, a Los Angeles nurse who had set up an illicit underground drug manufacturing operation. At the same time, I became a leader in a more libertarian cadre of patients, including Dave, Steven Wright, Barry and several others outside of San Francisco. We believed the underground violated reasonable laws essential to protecting public health, worse still, its products were generally useless or defective. Instead, we wanted AIDS activism to focus on pressuring FDA to approve legitimate drugs swiftly, thus making illegal underground knockoffs unnecessary. We sought Congressional legislation to scale back impediments to early access to AIDS drugs posed by FDA's rigid enforcement of the efficacy standard. Jesse died in September 1993, two years before availability of the drug cocktails that could have saved his life.

Steven Wright was a young emergency doctor at Stanford Presbyterian hospital in the exclusive Pacific Heights area of San Francisco. Incandescently bright with an inventive gay wit, he was full of fun and ever generous with his help. Like Jesse and many other AIDS patients, Steven had a powerful will to live. Unlike most others his survival drive was coupled with an experienced based and professionally trained grasp of how medical and drug research worked. Originally from Oklahoma, he came to the Bay Area to work as a researcher for a drug company, in his case Hoffmann-La Roche. As a result, he, like Dave, well understood the obstructive effects of FDA hyper regulation and its rigid efficacy standard.

In 1962 Congress, reacting to the thalidomide disaster, had passed the Kefauver-Harris Drug Amendments which instructed FDA to establish efficacy as well as safety before granting approval to a new drug. It was an ill-advised gift to FDA, an expansion of their bureaucratic power far beyond what was called for by the safety issues thalidomide raised. Safety was never controversial, however, the amendments left to FDA's discretion the standards for efficacy and their implementation. In subsequent years it became apparent that efficacy testing could be extremely slow and often inconclusive. Promising new drugs could languish at FDA waiting for more complete efficacy data while dying patients lacked access.

Cancer patients had long been frustrated with the growing FDA delays. But AIDS brought a new breed of activist patient skeptical of FDA's facile claim that the delays were needed to "protect" them. These impatient patients were unusually distrustful of government bureaucrats, especially those focused on victimless crimes. Dying AIDS patients wanted and began to demand a chance to try drugs whose safety was demonstrated but whose efficacy testing remained incomplete. FDA objected that early access would interfere with full, rigorous efficacy testing. Like Dave, Steve believed that behind FDA's resistance to modifying their approval practices for the dilemma of dying AIDS patients was an implicit devaluation of gay people arising from their unspoken contempt for and bias against us. After all, the rest of the government, along with society itself, discriminated with impunity against gays in employment and elsewhere. Discrimination was par for the course.

Those who did not have friends who struggled with AIDS in the early 1990s cannot appreciate how poorly the few available drugs worked and how desperate patients were for more effective, less toxic treatments. They will have difficulty understanding the anger many patients felt toward a callous society egged on by bigots who unjustly blamed gays for a disease caused by a retrovirus. The trials and persecution such patients faced are movingly dramatized in many memoirs as well as movies like "The Dallas Buyer's Club."

Steven Wright had failed AZT, was failing ddI, and he even tried some of the alternatives sold through the buyer's clubs. Desperate as he was to find effective treatments, Steve remained a committed medical scientist. As such, he was skeptical of underground drugs, and he distrusted the motives and competence of their hawkers. However, he was quick to recognize the value of combination therapies in impeding the virus's resistance to any one drug. He sharply condemned FDA's foot dragging on approving the combination therapies which seemed to him a no brainer. Understanding how medical research is done, Steve also understood the professional quirks and limitations of medical researchers. He criticized their habitual demand for data overkill, and what he termed virtuoso padding or featherbedding. "The more you do, the more you can ask to be paid," he explained, "regardless whether the overkill helps solve the problem. So you check out every possibility. It all takes time." He saw this overkill as afflicting FDA and the outside researchers alike: both gained by and became addicted to endless elaboration and re-confirmation. The losers were patients waiting for better treatments.

Initially he had hoped against the odds that Trichosanthin or Compound Q, an underground drug promoted by Martin Delaney, might play a role in a viable combination. He even wrote a scientific proposal for combining Delaney's drug with passive immunotherapy, another alternative that seemed promising to many doctors. However, Steve soon became disillusioned with the excess of hype, lack of scientific rigor and flickers of hidden agendas behind Delaney's claims for Compound Q and his other underground drugs. And like Dave, he knew that to be safe and effective pharmaceuticals had to be manufactured and distributed under carefully controlled and strictly monitored conditions. In the end, he dismissed Delaney as a charlatan and castigated the Washington officials who legitimatized him.

(Dr. Steven Wright in Demonstration at SF Courthouse)

Prior to knowing Steven, I had little understanding of the politics of the medical and research professions or the hard science of AIDS treatment and research. Steven was always ready, no eager, to explain everything to me. His explanations were wonderfully clear and, being a good teacher, he tailored them to my limitations.

Jim Foster was a long time gay activist whose activism began with his 1959 discharge from the army, as undesirable, for being homosexual. He moved to San Francisco where he co-founded SIR, the Society for Individual Rights in 1964, and in 1971 the Alice B. Toklas Democratic Club, the first gay and lesbian Democratic club in the country. Diane Feinstein credited Jim and SIR for her margin of victory in her 1969 election to the San Francisco Board of Supervisors, the inception of her long political career and of their friendship.

One of Jim's stories illustrated the strength of that friendship. When his partner Larry Ludwig died of AIDS Jim headed the San Francisco Health Department. Mayor Feinstein called him in for a meeting. A martinet about scheduling, she insisted that meetings be limited to fifteen minutes. As Jim left the meeting after more than two hours, her staff stood outside staring aghast—what new health disaster had befallen the city? None! It turned out that the mayor, herself recently widowed, spent the entire time giving Jim her Jewish mother advice on handling the death of a spouse.

The personal bonds of gay people with leaders like Diane Feinstein and Nancy Pelosi proved crucial to cementing the loyalty of a pariah community to the Democratic party. By contrast Republican elected officials, afraid of being publicly identified with known gays, kept their ties with the gay community and its leaders locked in dark closets. Gay Republicans knew the party leaders were embarrassed by them which humiliated them before the rest of the LGBT community. 'Welcoming' has never been a word LGBTs could apply to the Republican Party. Being welcoming, if only conditionally, gave Democrats a potent edge with our community; they continue to expand that edge unchallenged to this day.

Jim Foster was close to many other top Democrats including Ted Kennedy. Jim doubtless deserved some credit for Kennedy's emergence as a fearless and absolutely crucial champion of gay rights, and of the

AIDS cause. Jim had directed Kennedy's 1980 California primary campaign for the Democratic nomination. Jim won the primary for Kennedy, who failed to wrest the nomination from President Carter. Earlier, in 1972 during the McGovern campaign, Jim had become the first openly gay person to address a national party convention. The Republican party did not match Jim's precedent until Peter Thiel addressed the Trump convention in 2016. I was thrilled by both their speeches. The progress of LGBTs in the Republican Party since Thiel's speech has been less than thrilling, however.

Like everyone in the San Francisco gay community, I knew Jim by reputation, but did not actually meet him until 1989 when he became a consultant for Lyphomed, a pharmaceutical company that sold a drug for a common but deadly AIDS opportunistic illness, pneumocystis carinii pneumonia. I had written an article attacking FDA delays in *The Sentinel*, a gay community paper. Jim liked it and called me out of the blue to discuss creating political and media pressure for moving promising new drugs more rapidly through FDA's cumbersome approval procedures.

(Jim Foster, 1934-1990)

Because Jim had worked long and closely with the Democratic Party establishment, his alliance with me was unusual. At that time, I was a registered independent who had few connections with either party. Although Jim was a loyal Democrat, like Harvey Milk his first loyalty was to the gay community. Both men's top political priority was protecting our health, safety, and rights. I was heartened to learn that it was as difficult for Jim, as it was for me, to understand how gay individuals could put loyalty to any party above the needs of our own cruelly abused and ever threatened people who stood almost alone against the most terrible epidemic since the black plague. Jim, who died of AIDS in October 31 1990 at age 55, realized that the epidemic posed challenges that transcended party loyalties. He believed that gays must try to work with Republicans to speed HIV research and treatment development, especially to pressure and ultimately reform a congenitally obstructive FDA. Long before encouraging me, he had encouraged Ted Kennedy and other friendly democrats to reach out to the GOP to help our oppressed and endangered people.

The Republicans, he advised me, might be persuaded to support FDA reform, while the Democrats would continue to condone FDA foot dragging. Both parties considered open association with the gay cause a political liability, although the Democrats had credible exceptions like Ted Kennedy, Diane Feinstein, Nancy Pelosi, Barbara Jordan, and Jesse Jackson. AIDS made FDA reform a life and death issue for gays in the 1990s. I agreed with certain Republican positions, such as opposition to socialism and their distrust of big government and its unresponsive, self-serving, ever expanding bureaucracies, like FDA. However, I had deep reservations about working with a party that pandered to homophobic prejudice and disrespected gay people, and by inference myself and most of my friends

I had long believed discrimination against our people was deeply immoral, indeed a direct violation of the Judeo-Christian ethic. The intellectual dishonesty of "religious" rationales for homophobia, based as they were on deceptive cherry picking of scripture, appalled me. All too often throughout my life I had experienced and seen the terrible damage stigma and prejudice, along with guilt and denial, inflict on our people.

How did the homophobes consciences allow them to blithely mangle innocent lives in the name of a religion that claimed to be about love and truth? Were they irredeemably callous and dishonest?

Jim encouraged me to suppress my disapproval of GOP kowtowing to prejudice and expediency on gays and AIDS as a necessary sacrifice to help speed FDA approval of the drugs our people needed to survive. Someone had to sacrifice their pride to save people's lives. I knew that others had forfeited more for less throughout the history of our nation. Moreover, in Jim's opinion, as well as Dave's and Steve's, I seemed uniquely qualified by education, temperament, and I suppose stubborn intellectual audacity and moral tenacity, to become an effective voice against FDA abuses. Moreover, the cruel discrimination I had suffered at the University of Wisconsin left a potent chip on my shoulder, a high energy battery with the juice to power great exertions on behalf of justice for gay people.

Jim was a seasoned political operative who had endless informative and funny stories. Being a political naïf, I had much to learn from him. Like nearly all academics, I had some strong political opinions based on zero real world experience in how politics worked or of the difficulties with formulating effective policies and the obstacles to implementing them. Jim took me to Washington and introduced me to his contacts in government and industry, especially with Arnold & Porter, a law firm with many pharmaceutical companies as clients. Among them Hoffman-La Roche, a crucial AIDS player at the time. I was fortunate and honored to work with Jim on AIDS in the year before he died. He taught me much about how political people operate, and about the smelly sausage making behind public policies. Thanks to Jim, I learned the obstacles to effective change in the tortuous worlds of government and politics. Overall, there is one rule: **lasting change requires a compromise that respects the legitimate interests of all stakeholders. A viable compromise, means some like it enough to defend it, and none hate it enough to destroy it.**

Chapter 3
A Tale of Two Cities

All politics are local, as the saying goes. It applies especially to activist politics and activism in general. Activism begins in specific localities with community people talking about shared problems with their friends and neighbors. It's colored by the character of those communities and the peculiarities of the individuals in them. Activist leaders emerge out of a group of friends confronting common challenges.

AIDS conditions varied greatly across the country. The epidemic in New York was not the epidemic in Memphis which was not that in rural Kansas, which was not that in Miami or San Francisco. San Francisco and New York were the US cities hit hardest by the HIV epidemic in the 1980s and 90s. Other cities like Los Angeles, Washington, Miami, Atlanta, Dallas, Houston, and Boston were hit hard and became centers of AIDS activism. However, New York first and then San Francisco emerged as the thought leader communities. These two cities defined the nature and direction of treatment activism and stamped their character on its strategies, tactics, and consequences. For the media and the public AIDS activism became a generic term, but in reality its characteristics and initiatives were highly localized. New York and San Francisco, despite both being densely populated port cities with diverse populations, were quite different in their histories, cultures, demographics, politics, and economic structures. Their differences produced dissimilar activist approaches, leaders, goals, and results.

In 1988 I had lived in San Francisco for 14 years. Those years saw momentous changes in the status of gay people, changes that often began in San Francisco and the state of California. Since I hailed from San Francisco, I will focus mainly on it and refer to New York chiefly as it interacted, contrasted, and conflicted with my home town. The contrasts and conflicts of the two local activist movements were often important or even crucial to the development of the national AIDS treatment activism, its impact, and how it was perceived. They played leading but divergent roles in the activist struggle to expedite FDA approval of the antiviral cocktails, and especially in its denouement in 1994-1995.

The two movements, while sharing an overall goal of better treatments for AIDS, had different approaches in key areas, the most important being FDA. San Francisco activists stressed direct confrontations with FDA while attempting to secure cooperation with the pharmaceutical industry. New York activists sought cooperation with FDA, NIH, and NIAID, and tried to gain attention and clout by scapegoating and harassing the drug companies.

While San Francisco activists were more "radical," we nonetheless had much better working relations with our local political leaders, such as Representatives Nancy Pelosi, Barbara Boxer, Tom Lantos, and Tom Campbell of Palo Alto as well as Mayors Diane Feinstein and Art Agnos. With the help of Log Cabin Republicans, we established relationships with key people in the first Bush Administration. From 1991 to 1999, while Pete Wilson was governor of California, gay Republicans worked closely with his Administration. By contrast, the New Yorkers were confrontational with Mayor Koch and alienated from local political figures, especially their own Congressman Ted Weiss who adamantly refused to meet with them. Their influence was greatest with Federal bureaucrats, above all those in FDA who were quick to spot and nurture patient allies.

The San Franciscans were initially led by Martin Delaney, the ambitious, multi-talented co-founder of Project Inform, and later also by myself, a 1988 arrival on the activist scene. We developed a pragmatic strategy focused on creating incentives for the drug companies to invest in AIDS drug R &D. It required securing essential appropriations for basic NIH virology and immune research and for HIV specific NIAID research along with lowering drug development costs by pressuring FDA to approve AIDS drugs faster. Faster approval, Delaney and I realized, was a powerful incentive for the companies to invest in HIV research and develop new AIDS drugs. We knew that without corporate incentives better drugs would never be developed or approved in time to save our friends.

The differing perspectives of Delaney, the New Yorkers, and my local allies on the proper role of FDA in time diverged to produce conflicting strategies that sharply divided the activist movement. FDA worked behind the scenes to induce division, knowing that division strengthened the Agency's hand while it weakened those activists who sought fundamental regulatory reforms, such as accelerated approval of new drugs for life threatening conditions like AIDS and cancer. The activists nationwide were slow to grasp either FDA's divisive strategy or the full seriousness of the threat it's efficacy testing posed to accessing breakthrough drugs once they were tested for safety.

Major differences in the makeup of the heavily HIV afflicted gay male communities in the two great metropolitan centers impacted the character of their activist movements. The New York movement, always centered in Manhattan, had more professional people, in theater, the arts, and advertising. In San Francisco these sectors were smaller and employed fewer gays. Heavily influenced by the hippy-flower children phenomenon in the late 60s and early 70s SF was more Bohemian. Many SF gays were stuck at the bottom of the employment ladder as drivers, cleaners, landscapers, security guards, handymen, waiters, and personal servants to the wealthy. Over qualified gay refugees had to take what they could get. I was typical, working as a night watchman in an exclusive cooperative where other co-workers and servants also had advanced degrees. These differences made the New Yorkers outlooks more conventionally liberal, while the San Franciscans tended to be pragmatic and libertarian.

A critical difference was the larger portion of San Francisco gays who were refugees from oppression for being gay. Gay people who had been deeply hurt or impaired by the pervasive anti-gay discrimination and abuse in the 60s and 70s came in droves to San Francisco, the one place in the country where they felt safer and freer to live as who they really were. Indeed, San Francisco was the original sanctuary city, not for undocumented migrants but for gays fleeing homophobic oppression. In Tony Kushner's *Angels in America* set in Manhattan, heaven is portrayed in the image of San Francisco. Before AIDS, that portrayal seemed on the mark for gays who'd fled a hell of stigma and discrimination elsewhere.

Because gay San Franciscans had suffered more bias than our counterparts in New York and other large cities, we were more rebellious, distrusting of authority, and open to new methods of activism. Status usually didn't impress us, and we were less concerned about what "they think," especially if "they" meant inflexible bureaucrats or an unresponsive liberal establishment. We were quicker to show our local establishment figures how things really were and tell them what they should be doing. They in turn were more willing to listen to activists with fresh approaches and ideas. Nancy Pelosi, in particular, was ready to listen to us, and we were ready to confront her when needed. Unlike important politicians outside the Bay Area, she listened conscientiously and took our criticisms with grace and class.

Chapter 4
The Politics of AIDS

The politics of the AIDS epidemic illustrate a basic rule of politics that is crucial for LGBT people to understand, yet is usually overlooked: *the interests of any segment of the population will never be permanently or entirely aligned with one party.* Individuals must beware of putting loyalty to a single party above loyalty to their own people. Since each political party is a coalition of groups whose interests alter over time and sometimes fall into conflict, no group can ever be certain that its interests will not be sidelined because they conflict with those of other more powerful factions within the party. The party will always side with those who best serve its *raison d'etre*, to win and maintain political power. It is never wise or safe to let politics trump personal loyalties or cause you to forget who you are or where you came from.

During the height of the AIDS epidemic many Republicans courted groups, like Focus on the Family and Family Research Council, who turned promotion of anti-gay stigma into a thriving industry. But the Democrats were allied with consumer protectors and trial lawyers who backed ponderous FDA drug approval procedures that delayed development of and access to drugs for AIDS and killer diseases like cancer. Most gays did not realize it, but our two parties taken together were offering us a lose-lose proposition. Gay rights issues were more urgent then, and violations more brazen than now. The Republican record on LGBT rights was a travesty. Democrats championed our basic civil rights, if not always consistently or effectively, yet they stood ready to compromise our right to try medicines that might keep people alive and well longer. Too often our options amounted to pick your poison.

Rights issues notwithstanding, in the 1990s Republicans managed to score a credible record on funding HIV research, especially Senators Mark Hatfield and Arlen Specter, Chairs of the Senate Appropriations

Committee and Representative John Porter in the House. Senator Orrin Hatch joined his friend Ted Kennedy to write the indispensable Ryan White Care Act. On research and care issues the two parties displayed commendable bipartisan cooperation for the most part. Nonetheless, the noisy demagoguery of Jesse Helms and fellow travelers got the press and made "Republican" a bad name among gays. President Reagan's silence on AIDS was also deadly, as the ACT UP slogan "**SILENCE = DEATH**" said.

While the Democrats' alliance with FDA posed a threat to drug development, its gravity was poorly understood by the media and the AIDS and gay communities. Moreover, since FDA regulated food and drugs, a huge swath of the US economy, currying FDA's favor could boost fund raising from the regulated---as the New York activists and Delaney well understood. The gay community, grateful to the Democrats for support on rights, was reluctant to pressure them on FDA, and unwilling to work with Republicans for FDA reform.

That's where I came in along with my AIDS patient allies, and the Log Cabin Republicans. Despite sympathies with Democrats on rights issues, I have always been an independent minded intellectual who tries to evaluate all issues on their own merits rather than choosing sides on the basis of political allegiance or ideology. I had voted for McGovern and strongly opposed the Vietnam war, and in 1980 voted for John Anderson, the first Presidential candidate to openly support gay rights. I voted for Reagan in 1884, but supported Clinton in 1992 for gay rights reasons. So I became what was sometimes called a yellow liner, one who drove down the middle of the political road.

The catalyst suggestions on where and how to start working with Republicans on FDA and AIDS came from Jim Foster and an unlikely source Jim introduced me to, Tim Westmoreland Legislative Director for Rep. Henry Waxman of the Energy and Commerce Committee. Tim was also the key Congressional staffer on AIDS. Tim explained that the AIDS movement, had failed to tap the potential of working with Republicans. Tim said I seemed a very reasonable person who could talk and work with Republicans and stood a chance of getting results, including by getting them to pressure FDA where Democrats got cold feet. He gave me the names of a number of staffers I could work with, chief among them Kim Belshe in Senator Pete Wilson's office, who later headed the California Department of Health when Wilson became governor. I had also received similar encouragement from another unlikely place, the office of Congresswoman Barbara Boxer which worked closely with one of my AIDS doctor allies, Marcus Conant. Bipartisanship was a fully acceptable option even for Boxer in those days, long before Donald Trump and his Resistance.

The Waxman link became particularly interesting two years after my initial discussion with Tim. The March 6, 1991 *Wall Street Journal* ran my opinion piece defending the laws promoting orphan drugs, a cause I 'd inherited from Jim Foster. I criticized Tim's boss for attempting to weaken incentives to develop orphan drugs. They titled it "Consumer Protection Could Kill AIDS Patients." The *Journal* added a drawing of Waxman to make sure no one missed their title's target. The piece garnered wide attention in Washington among those interested in AIDS and drug approval. Here are some of its key points:

> *Many AIDS Activists are coming to the realization that the fastest way to develop new treatments is through regulatory reform and research incentives for the pharmaceutical industry . . . Where AIDS activists seek the bread of new treatments, Mr. Waxman has offered them the stone of his anti-research, ant-business amendments to the Orphan Drug Act. . . . Mr. Waxman maintains that his amendments will curb excessive corporate profits: in fact, they will curb the development of new AIDS treatments. . .. AIDS activists, especially the pragmatic California species, are comprehending that stable incentives are needed to make sure new drugs for AIDS are developed. We are worried that drug companies will look at potential new drugs for AIDS and decide not to develop them because the incentives are undependable, while the political hassles are a sure bet. We are concluding that the country cannot afford ideological legislation that removes incentives from drug companies . . . Instead we want regulatory reform . . . Supporting private sector incentives for AIDS drug research and expediting approval of those drugs may well cut against the grain of Mr. Waxman's old-style consumer protectionism. But*

*we hope that he will update his thinking and begin, now, to help
rather than hinder the struggle to get new treatments to patients
who desperately need them.*

A tsunami of horrified condemnation swept the AIDS activist
community upon publication of the piece. The target was not Mr.
Waxman, it was me. That might be expected from people who were often
that era's version of "woke" Democrats. What surprised me was that no
one defended Mr. Waxman's position, or bothered to object to my
criticisms of it. They just attacked me personally for daring to say what
most of them believed, for pointing out the Emperor Waxman's sartorial
deficiencies. Political allegiances and ideology can do strange things to
otherwise seemingly rational people.

AIDS lobbyist Tom Sheridan pleaded with me, 'not to destroy my
relationship with Henry Waxman,' and I was roundly attacked by the New
York group and their fellow travelers around the country. But many of the
San Franciscans seemed bemused that one of their own, an ACT UP
Golden Gate founding member and a familiar figure in their meetings and
demonstrations, had actually placed an opinion piece in the prestigious
Wall Street Journal. Martin Delaney was publicly horrified, yet privately
amused and supportive.

Waxman met with the activists. I was excluded, not by Waxman
himself but by the irate New Yorkers. However, Tim Westmoreland, a
shrewd political observer, spied opportunity where the less imaginative
saw only a threat. Tim again offered to give me tips on working AIDS and
FDA angles with Republicans. I often disagreed with Waxman's positions
in those early days, but he and his office always displayed a level of
professionalism that, sadly, has become less common in Congress is this
era of Trump and his Resistance. I felt that their professionalism deserved
mine in return. So over the years I continued to work with his office; in
fact, during the 2006 re-authorization of the Ryan White Care Act some
of the groups made me their liaison to Waxman's office at the suggestion
of that office. In Washington, as in life, it is unwise to turn this season's
opponents into mortal enemies. Someone who is your prime adversary
today may be an indispensable ally on a different issue two, five, or ten

years down the road. Where human lives are at stake, ethics instruct us to prioritize flexibility over ideological purity.

The *WSJ* piece, followed by similar pieces critical of FDA in *WSJ* and other papers got me noticed and opened doors among Republicans that had not been open to anyone in the AIDS or gay movement before. To the shock of many, those doors included the one to the office of Vice President Dan Quayle.

The other gay Democrats in San Francisco were, like myself, more flexible and less ideological than the New Yorkers. As a result, we were successful working with local Democrats. At one point Larry Kramer remarked that the San Franciscans got frequent meetings with Nancy Pelosi and Barbara Boxer. All the while their own congressman Ted Weiss, his ears plugged against even the mildest criticisms of FDA, bolted his doors and locked up his casements against all members of New York ACT UP. We also met with holocaust survivor Tom Lantos, a man who always seemed to know and do the right thing; he wanted to speed approval of AIDS drugs as well as other drugs for life threatening conditions.

The meetings with Pelosi were not all flattery and hugs, in fact they were at times quite confrontational, though never hostile. At one early meeting, organized by Hank Wilson for ACT UP, an emaciated patient in a wheelchair and on oxygen feed rolled right up beside her desk. Pelosi had been explaining that Henry Waxman was the party leader on FDA and AIDS issues, so she had to follow him.

"You represent us. Henry Waxman did not elect you, we did," the patient asserted. "Our lives depend on faster drug approval from FDA. I will die soon, but others here may be saved if we can move drugs through FDA. I'm not leaving until you promise you will represent us on our life and death issues. Otherwise, you'll need to call security to haul me out bodily!" Pelosi said she understood and would tell Waxman she had to represent her own constituents on AIDS drug approval matters. We wanted more action than we got from her on FDA, but we did get respect which was very useful and badly needed. One young man cried after one of the first meetings with Pelosi because he was so moved that someone in her position would shake hands with an AIDS patient like himself. It's painful to recall scenes like that. Thankfully, we progressed quickly to where Pelosi's openness was no longer unusual.

While Republicans have been critical of Pelosi's leadership in the last 15 years, she has been a key champion of the AIDS cause and LGBT rights from the beginning and remains so to this day. She listened to us, was always compassionate, outspoken in our defense, and at times even courageous, all rare qualities in a politician. Her open door and warm acceptance of AIDS patients, who otherwise could be made to feel like untouchables, meant more to them than she realized. All LGBTs owe a debt of gratitude to Nancy Pelosi for her moral leadership on our rights and on AIDS. Nancy often delivered politically, and she always delivered morally.

Many Democrats followed Pelosi to embrace the AIDS cause, although, like her, most dragged their feet on FDA reform. The respect for Pelosi, however, did not prevent ACT UP from demonstrating against FDA in front of the Federal Building where she had her office, or from waving placards censuring Pelosi for bowing to hardline FDA promoter Ted Weiss. Pelosi's bowing to Weiss particularly nettled Dave Olson who demonstrated with a placard he made (I persuaded him to amend it, compare photos below) and he attended Pelosi's community meetings to protest personally her kowtowing to Weiss and to condemn FDA's never-ending delays.

Although the activists, even Dave, liked Nancy, still we wanted her to do more. That was the big problem with all the Democrats, they could have done more, much more, on FDA reform. By doing something on gay rights, they got an undeserved pass for failing to take a stand to save gay lives endangered by FDA delays.

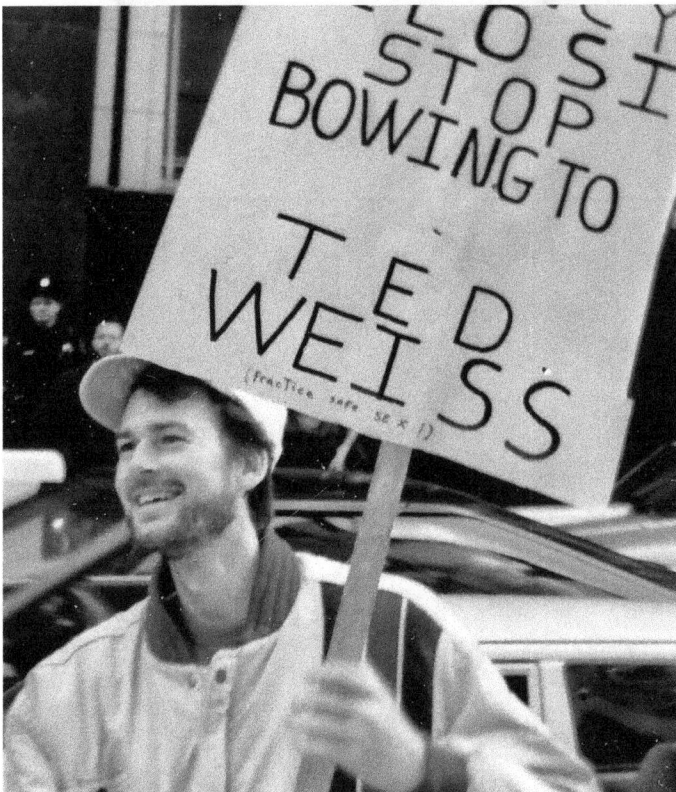

(Jim Driscoll holding Dave Olson's original unexpurgated placard;
Dave in demo, placard sanitized. 1990)

Chapter 5
Trailblazers in Identity Demagoguery

"Liberty, equality, fraternity, or death;
- the last, much the easiest to bestow"
Charles Dickens

Identity politics increasingly infiltrated AIDS activism. Before 1990, when ACT UP SF was a small band whose most visible leaders were Jesse Dobson and myself, the group focused exclusively on treatment development and access. We were survivalists. The influx of new people attracted by the publicity around the 6th International AIDS Conference scheduled for San Francisco that summer brought in interlopers focused primarily on identity politics and only incidentally on AIDS.

Even at that early date, identity politics was not confined to knee jerk leftists. It was already making inroads on the thinking of traditional liberals. Consequently, AIDS credentials became inordinately important that year. The best credential was having HIV yourself, and that was burnished by being a woman or minority, with points subtracted for being a white male. The next best was to have a spouse, lover, or close friend or relative with AIDS. Pain and suffering can give moral standing. The closer you are to AIDS yourself or to someone with the disease the greater your pain and suffering. Hence, these rankings made sense, as long as they were not carried too far. They didn't keep opportunists from muzzling in, their sole credential being self-proclaimed champions of women and minorities, and relentless critics of this world's uber-evils, "white male oppression" and corporate "greed."

The time ACT UP devoted to AIDS activism was increasingly dissipated in identity contention. Patients I worked with had no time to waste. They resented distraction created by identity leftists whose primary aim was power for themselves, not treatment for the dying. Overall, the far left created chaos and division which often drove away people with more legitimate reasons to be fighting AIDS. The left provided bodies and noise for demonstrations, but little else of value.

Then as now the *modus operandi* of the radical left were to infiltrate new groups and causes to secure their commitment to the left's main agenda. Gays with AIDS were always expendable when in conflict with higher priorities on their agendas. Relativists philosophically, the far left's fundamental rule was: ***power to the people who manipulate the people, power at any price.*** The far left in San Francisco was already potent in the early 1990s, but only a shadow of the political dominance it would later attain in that hapless city and the state of California.

A sticking point for the leftist infiltrators was their insistence that women and minority issues must be brought up at every meeting and be part of every serious proposal. Identity politics became a club to bludgeon the group into submission on all matters. Increasingly, the HIV positive white gay men who had formed and dominated the first incarnation of ACT UP San Francisco felt marginalized and harassed. Jesse Dobson was particularly targeted because he was not just any white male, he was a blond, blue-eyed white male from South Carolina. If that weren't enough, Jesse was not disposed to take guff from HIV negative, leftists whose primary objective was never his survival or that of our friends. Later in 1990 Jesse, Barry Freehill, Dave, and myself, along with nearly all the HIV positive men split from the main group to form ACT UP Golden Gate. The new group leaned liberal reflecting the community, but not ultra-leftist. Its goal was to avoid distracting social issues and focus on expediting AIDS treatment development and access.

The Sixth International AIDS conference that summer was from day one an extremely tumultuous affair, and at times became violently disruptive. President Bush's HHS Secretary, the venerable Louis Sullivan, was shouted down in his speech before the entire conference. Dedicated researchers, such as Drs. Thomas Merigan of Stanford and Doug Richman of UC San Diego, were hung in effigy and burned. Merigan, a renowned cancer researcher, had run several key trials applying to HIV what he had learned about cancer cocktails. His work spurred interest and then support for the idea of the multi-drug cocktails. But the leftist activists refused to consider, let alone support, the FDA reform legislation that offered the ready and easiest way to speed development and approval of the cocktails. For them AIDS was about fame and power for themselves; and FDA was big government with a capital B, which they adored on principle. So instead of supporting legislation to speed the work of researchers, they blamed and attacked them personally! It got the professional leftists media attention, making them seem like leaders, and that's what gratified them most of all.

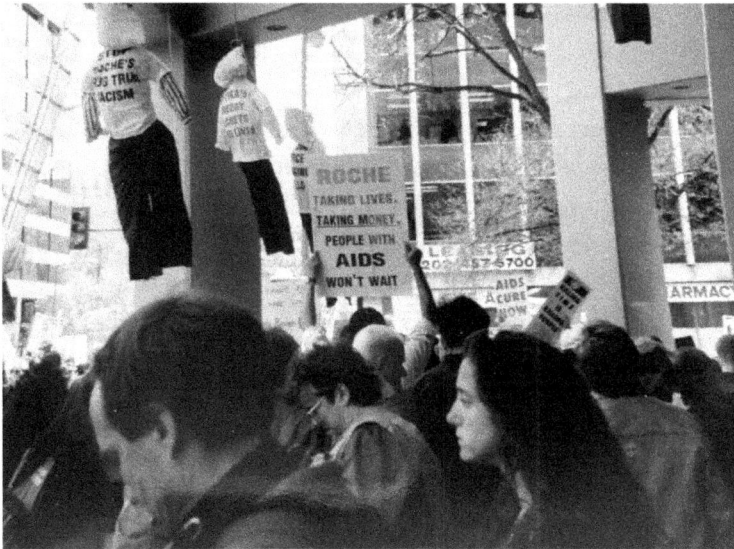

(Researchers hung in effigy at IAS 1990)

The perpetrators of travesties like that pictured above were not San Francisco people, but a group within ACT UP New York some of whom later formed TAG, or the Treatment Action Guerillas. Among the group's better known people were Peter Staley, Garance Franke-Ruta, David Barr, Spencer Cox, Derek Hodel, and Mark Herrington. As we San Franciscans saw it, these New Yorkers fashioned themselves *the* true AIDS activist leaders. Although community politics forced them to make an exception for Martin Delaney, they dismissed the other San Franciscans as parvenus. After all they were the geniuses who founded ACT UP, or so they claimed, the obstreperous figure of Larry Kramer to the contrary. To their credit, they were among the first highly visible AIDS activists; as such they did make critical contributions to public awareness of the horror of AIDS, and of the disease's initial neglect by the Federal and local authorities. Their early contributions to trial design, while sometimes problematic, did add further urgency. Yet they were far from being the only activists; and by the end of 1990 few, other than themselves and their buddies in FDA, believed they and they alone were the best and brightest of the entire movement.

The New Yorkers had the advantages of living in the largest center of the AIDS epidemic, being near Washington DC the apex of bureaucratic power, as well as close to the pharmaceutical industry, many of whose major players were headquartered across the Hudson in New Jersey. They also enjoyed, some of the time at least, the favor of the incandescent but ever erratic Larry Kramer, the real founder of ACT UP whose pronouncements were always widely publicized regardless of merit. For all his faults, Kramer had headlined the desperate plight of people with AIDS. His prime culprit was never FDA delays, but ever drug company "greed." Yet he always had a bogeyman du jour; at that conference it was the researchers struggling to find viable treatments for AIDS.

The San Franciscan activists were more flexible and resourceful, and more open to cooperative relations with industry and researchers. Unlike the New Yorkers, they did not regard Republican officials as morally comparable to Nazis or purveyors of child pornography. Delaney and I were proving more adept than the New Yorkers at getting favorable press especially from the media that counted most, The *New York Times* and the *Wall Street Journal*. This did not endear us to our rivals in the Big Apple. So they came to Bagdad by the Bay in the summer of 1990 determined to make a big splash. They would show us who the real activists were. They would burn the top AIDS researchers in effigy! Only they were clever enough to think of that, and gutsy enough to actually do it!

My chief allies then, Dave, Steve, and Barry had their native Midwesterners' almost instinctive distrust of the "snobby" New Yorkers. At the insistent urging of Dave, I wrote off the New Yorkers knowing I did not have time to waste on their ideological rigidity, egoism, and immaturity. Instead of hassling with ideologues, I forged alliances with women's cancer groups and African-Americans whose ruling concerns were their survival.

The San Franciscans, at my urging, mounted more anti-FDA demonstrations, and I repeatedly attacked FDA's dilatory procedures and implicit biases in opinion pieces in a wide range of newspapers. Delaney, with more ambition than realism, saw himself as a bridge over these troubled waters. Yet the LGBT community was too individualistic to want a unifier. Reflecting America itself, LGBTs are extremely diverse. Every race, religion, ethnicity, culture, and class is represented. We come from every part of the political and economic spectrums. The strongest things that unify us are persecution, stigma, and an often desperate need for respect. At that time, the entire national gay community had a loose consensus that FDA needed to approve drugs faster, but we couldn't agree on how to do this politically or who should lead. Separate strategies and leaders were inevitable. These led to separate actions that often fell at cross purposes. Cross purposes are ever the serpent's egg of open conflict, and that would come soon and grow bitter over the rise of the AIDS drug underground.

(Martin Delaney at San Francisco DDC Demonstration.)

My allies and I told everyone that the single area where activists could have the most impact was regulation, specifically FDA. After all, you could pressure regulators to expedite approval of a drug, but the New

Yorkers strategy of pressuring research scientists and companies to hurry their discoveries was a non-starter, and it could easily become counterproductive. The critical question was whether to change the clinical trials to speed getting the data FDA demanded, or lower FDA demands to speed acceptance of the data the trials could provide. Human trials took time to set up, enroll, and run; they could seldom be rushed. You could instill a sense of urgency, but since the researchers were human most of them had this already. Certainly Tom Merigan did, which was why the San Franciscans, even Jesse Dobson and Delaney, were appalled when the New Yorkers burned him in effigy.

To us it initially seemed that our New York rivals were naïve about the business side of drug development. As we learned more about them, we came to see some of them as opportunists bent on using AIDS and their own connections with FDA to promote themselves and secure their groups financially. Steve observed that in them resentment against marginalization was yoked with pretentious snobbishness. Whatever they truly were, pretentious snobbishness and ideological rigidity were the sides of themselves they showed us and they never bothered to make a better impression. Barry and I raised similar charges against Delaney, though in retrospect they seem less justifiable. Delaney was more experienced, flexible, and insightful than the New Yorkers. In the context of the Democrat Party and the left today, Delaney might be seen as a rare moderate and a comparatively selfless advocate for the AIDS cause— something he became at the one point in 1990's activism where it mattered most. But I am getting ahead of my story.

Chapter 6
Paths to Nowhere and Byways of Denial
(1991: 35,690 deaths from AIDS)

Proliferation of experimental treatments was a striking, innovative feature of AIDS treatment activism prior to the introduction of the protease based cocktails in late 1995. Under a death sentence, young people are often ready to try almost anything to stay alive a little longer. This was and remains especially true in the iconoclastic, experimental LGBT community where interest in gender choice and life extension is strong today.

John James's *AIDS Treatment News* reported new alternative treatments as they came out. Thousands of patients, including most of my patient friends, awaited each issue of *ATN* for something new to try or at least some reason to hope. *ATN* was a respected publication, always well-written, carefully researched, and unbiased. Sadly, none of the initially promising alternatives panned out. Nonetheless, *ATN* helped sustain hope and it encouraged patients to take charge of their health. Patients trying alternatives created a sense of urgency, thereby pressuring NIH to move orthodox research and FDA to speed approval of HIV drugs. In turn, pressure on these bureaucracies created incentives for drug companies to invest in R & D. Few, if any, of the alternatives, usually herbals or nutraceuticals, did significant damage to patients or their pocket books.

On behalf of friends, I was drawn into the controversies around two of the alternatives, Trichosanthin or Compound Q, a Chinese abortion drug that killed HIV in the test tube, and PATH or passive immune-therapy. While most of the alternatives were harmless and useless, Compound Q was not harmless though it did prove useless. In 1989 Steven Wright, Dave Olson and I attended an early Compound Q community meeting put on by Project Inform. There I met for the first time, the drugs' promoter Martin Delaney, who was Project Inform's Executive Director and co-founder.

Though Steve hoped that CQ might pan out, like other experienced researchers he saw Delaney's research methods as defective and the results misleading and inconclusive. Dave reached the same conclusions, and objected particularly to Delaney hyping the drug. The meeting turned both of them against Delaney and his underground movement. The controversy around CQ dragged on for years, but there never was reason to doubt either Steve and Dave's initial negative assessments of the drug or dismiss their concerns about Delaney's promotion tactics.

However, a community desperate for hope, any hope, was primed to follow a pied piper, a role Delaney seized and played with panache. His CQ hype quickly made him the most visible, if highly controversial, leader of the SF AIDS treatment community. He soon rose to national prominence cultivating ties with the media, NIAID's Director Anthony Fauci, and the almighty FDA. Although critical of Delaney's methods and hype, established researchers were also wary of his influence with government officials. A few of them blasted Delaney as an unscrupulous pitchman. Yet none ventured to extend their criticisms to the FDA and officials like Fauci who legitimized Delaney by working closely with him.*8*

Jesse Dobson put aside his doubts because the chaos in ACT UP convinced him that the AIDS movement needed a leader; that, he believed, had to be Martin Delaney. The skeptics and mavericks were numerous, however, and I, as much by default as by assertion, became the most prominent of the skeptics. Thus began a split between Jesse and myself that became one of the notable fractures in a rapidly fragmenting national AIDS treatment activist movement.

Among my friends Steven, Dave, Jim and several others refused to try CQ. When Barry Freehill tried it he went into anaphylactic shock collapsing on his kitchen floor. Fortunately, he lived a block from the Davies Hospital emergency room: that proximity may have saved his life. Two other patients whose deaths were linked to CQ were less fortunate. Barry's close call left him angry, feeling that he had been conned by

Delaney. Barry was not one to forgive readily being conned: his intellectual pride would not allow that. He began to refer to Delaney as Bhagwan, after Bhagwan Shree Rajnesh, a Hindu cult leader notorious for misleading, shagging, and fleecing gullible American youth. Steven, Dave, and a number of others also started to refer to Delaney as Bhagwan. Our skepticism infected members of the press leading to detrimental consequences for Delaney, as well as for the FDA which, out of political expediency, had turned a blind eye to Delaney's violations of their rules on the safety and legality of the underground drugs he was promoting.

Skeptics like my friends rested their hopes on properly tested and manufactured drugs developed by legitimate pharmaceutical companies and formally approved by FDA. Approval was essential, otherwise insurers would not reimburse and only a privileged few would benefit. Notwithstanding, these skeptics were attracted to passive immunotherapy, or PATH as we called it, because it made sense to them scientifically, and had no toxic side effects. PATH transferred HIV antibodies from still healthy patients to advanced patients who, because HIV attacks the immune system itself, had lost their ability to produce sufficient antibodies to keep the virus in check. It appeared to give extra time to the few patients who were able to try it. Abbott Labs experimented with a version they called Hivid, though they never developed it commercially. Otherwise there were only small trials run by individual physicians.

(Dave Olson as skeleton tied in red tape at PATH demo.)

I spent from late 1988 into 1991 heavily involved in community efforts to make PATH available. I trusted Steven, Dave, Jesse, and Barry's judgment that it held promise for extending their lives. Also, I had begun to work on PATH with Dr. Marcus Conant and his office manager Joe Robinson. Conant was San Francisco's best known AIDS clinician, a role detailed in Randy Shilts widely read chronicle of the early epidemic, *And the Band Played On*. Conant believed that PATH could help patients stay alive until better drugs were available. (Conant, was privately critical of Delaney and Compound Q, and worried about the safety of underground AIDS drugs.) 7

After a small demonstration in San Francisco, an audacious ACT UP member spray painted in huge letters "PATH NOW!" across the pavement of Castro St. at its intersection with Market St. The *San Francisco Examiner* ran a photo of his graffiti in a front page story on PATH. Thus motivated, the California regulatory authorities in Sacramento set up a meeting with us that Dave and Steve attended. Afterwards, the regulators were quick to meet our requests. Successful in overcoming the California regulatory impediments to implementing PATH, we congratulated ourselves prematurely.

Passive immunotherapy could not be patented, so little money was to be made. The medical establishment had scant interest in a brief and unprofitable stay of execution. But the patients were desperate, as were the friends that cared about them. Consequently, many of us put much time and energy into PATH. In the end its only lasting value, aside from comradery in struggle, was to teach us a crucial lesson: ***treatments that fail to offer significant profits for the drug companies and the healthcare industry will not be developed***.

Writing about our futile struggle to implement passive immunotherapy fills me with sadness as I recall the faces and voices of the many desperate young men in the PATH group who struggled in vain to secure a few more months of life. Most of them were, smart, attractive, educated, guys with promising careers, and everything going for them; their futures looked bright, until suddenly it all went dark. Except for Barry Freehill, none of them lived to benefit from the protease based cocktails. Perhaps there were 30 to 40 people seriously involved in the group over time. All the patients were advanced cases, desperate for more time. It was terrible to watch those bright, talented, kind, beautiful young men wilt and die, sometimes slowly, but often in only a few months or weeks. You were laughing, planning, and sharing ideas with them one week; a month later you were attending their memorial service.

Dying and death was everywhere you turned in the San Francisco gay community during those years. The sadness of the survivors was palpable. Working on my book *The Unfolding God of Milton and Jung* at that time, a grand passage in *Paradise Lost* seemed to capture the ambiance of desperation in that plague ravaged world:

> *The dismal situation waste and wild,*
> *A dungeon horrible, on all sides round*
> *As one great furnace flamed, yet from those flames*
> *No light, but rather darkness visible*
> *Served only to discover sights of woe,*
> *Regions of sorrow, doleful shades, where peace*
> *And rest can never dwell, hope never comes*
> *That comes to all; but torture without end. Book I, 60-67*

Although Tony Kushner's *Angels in America* presents San Francisco as the image of heaven, by the AIDS ravaged 90s the paradise of new found freedom that was San Francisco in the 1970s had turned into the other place. During those years, denial was often the only way to retain sanity in the dismal dungeon of anguished hopelessness where people with AIDS and those who cared for them were confined. Death has a thousand doors. For those whose door was AIDS, denial offered a thousand byways to reach that door. The story of all our lives then was about each person's preferred byways, and our denials du jour. I did not think myself in denial, I felt I was a realist and so were most of my closer friends. Not until I almost died from an extreme bout of Crohn's disease in 2009, and then again from a heart attack on an airplane flying to the 2012 AIDS conference in Washington DC, did I realize that every person lives in denial of death until they confront the grim reaper personally. It was a psychological truth whose profound significance Carl Jung himself appreciated only after his first heart attack. Although I understood intellectually that my friends would die, I never fully accepted it emotionally before their deaths and sometimes not until long after.

And so we all resist recognition of inevitable death, the deaths of those we love and our own, in our individual ways, courageous and cowardly, beautiful and base, and all shades between. Yet denial had its common patterns and comes in degrees. Many just went on with their lives pretending their disease was a nuisance like a bad cold, or a dangerous but not necessarily deadly condition like high blood pressure. People complained about how the disease was damaging their careers, as if AIDS patients should expect a normal career trajectory. Some stopped working if they could afford it. Many who could not went on welfare to get Medicaid and the drugs and care it provided. Others continued working as long as they were able just to keep busy and avoid thinking about their hard fate. Those who stopped would sometimes take multiple vacations, buy the car or whatever else they always wanted, or spend time visiting the people who mattered most to them. While nearly all knew intellectually that they were going to die, they nonetheless were usually shocked when they heard death's first determined knocking at their door. Few were ready, but who could blame them? The old have time to prepare for death and sometimes do, the young are too busy planning for life and living it.

In retrospect the underground treatments, even credible approaches like PATH, were byways of denial: not outright denial like stubborn refusal to accept the facts of HIV disease, but a way to purchase time or borrow hope. Outright denial did have its many followers, and those who exploited them. Healer-entrepreneur Louise Hay taught thousands of desperate men that their lack of self-love caused their illnesses and, therefore, they had the power to heal themselves. David Groff wrote in *Slate* on Hay's death at age 90 on August 30, 2017:

> She ascribed physical diseases and syndromes to lack of self-love and other psychological causes. You had to take responsibility for your "dis-ease," as Hay dubbed it, because you caused it. And if you dealt with your "dis-ease," you could cure your illness. . . .. To these desperate people Louise Hay offered open if judgmental arms; emotional group encounters known as Hayrides; teddy bears to cuddle; mirrors in which

you could affirm your worth no matter how bad your Kaposi's
sarcoma lesions looked. . .. The people celebrating Hay largely
ignored or brushed past the pernicious side of her
prescription—the place where self-love slides into self-blame.9

Hay left an estate of $118 million, a testament to the desperation of those times and the high price many will pay to enjoy a respite into denial.

Of course everyone buys time all the time, even the young and happy. Denial of death is as universal as death itself. Today I want to buy enough time to finish this and other books I plan. My activist friends hoped to buy enough time for science to discover treatments far better than AZT and the other sorry nukes, and a few lucky ones such as Barry did. For them it was not a vain effort. For others, like myself, the activist struggle gave a sense of purpose and fleeting savors of optimism. Life always feels better anticipating an open future and working toward a goal than trapped in paralytic despair. So these efforts made life more tolerable even if they failed to extend it.

The belief that AIDS would remain incurable made the virus seem an almost supernatural evil. It fed the poisonous notion that AIDS was a judgment of God against wicked sodomites. It thereby emboldened anti-gay demagogues who spread guilt, shame, and stigma making patients' lives harder and more painful. AIDS stigma, the direct effect of anti-gay stigma, rationalized denial of the compassion enjoined by the Golden Rule. Everywhere AIDS struck, denial inhibited charity while fear paralyzed common sense.

Denial infected the political realm thwarting action, misdirecting policy, quelling hope, and instilling terror. Liberal AIDS patient leaders and activists were often in heavy denial about the ability of their community to bring the social and political changes needed to combat AIDS more effectively. They denied it could ever be productive to work with Republicans. Their denial slowed AIDS research and FDA reform by impeding communication and missing opportunities for support. Equally detrimental, they were in denial about the seriousness of the obstacles posed by the Democratic Party's alliance with consumer protectors and FDA itself. This denial fed support for the useless and sometimes dangerous drug underground as our only viable option for speeding access to new drugs. No, they could not, would not take on FDA against the Democrats or work with Republicans who wanted to reform FDA. Their denial was at bottom a deficiency of moral courage, imagination, and simple common sense.

The foot dragging notwithstanding, work with Republicans by only a tiny segment of our community in the end proved critical to speeding access to the lifesaving drug cocktails coming down the pipeline. Another truth lost in denial was that some Democrats would likely have done more to help, had the community been willing to pressure them, or even to ask them. Overall the Republicans weren't monsters and the Democrats weren't fools, despite numerous instances to the contrary in both camps. Yet all but a small fragment of the community was in denial of the political realities. Much of that denial was understandable if counterproductive: we were a pariah group that no politician wanted to be included in, mistakenly or otherwise. Prejudice, discrimination, and ostracism gave rise to destructive fatalism and guilt, sometimes repressed but always there, making people feel accursed and doomed. It drove them to exploitative gurus like Hay, and to panaceas like most of the underground drugs. The sense of being accursed, fed by guilt for being gay, was one of the most destructive manifestations of denial. It indirectly sanctioned a denial of responsibility in society itself that delayed effective public health response to the epidemic thereby increasing the suffering.

America has yet to come to terms with the AIDS epidemic. Our society is left with its own insidious aftermath of denial. Denial is evident in our failure to hold FDA accountable for its delays and problematic actions and inactions wherein it still prioritizes its sclerotic procedures above human life and the right to free choice. Denial is evident in America's continued refusal as a nation to acknowledge the damage done to millions of LGBT people by cruel stigma perpetuated through anachronistic bigotry cloaked as religion. Denial is evident in our stiff-necked refusal to recognize that bigotry and stigma violate and pose a dire threat to the moral foundation of our laws and civilization, the Judeo-Christian ethic itself.

Chapter 7
A City Riddled with Denial

Denial was not confined to patients and their friends, it became an epidemic pervading local society. Most San Franciscans without close ties to the gay community lived in denial dismissing AIDS as someone else's problem, at least until someone close, a son, a familiar neighbor, a fellow worker, became suddenly ill and fell into swift decline. Although AIDS was rarely more than two degrees of separation from anyone, denial and its consort fear made it easier to withhold help and sympathy, to say nothing, or even forget altogether.

While the political elite of San Francisco was usually responsive, sometimes generous, and even compassionate, the financial elite was a different story. In a capitalist society the political elite, like everyone else, is beholden to the financial elite. Because of the power of their money, a callous financial elite can set a tone that hardens and debases an entire society. This happened in San Francisco. By the 1980s the flower children were fading memories, money grubbing was again the vogue. Despite the gay service people who labored to make the lives of the rich pleasant and comfortable while they themselves were sick and dying, with a few notable exceptions like the Levi Strauss Co., the financial establishment remained largely oblivious to the burgeoning HIV epidemic.

To the San Francisco wealthy in the 1980s and 90s, gays were a servant class. Like indentured workers kept for menial labor and sometimes sex, they could be discarded when no longer useful. Today the wealth of the city of San Francisco is on a scale unprecedented in human history. Yet homelessness and dereliction are rampant; vagrants and addicts strew the sidewalks with litter, human feces, and used hypodermic syringes. The rich are annoyed, but too few of them care enough to make a difference.

In an angry depression following the death of yet another close friend, I wrote my own Kramer style Jeremiad for the December 22, 1993 *San Francisco Sentinel*. The San Francisco AIDS Foundation later told me the piece offended many big donors and caused a substantial drop in donations over the next year. They asked me to please consider the consequences if I intended to write anything like that again. Re-reading it, I reflect that the San Francisco wealthy did not like or respect their gay workers and servants. That happens where a scorned minority becomes numerous, and its peculiarities are highly visible: after all, it is the prerogative of the wealthy to be the visible ones--when they want to be visible in the ways they want!

San Francisco has often blazoned paths other cities follow, but since the gold rush it's been a place chiefly about two things: freedom and money. Forget excellence, responsibility, compassion and real class, especially the latter. In the sixties and seventies, the city by the bay was chiefly about its promise of freedom. In the eighties and nineties, it became more and more about just money; though AIDS and gay activists continued to carry the torch of freedom. Today money, far more than freedom or outstanding creativity, defines the city and the entire Bay Area. My December 1993 article, "San Francisco's AIDS Scrooges" prefigures much of what San Francisco has increasingly become, a city of virtue signalers who hide from their biggest problems and deny pressing evils at their doorsteps.

> *Other cities have their AIDS angels, wealthy people who give generously of their time, their money, and themselves. San Francisco's "A-list" is notable only for its apathy. Our rich rely on gay workers to serve them, but dismiss AIDS as someone else's problem. Their rule seems to be AIDS is a gay disease, let them take care of it.*

> *The roster of AIDS angels in New York and Los Angeles is impressive. It includes many who give hundreds of thousands. It includes socially prominent straight women like Joan Tisch, Jane Natanson, Judy Peabody, and Blaine Trump. Not content with giving money, they shoulder the heartbreaking tasks of providing physical and emotional care for people dying of*

AIDS. No one has had to "approach them the right way;" they just saw a need and volunteered.

Instead of angels, San Francisco has a depressing roster of Scrooges. One recently re-furbished her Pacific Heights Palace for $25 million plus, but leaves AIDS to lesser mortals. Another has a private Boeing and multiple mansions maintained by a small army, gays well represented, yet can't be bothered with AIDS. Many have hundreds of millions for themselves, but not one penny for people with AIDS. The fabled Bohemian Club, that bastion of corporate power (immensely rich, steadfastly homophobic) has been a gallery of Scrooges.

I won't name names. In a single night the benefactors of the opera raised millions to upgrade its scenery. But for one major AIDS fundraiser, San Francisco society had to be coaxed with Elizabeth Taylor as a draw. Nobody has bothered to coax them again: Even for Liz, they gave, comparatively, a pittance.

The upper crust of San Francisco depends on gay labor to run its art, fashion, culinary, and décor industries. From hair dressers to florists, chauffeurs, decorators, waiters, handymen, janitors, guards, and secretaries, gays are at the beck and call of wealth. As in New York and Los Angeles, among the myriad gays attending the rich, countless individuals get sick, suffer and die of AIDS.

Nearly 20 percent of the gay male community of San Francisco has died in the AIDS epidemic. Another 20 percent may die during the next decade. San Francisco's per capita AIDS death rate is 100 times the national per capita death rate in the Vietnam war. In the gay community itself the death rate now approaches that of the bubonic plague. Before the end of the decade the percentage of San Francisco gays who perish may surpass the percentage of Jews lost in the Holocaust.

[Comment: Had the FDA succeeded in delaying the cocktails, the percentage of San Francisco gays lost to AIDS would have surpassed the percentage of Jews lost in the Holocaust. JD]

In San Francisco, as in New York and Los Angeles, AIDS has become a holocaust for gays. But San Francisco's privileged elite, like "good Germans," keep their eyes sealed. Open your eyes and you can see the San Francisco model collapsing around you. Funds and volunteers can't meet the demand, despite monumental efforts from the gay and lesbian communities. Worthy AIDS organizations starve while the rate of new infections rises. The ranks of the homeless people with AIDS are swelling.

Liberal, enlightened San Francisco, "Baghdad by the Bay," is a myth. San Francisco has become a citadel of the hard hearted rich. To change, San Francisco's Scrooges need to learn some elementary truths: AIDS is not a gay disease; AIDS is everyone's problem; you can make a difference to someone with AIDS. And finally, callousness is the lowest form of vulgarity---caring is the essence of class.

Why do I resurrect this angry Jeremiad which, I dare say, seems worthy of Larry Kramer himself? Because it shows how it felt to be a gay man living in that era and place. Gay men in San Francisco contended with more than just an implacable killer disease, they contended with pitiless indifference and its underlying contempt as well as with unchecked bias and unpunished discrimination. The tension of that dark time is almost unimaginable today. By the end of 1993, 23 percent of San Francisco gays had died of AIDS, another 12 percent would die before the protease cocktails became widely available, and there was no hope in sight. At the same time, gay people were despised and suffered discrimination that shocks memory when it is not repressed and forgotten, as it usually is in these so much easier times.

There are lessons from that time for future dark eras. The heroism, the nobility, and the crucial sacrifices will come from a minority of people, often a small minority. Too many of those who can get away with it will say, "it's not my problem," or even, "you brought it on, take care of it yourself," until of course it becomes their problem at which time they will usually retreat into deeper denial. Yet there may also arise great heroism, nobility, brilliance, and sacrifice, for these too are part of our ever varying humanity along with intellectual sloth, dishonesty, cruel indifference, and moral cowardice.

We won't know where resolutions to our dilemmas will come from and can't be sure they will ever come. Tragedy is inherent to the human condition as it is to life itself. But we must remember, when relief comes it's often from unexpected places at an unpredicted time brought by unorthodox heroes. We must never give up hope, never stop trying, never cease to work for a better life for ourselves and others. Giving up, we trade the best part of our humanity for the worst.

PART II: Struggles & Conflicts

Chapter 1
The DDC-DDI Petition:
A Fast Lane for AIDS Drugs

In 1990 it became increasingly apparent that the New York activists were too readily satisfied with baby steps and always wanted to handle FDA with kid gloves. Dave Olson complained that the New Yorkers insisted on being the leaders, yet refused to lead. "They suffer a kind of selective dementia that takes over on the subject of FDA causing them to credit all FDA's lies and blinding them to their chicanery. If the New Yorkers can't lead, they should get out of the way of those who can." Dave repeatedly made it clear that the leader he had in mind was me. My answer to Dave's demand for leadership was the San Francisco Citizen Petition of FDA.

The petition called on FDA to expedite a decision on approval of both ddI and ddC so that they could be used in combination with AZT. Beyond that, it laid out the legal basis and medical arguments for accelerated approval, rather than traditional full approval of AIDS drugs. Since the petition all AIDS drugs have been given accelerated approval. Written by Barry Freehill in conjunction with Dr. Donald Abrams and myself, it became one of the most impactful activist initiatives of 1990-91. In retrospect, it appears to be the watershed event of that period.

As a result of our shared opposition to Compound Q, Delaney's methods, and his burgeoning underground drug operation, Barry Freehill replaced Jesse Dobson as my chief activist compatriot. Contrariness was a common trait among gay men in San Francisco then, and still is. Barry Freehill, however, did not otherwise fit the gay stereotypes. An exceptionally bright University of Illinois trained chemical engineer, Barry had a business background and was the son of an executive in a major multinational corporation. Handsome and buff, he could be articulately contrary whenever he chose, but also as easily nice and charming as otherwise. Often he was notably insightful and full of mischievous fun. Barry was struggling with advanced HIV, had lost a lover and many friends to the disease, and was determined to use all his wits, savvy, and contrariness to stay alive. These proved to be prime assets for activism.

(Barry Freehill, Amsterdam 1992)

Barry had made his own underground version of ddC but knew that others needed the safety and efficacy afforded by the legitimate, properly manufactured Roche drug. Dave also wanted the Roche drug, but refused to settle for the underground alternatives. Working with Jim Eigo of New York ACT UP, I initiated the national movement for ddC expanded access in late 1989. It took until May 1991 for FDA, under intense pressure from the community, to allow a small expanded access program that was woefully inadequate to the burgeoning demand for the drug. That demand was spurred and validated by ample data from clinical trials showing that combination therapy, specifically ddC combined with AZT, was more effective and longer lasting than AZT monotherapy.

The petition was a big step beyond what the overly cautious consumer protectionist New York activists were seeking in that it called for accelerated approval of AIDS drugs, rather than just expanded access. Barry researched all the relevant legal backgrounds and documentation about FDA petitions so he could lay out in detail the lawful basis for our requests. Reporter Dave Gilden wrote in the *B.A.R.* Jan. 5, 1991:

> *The petition's importance is that it is an official legal document to which the FDA must respond. Its prestige is heightened by the fact that professional medical groups drew it up. . . AIDS activist Jim Driscoll, another of the petition's individual signatories feels uncomfortable with the whole expanded access process. "With expanded access the drugs are distributed for free and companies are not going to develop treatments if they can't make any money off them," said Driscoll. "They'll just bury them rather than spend $2 million a month on expanded access programs like Bristol Myers is doing. (for DDI).*

At that time Dr. Ellen Cooper, a big favorite of the New Yorkers who almost seemed to conduct a group love affair with her, headed the antivirals division of FDA. The first woman in that position, Cooper of course became an automatic heroine to the politically correct. I became a villain to them by referring to her as the ice queen in one of the newspaper accounts. Not wanting to further antagonize the New Yorkers, I faxed Cooper a copy of the petition prior to filing it. She immediately resigned sparking anguished wails from her Manhattan fan club. The petition demonstrated that she had the power to move AIDS drugs faster, but had failed to use it despite the desperate need.

Because the petition represented a radical shift in activist demands and strategy, as well as leadership, it got wide attention outside the AIDS treatment community, including from staff of Vice President Dan Quayle. In many ways it prefigured the issues in the momentous 1994-95 struggle to compel FDA to grant accelerated approval to the protease based antiretroviral cocktails. Since *New York Times* and other major papers covered it in scrupulous detail, it created a sensation in national AIDS treatment activism. Here are excerpts from the front page Dec 21, 1990 *Times* account by science reporter Gina Kolata:

> *Using a legal tool previously employed to drive dangerous drugs off the market, doctors and advocates for people with AIDS are petitioning the Federal Government to put two new AIDS drugs on the market.*
>
> *About 200 of them have signed a citizen petition, a tactic that consumer advocates have used for years to prod the Food and Drug Administration to regulate drugs more stringently. But this petition is asking instead for quick review for two experimental drugs, dideoxyinosine, or ddI, and dideoxycytosine, or ddC.*
>
> *It is believed to be the first citizen petition to call for the agency to move quickly to approve drugs. The petition is to be submitted to the F.D.A. today, if the group reaches agreement on its final draft, or just after Christmas otherwise. If the F.D.A. decides not to comply with the petition, the petitioners can sue the agency.*
>
> *The idea for submitting the petition came from Dr. Sidney Wolfe, the director of Public Citizen, a consumer advocacy group, who has spent years petitioning the F.D.A. to remove various drugs and devices from the market or to regulate them more closely.*
>
> *Although the advocates for people with AIDS were surprised to get help from Dr. Wolfe, who they thought would oppose speeding up drug approvals, he said that he has always believed in using the F.D.A's own rules to force the agency to act in the best interests of patients. The petition "is exciting to me," he said. "I hope the F.D.A. takes it seriously."*
>
> *The petition demands that the agency ask drug companies that are testing DDI and DDC to send in their data for review and apply for marketing approval. It also demands that the F.D.A. expedite its review of the data and use laboratory test results, like increasing numbers of immune system cells, as evidence that the drugs are working, rather than requiring extensive, long-term evidence of patient survival.*

The petition notes that the agency's own regulations say that drugs for life-threatening diseases like AIDS are not bound by rules as strict as are drugs for diseases that are not life-threatening.

The collaboration with Public Citizen began when James Driscoll, an advocate for people with AIDS who lives in San Francisco, suggested that he and other advocates meet with the Dr. Wolfe.

"He's the key consumer protectionist and I felt we should touch base with him to make him understand our point of view," Mr. Driscoll said. He said other advocates were initially opposed to the idea and some had even wanted to occupy Dr. Wolfe's offices to protest what they said were his policies of trying to keep promising drugs off the market.

But when Mr. Driscoll and seven others met with Dr. Wolfe early this month, "We discovered that he understood our point of view better than we had thought," Mr. Driscoll said. Dr. Wolfe then proposed that the group file a petition.

To gain support for the petition, the advocates enlisted Dr. Donald Abrams, an AIDS researcher at the University of California in San Francisco and a member of an advisory committee to the F.D.A.

Dr. Abrams in turn presented the petition to the Community Consortium, a group of 180 doctors who treat AIDS patients in the San Francisco area. The group voted to sign on.

Dr. Abrams said that he and others who treat people with AIDS have become increasingly distressed by the dearth of drugs on the market. The FDA has approved only one anti-AIDS drug, azidothymidine, or AZT; many patients either cannot tolerate it or are no longer responding to it.

Barry Freehill, a member of Act-Up, or the AIDS Coalition to Unleash Power, in San Francisco who scrutinized the F.D.A.'s regulations and wrote the citizen petition, said he and other advocates were concerned that data being gathered in trials of the two drugs will not provide definitive answers any time soon. The studies, which compare the drugs to AZT, were designed to see whether people with AIDS live longer if they take DDI or ddC than if they take AZT. But it could take years to show this, Mr. Freehill said.

He and other advocates as well as many researchers say the F.D.A. instead should consider clinical markers like an increase in immune system cells and declines in viral proteins as evidence that disease progression is being slowed.

These could give a faster demonstration of efficacy because they do not require investigators to wait for patients to sicken and die. But some researchers, and the F.D.A., say they are not yet convinced that these clinical markers are reliable enough.

In retrospect, the citizen petition was a brilliant strategy which I could never have been able to implement without the ideas and research of Barry Freehill and the wholehearted support of the Bay Area AIDS doctors. While Barry manned the pen that wrote the petition, I wielded the whip that got it done and Barry often felt its sting. I put intense pressure on him and our community supporters, including doctors like Donald Abrams, a local head researcher in HIV and, what was crucial, a member of the FDA Antiviral Drug Advisory Panel, to get it filed before Christmas 1990. If it dragged on into 1991, the impending hostilities of the Gulf War in Iraq, would take up all the media air relegating the petition to back pages of the papers where FDA could more easily dismiss and ultimately ignore it.

The petitioners were the Community Consortium of healthcare providers who treated patients with HIV disease and the Bay Area Physicians for Human Rights (BAPHR). The Consortium had more than 180 physicians, nurses etc., and BAPHR was an organization dedicated to quality health care for lesbians and gay men. Both organizations were influential and respected. The petition demonstrated that FDA had the legal power and regulatory mechanisms to give AIDS drugs accelerated approval and that the agency was not required to wait for data for full approval. Among the petition's other crucial points were: the need for alternatives to AZT, the inadequacy of expanded access programs, the manageability of ddI & ddC toxicities and the drugs' therapeutic benefits, the proven value of combination therapies, and the lack of any clear FDA criteria for approving antiretroviral drugs. The most significant of these was a consideration Freehill developed with a scientific clarity and precision seldom seen in activist writings. Let me quote from the conclusion of the petition:

> *The criteria for approval should recognize the need for medical risk benefit judgement and permit broad flexibility in their application. The criteria must satisfy the statutory standards for approval which require that the therapeutic claims for the drug be supported by reliable pharmacological and therapeutic studies. Proof of prolongation of life is NOT a statutory requisite for approval. Furthermore, it is neither necessary nor expedient to require evidence that the new drug is superior or even equivalent to other approved drugs.*
>
> *Finally, we strongly urge that the criteria for approval incorporate the use of clinical data demonstrating therapeutic effect on appropriate surrogate endpoints (e.g. CD4 cell counts) as well as improved quality of life.*

Thanks to the development of PCR technology by Hoffman La Roche, shortly after the petition doctors were able to measure patient viral load, a more reliable indicator of treatment efficacy than CD4 count. PCR could directly measure the disease and its progression, as Barry and I along with top researchers, like Drs. David Ho and Tom Merrigan, quickly grasped. Relying on viral markers, rather than on improved longevity, became the key to earlier approval of HIV drugs. The argument about the markers dragged on for years until 1995-96 when the first protease drugs were approved on the basis of viral markers.

But the seeds for that victory were first planted by Barry Freehill in our 1990 petition of FDA. The petition had set a template for HIV drug approval policies that could save countless lives, and speed the day when AIDS was no longer a death sentence. Moreover, it had given FDA the legal and medical grounds for doing what was morally right and medically necessary. The rest was up to FDA, and to the massive forces that had to be marshalled to overcome FDA resistance to doing the right things. That proved to be an extremely formidable task requiring a long painful struggle whose success hung in the balance until late 1995.

It was my idea to approach Sydney Wolfe, and a very ingenious idea it proved to be. The pharmaceutical industry regarded Wolfe as the

Dark Prince of Consumer Protectors, the King being Ralph Nader himself, whom I met years later and also liked. The industry people were astounded when I persuaded Wolfe to cooperate with the activists to speed approval of HIV drugs. Wolfe's support was essential to wide publicity and impact. Without it the *New York Times* would not have been likely to run the article on their front page. FDA, along with the rest of Washington, would have ignored the petition. To his credit, Wolfe not only supported the idea of a petition, he suggested it!

All of the key SF activists, including Martin Delaney, and all the key AIDS doctors, supported the petition. It was clearly a San Francisco initiative, few in New York were involved in any way. The New York activists seemed shocked; they assumed, and assured FDA, that they, and they alone, were the bona fide thought leaders of US and global AIDS activism. The other activists were just a bunch of no count bumbling bumpkins. Locals, even the San Franciscans, should wait to get their cues from the geniuses in Manhattan.

The only outside activist they would listen to was Martin Delaney, and there his road was usually rocky. Delaney wanted to maintain working relations with the New Yorkers, and especially with FDA where the New Yorkers had pivotal ties. But the New Yorkers castigated the SF activists for initiating demonstrations against FDA, for criticizing their beloved Ellen Cooper, and me in particular, for disparaging FDA in my op eds in the *Wall Street Journal*, hated for its ties to Republicans. We were not to take the lead, that was their prerogative. They were especially dismayed and chagrined because of the petition's support from the medical profession, Syd Wolfe, and, implicitly, the *New York Times*.

From the petition on, San Francisco became as influential a center of AIDS treatment activism as New York, and a more important wellspring of activist thought and innovation. An unsung, and unintentional, hero on the petition was Nancy Pelosi. By meeting and working with us on FDA and related matters she gave us recognition and status. Like Pelosi, Republican Congressman Tom Campbell of Palo Alto soon gave us similar support further raising our profile. At that time actual leadership within the gay community was insufficient to secure recognition outside of it. To get recognition as a gay leader one needed to be legitimatized by straight leaders willing to meet and work openly with you. The New Yorkers, spurned by their politicos, especially their obdurate ideologue Congressman Ted Weiss, were ever left out in the cold. Hence, they desperately need legitimatization from FDA officials, but that came at the cost of condoning FDA delays.

Ironically, Wolfe and the liberal media embraced more whole heartedly than the NY activists the medical and emotional concerns voiced by Donald Abrams:

> *"We have nothing for this ever-expanding group of people,"*
> *Dr. Abrams said. "We are in the same quandary we were in*
> *before AZT became available." It has been five years since AZT*
> *was approved, and since nothing else has been marketed,*
> *people get a little frustrated," he said.*

The San Francisco AIDS patients were more than a little frustrated, they were desperate. Dealing with so many distraught, heart rending patients profoundly affected SF AIDS doctors like Abrams. They acquired the urgency of the activists and suffered through the despair of their doomed patients. Many were also gay. These AIDS doctors gained an importance doctors rarely have in any community. The saying "in the country of the blind the one eyed man is king" seems apropos: *in the country of the sick the doctor is king.* The AIDS activists also gained a degree of community support few activists for subsequent causes have enjoyed—understandable considering the merit of our cause and the commitment of the activists compared to that of many of today's problematic causes, and their too often transparently self-serving proponents.

But let me return to ddI and ddC. As a result of pressure from the national AIDS community led by New York activist Jim Eigo, FDA had approved didanosine, or ddI, for "expanded access" in September 1989. The term "expanded access" was a cruel misnomer as only 2500 people were allowed to enroll in the program, a tragically inadequate number. ddI was not formally approved until October 1991. However, like the other nucleoside analogue drugs, AZT, D4T, and ddC, ddI was toxic to many patients, among them Dave Olson and Barry Freehill. Such patients frequently developed pancreatitis, neuropathy, and other grave debilities.

Needing something new, they turned to ddC. Both the FDA and the drug's sponsor, Hoffmann-La Roche had serious concerns about ddC's tendency to cause severe neuropathy. But patients were running out of options and those who were my friends and allies were unwilling to rely on underground ddC, except for John Dolan who did so reluctantly out of sheer desperation.

ddC was not finally approved by FDA until June 22 1992. A year earlier an obstinate FDA had caved to unrelenting pressure from dogged San Francisco activists to allow a limited ddC expanded access program. Not even this small program would have been launched but for a shocking, bloody demonstration in the plaza before the Federal Building where Nancy Pelosi had her local office. Here is a newspaper account of the events up to and surrounding that demonstration:

> *Jim Driscoll, a San Francisco Shakespeare scholar turned-AIDS organizer had two friends dying of the disease who couldn't tolerate the side effects of AZT. As Driscoll saw it, ddC was the only hope for his friends and for the many others in the same condition. That opinion was confirmed in extensive private conversations with outside scientists testing the drug. With ACT UP backing, Driscoll cajoled and threatened Hoffmann-LaRoche into having a meeting with him and other San Francisco activists. At the session, held in February the company agreed to explore the idea of releasing ddC to patients outside the official tests. . . . But then when Driscoll thought the company was moving too slowly, he organized a demonstration at the San Francisco Federal building. Photographs including a particularly bloody police arrest were sent to corporate headquarters. Also sent were calmer appeals such as a supporting letter from a mainstream religious group, and a newspaper story, arranged by Driscoll, in which one of his friends made a plea for ddC. (San Jose Mercury, June 18,1991)*

The activists' victory from this demonstration is an instance of one picture being worth a thousand words.

At the time Barry and I were still active in ACT UP Golden Gate which had organized several demonstrations against FDA where patient-activists were arrested. James Olson, the patient in my photograph, played a crucial role in forcing FDA to make ddC available. Before the demonstration Olson approached me at an ACT UP GG meeting. His doctors told him he had only a few months to live. He asked me if I really believed that ddC could help anyone. He wasn't looking for himself because he had severe neuropathy already and couldn't risk worsening it. He just wanted to know if he could help others. "Yes," I told him, "some patients would be helped by ddC, not that many, but some." He looked me in the eyes declaring, "Then I'm going to demonstrate, I'd like to help the others." At the demonstration poorly trained security police got out of hand attacking some demonstrators, an emaciated James Olson chief among them. I photographed the cops beating on Olson with their sticks, Olson's head on the pavement pinned against his placard blasting FDA and DDC's sponsor, Hoffman La Roche.

(James Olson, left on ground, with police clubbing him. The more graphic photograph sent to FDA and Roche has been lost.)

Early the next morning, I faxed the pictures to Roche and FDA Commissioner David Kessler, warning them that unless they acted immediately, the pictures would be in the papers tomorrow. They called back that afternoon to promise a pilot expanded access for ddC. Although it was too small, it enabled some patients to benefit from DDC without risking the dangers of the faulty underground drug.

Barry Freehill's work on the ddC/ddI petition became a critical factor in the long push to compel FDA to grant AIDS accelerated approval on the basis of surrogate markers, particularly viral load. For his brilliant work he was never formally recognized or thanked by FDA whose behinds he helped rescue. Evidently, the FDA hard-liners were too busy extolling the New Yorkers nonpareil intellectual brilliance while bussing their fragrant behinds. The New Yorkers had to be smarter than Barry, after all one of them was a graduate of Harvard!

Chapter 2
The Real AIDS Drug
Underground and its FDA Enablers

Of all forms of government, those administered by bureaus are the least satisfactory to an enlightened people . . . Being irresponsible they become autocratic, and being autocratic they resist all development. Unless bureaucracy is constantly resisted it overwhelms democracy. It is the one element in our institutions that sets up the pretense of having authority over everybody while being accountable to nobody.

Calvin Coolidge, 1926
speech at William and Mary College

In November 1991 *Beta*, the treatment publication of the San Francisco AIDS Foundation, ran my opinion piece titled, "Why We Need Congressional Legislation to Speed Approval for AIDS Drugs." I had written similar pieces in several different papers, including the daily San Francisco papers and the *Wall Street Journal*, but the *Beta* article was the last and most thorough of them. It reviews the arguments for legislation to expedite AIDS drug approval and stresses the unfairness to the disadvantaged of dilatory FDA practices. Legislation was necessary to force the FDA to do what our petition would show they had the power to do yet refused to do. Let me quote selectively:

> *The current regulatory impasse of ddC/AZT combination therapy underlines the need to reform the efficacy standard. Margaret Fischl and Douglas Richman's study of different regimens of ddC/AZT combination therapy (ACTG 106) has given weighty evidence of its superiority to monotherapy, but the weight of evidence is not enough for FDA which demands the proof of degree of efficacy that only a lengthy large-scale study can give. ACTG 155, a combination study with more than 1000 patients, will probably offer exact proof of efficacy, but only after its completion in late 1992.*

Desperate patients not lucky enough to get into ACTG 155 have turned to underground sources for ddC to use in combination with AZT. FDA has quietly sanctioned an illegal and unmonitored black market for ddC. The FDA's grip on the underground ddC lifeline gives it the power to curb community demands for regulatory reform. Equally detrimental, the ddC underground protects FDA from activist protest at the cost of discrimination against disadvantaged patients. Since no insurance covers underground drugs, disadvantaged patients cannot afford them. And the knowhow to access the underground is rarely found outside the privileged elite of well-educated gay white males. Thus, the poor, unexperienced people of color, and those living outside major cities must bear the brunt of FDA's rigid consumer protectionist efficacy standard. . ..

The shortcomings of our present Band-Aid system of "expanded access" . . .. have failed to provide early or wide access to breakthrough treatments. Because it is easily accessed only by well-educated, affluent patients, "expanded access" like the elitist drug underground discriminates . . .. Responsible public policy demands faster approval based on the probability that a drug will prove efficacious. Furthermore, AIDS patients have a right to attempt to save or improve their lives with promising new treatments whose efficacy is not fully tested. . .

In retrospect my position then was on the mark. Its pertinence becomes apparent as the story of the underground unfolds. If anything, the moral and scientific case against FDA was stronger than what I laid out in *Beta.* Earlier it was made stronger legally and politically when we filed the citizens petition. Yet at the time my allies and I were subject to fierce castigation that extended to threats of violence for daring to call for FDA reform legislation.

To assess morally and legally FDA's delays in approving AIDS drugs, one must keep in mind that the law does not instruct FDA to delay approval of drugs for reasons other than safety. The degree of efficacy was up to the discretion of FDA who had never published their standards, even though they were required to do so. It was FDA, not Congress, that made the efficacy requirements increasingly strict. On efficacy Congress gave

FDA an inch and, like a true bureaucracy, it took a mile. Pulling off the market dangerous and illegal knockoff pharmaceuticals should not be a decision based on agency politics. FDA imperiled countless AIDS patients by making their enforcement on underground drugs discretionary, and baldly political. Discretionary meant discriminatory because selective non-enforcement denied all patients the protection they were entitled to under the law, and it impacted disadvantaged patients more severely than others.

The AIDS drug underground was the most sensational and misunderstood facet of AIDS activism in the early 1990s. Today the FDA and its activist allies would very much like the underground to be forgotten. But in its heyday these same activists painted the underground as heroic, its leaders romantic Robin Hood figures appropriating intellectual property from greedy drug companies to give lifesaving medicines to dying patients. Those of us who saw the underground up close and bore the brunt of its ruthless tactics knew otherwise. Doctors on the front lines were privately reporting serious safety issues with the knockoff drugs. With ddC in particular, patients experienced a shocking difference in safety and efficacy between legitimate ddC and its underground knockoff. Facing recriminations from the underground drug lords, few doctors dared admit publicly that the underground was an emperor with no clothes.

The most important lesson of the AIDS drug underground is usually missed: ***The story of the underground shows how the FDA places protection of its turf, policies, practices, and the source of its power, the sacrosanct efficacy standard, above protecting public health and patient lives***. It reveals an FDA ready to play fast and loose with selective enforcement for its own political ends. The public may think of FDA as a benign bureaucracy compared to the DEA, CIA, IRS, and FBI, but in the 1990s it was a loose cannon. Make no mistake, FDA was and still is, in power, culture, and lack of transparency, a full-fledged denizen of what conservatives now call the deep state.

From its beginning, the AIDS drug underground that produced illegal knockoffs of patented drugs existed with the full knowledge of the FDA, and, what will surprise many today, with its clear acquiescence. The major underground players, Martin Delaney, Jim Corti, and their New York allies, had colluded with FDA Commissioner David Kessler in an illicit arrangement whose purpose was to reduce community pressure on FDA to give accelerated approval to ddC.

Although the AIDS drug underground was complex and chaotic, it was largely controlled by the players who colluded with and were sanctioned and protected by FDA. Nonetheless, there were numerous outliers, libertarian underground players who did not cooperate with FDA and wanted legitimate AIDS drugs expeditiously approved. The outliers had reason to worry: they could be targeted by FDA selective enforcement, and they were harassed by FDA's covertly sanctioned players. Ron Woodruff, the most famous of the outliers, was hit by FDA raids and legal actions several times, as is dramatized in the popular film *Dallas Buyer's Club*. The New York and SF operations were spared such measures. Besides Woodruff, there were a number of other local operators. Jack Girard of Spokane Washington became the best known thanks to *San Francisco Examiner* reporter Lisa Krieger.

The film won an array of awards including three Oscars. It made Ron Woodruff a folk hero, a distinction he deserved, more or less. Woodruff, however, was essentially a local actor in a much larger scene dominated by a budding syndicate controlled by Martin Delaney, Jim Corti, and the New Yorkers and covertly sanctioned through collusion with the FDA hierarchy. The film overlooked the national scene, although that scene had far more important consequences for AIDS drug development, the AIDS patient community, and the course of the epidemic.

Although Delaney and Corti were the kingpins of the underground, they had close operational ties with the New York Buyer's Club headed by Derek Hodel of New York ACT UP. Delaney and Corti worked in tandem but never acknowledged a formal business tie. Jonathan Kwitney's book *Acceptable Risks* offers a glowing account, authorized by Delaney and Corti, of the pair's "heroic" efforts to set up a drug smuggling and manufacturing operation that allowed their AIDS patient customers to circumvent the law and pharmaceutical patents to obtain "lifesaving" knockoff drugs.*10*

FDA escapes the brunt of criticism in Kwitney's book which blames those perennial scapegoats the "greedy" drug companies, especially Hoffmann-La Roche, along with researchers who fell out of favor with Delaney. The public image Delaney liked to convey was captured in a December 5, 1989 piece in *The Advocate* titled: *Martin Delaney: The Man Who Bucked the FDA.* However, the image Kwitney's book presents is more in accord with critics like Jack Girard who saw Delaney as: *"The Man Who Colluded with FDA."*

It is dubious indeed that the knockoff drugs saved many or even any lives, but they likely had a placebo effect on some and may well have had more than that on the bank accounts of their hawkers. Corti and Delaney enjoyed boasting about their adventures "saving lives," but denied they profited financially. I was never chiefly interested in whether there was significant financial profit in their illicit trade. My focus was on their collusion with FDA and on the knockoffs public health dangers. Barry Freehill stressed the similarities between the Delaney-Corti-New York operation, tacitly green lighted by FDA, and familiar quasi-criminal syndicates. In meetings with FDA and the drug companies Barry and I laid out our concerns about conflicts of interest in their back room dealings with Delaney and the underground. In a powerful, no holds barred November 5, 1992 letter to the editor published in *QW* M*agazine* Barry summarized our concerns:

> *Martin Delaney seems to personify most of what is rotten in professional AIDS activism. Delaney publicly acknowledges accepting drug company largess through Project Inform . . . He maintains that drug company money does not affect which treatments he recommends or pushes the FDA to approve, or which trials he lobbies NIH to subsidize, or which drugs he decides are over-priced. . .. His pet nostrums of the 80s [were] Ribavirin, dextran sulfate and compound Q. For years Delaney touted these treatments, which have proven to be worthless and highly toxic, while his associate Jim Corti imported and sold them in large quantities.*
>
> *Behind closed doors Delaney and cohorts meet with Burroughs Wellcome, Bristol Myers, Roche and other pharmaceutical dreadnoughts. Then they meet again behind closed doors with*

NIH officials who decide which drugs will be tested at government expense, and he moves on to meet with FDA officials who decide which drug will be approved, and which delayed. Were that not enough he also works secretly with underground drug lords whose business booms whenever FDA stalls an AIDS drug. Who knows what bargains Delaney cuts, whose interests he really serves or what's in it for him?

Being on the Board of Directors of Healing Alternatives, the local San Francisco buyer's club, gave Barry standing with the underground. Several individuals who had direct knowledge of the underground as a business confided in him: among them were Jack Girard, John James, Steven Fowkes, David Blanco, and Paul Sergios as well as other insider sources who preferred to keep a lower profile.*11* These sources reported that Jim Corti entered the nascent bootleg ddC trade in 1990 with purchases from John Morgenthaler of bottled ddC tablets for $19.50/ bottle. Soon the deal was altered so that Corti bought bulk ddC from Morgenthaler for $10.00 / gram and paid $4.60 to have it bottled giving him a finished product that cost $14.60/bottle. David Blanco, a figure in the Southern California alternative therapies scene, reported that Sherman Patel, who had run Corti's "secret pharmaceutical lab," showed him invoices revealing that he prepared Corti's bulk ddC for $4.60/ bottle. Blanco was unable to determine how Corti measured dosages for his ddC, dosage being the crucial safety factor. Through July 1991, Corti's wholesale price to the buyer's clubs averaged $45.00/ bottle giving him a 300% markup. In July Corti found a cheaper bulk source dropping his product cost to $10.60/bottle and raising his markup to 400%. All of this was known to FDA's bureaucracy, and more, much more.

In the summer of 1991, while Barry was still a director of the Healing Alternatives Buyer's Club in San Francisco, the club's sales reached 800 bottles /month. When another director, Bart Casimer, learned that the club had accumulated over $100,000 in ddC profits, he asked the club to undertake minority outreach. Bart was concerned because too few African-American patients could afford or knew about the underground product. He resigned in protest when the club refused.

According to sources in the Dallas Buyer's club, it sold over 1100 bottles/ month at a somewhat higher price and profit margin than Healing

Alternatives. Jack Girard, Steven Fowkes, and John Morgenthaler estimated that in 1991 alone Corti sold over 65,000 bottles at a profit of more than $1,700,000. We do not know how accurate this is since Corti's operation was never audited. We can be sure, however, that people with AIDS paid for Corti's often defective, mismeasured ddC out of their own pockets. The main conference room at FDA headquarters had a picture of a Victorian woman handing her last dollar to a snake oil salesman. A picture of an emaciated AIDS patient emptying his wallet to Jim Corti would have been a more up to date reminder of the moral challenges facing FDA.

My friends with AIDS were afraid to use drugs whose sources and manufacturing conditions were unknown, and they were opposed to subsidizing an illegal operation. In fact, Dave Olson said he'd die before he'd take underground drugs, but Dave was given to overstatement on the need for drug quality controls since he had worked in that area for a drug company. The focus of his anger, however, was more on the FDA's tolerance of the underground than on the underground itself. He was outraged that FDA would collude with Delaney, Corti and the New Yorkers to relieve community pressure on the agency to approve new drugs. It further deepened his conviction that FDA was a loose cannon agency. That view, implicit in Kwitney's book, was confirmed in our meetings with FDA officials and confidential discussions with researchers and industry. To Dave and many other thinking community people, FDA's strategy evidenced a criminal disregard for people with AIDS, rooted in their officials' ignorance of and conscious and unconscious disregard for gay people. Only one of 31 FDA regional AIDS coordinators was gay and open gays were non-existent in FDA's upper hierarchy. The gap between FDA and the AIDS patients was vast and unbridged. As Dave put it: "People with AIDS suffer under regulation without representation."

In the eighteen months before ddC's approval we met often with FDA. In retrospect it seems we were duped by FDA into believing that meetings alone represented progress, a trap for all activists dealing with government bureaucrats. Hindsight shows we accomplished little, though the meetings made us feel important, and that sop was all FDA was willing to give us. The meetings were run on the community side by Barry and myself, others who attended regularly were Hank Wilson, Bill Thorn, Steve Fowkes, and John Dolan. Some of the meetings were in San Francisco, others in Rockville, Md., at the FDA Parklawn building, AKA "The Castle," as in Franz Kafka's novel. The stances of the West Coast groups toward FDA were always aggressive, especially so on underground drugs.

In 1990 Jack Girard and the underground outliers first began to impact San Francisco activism by giving its gay activists information on Corti's operation. Early in 1991 Girard called me after reading about my efforts to secure faster FDA drug approval. Barry and Girard had a common interest in the chemistry of drug production, and Barry and I soon developed a working relationship with him. Girard was a rogue operator with a personality to match. He and his wife Cindy had an infant daughter, Jackie. Both Jack and Cindy had full blown AIDS, Jackie was negative. They lived on a farm forty miles from Spokane Washington and worked with distribution and social networks outside Corti's purview. These included Steven Fowkes, David Blanko, Troy Dickerson, Saul Kent, Bill Faloon, Paul Sergios, Michael Onstott, and Jarrow Rogovin along with a number of physicians who stressed nutritional approaches. The group had some gay people, but was dominantly heterosexual-bisexual, as were Girard and Ron Woodruff.

They regarded FDA as a power-hungry, loose cannon agency that casually disregarded its own rules and US law. FDA got away with their infractions because they enjoyed political cover from consumer protectors in Congress, and an uncritical media. Moreover, it was costly to challenge them in court. When they were challenged, as with the supplement Coenzyme-Q10, FDA usually lost. I was a witness for Saul Kent's case in Florida. Kent's lawyers contended that FDA enforced its rules on a selective basis against their critics, like Kent, while they turned a blind eye to the illegal activities of their friends like Delaney, Corti and the New Yorkers. FDA lost that case.

The outsiders deeply distrusted Delaney, Corti, and their east coast allies. Their close relations with FDA made them seem like quislings. They believed that Corti's underground drug products were defective, and with reason since they knew the problematic conditions of their manufacture. They regularly accused Corti and his partners of promoting useless nostrums for profit. They dismissed Delaney's Compound Q promotion as a dangerous scam that gained publicity for Delaney at the cost of serious risks for vulnerable AIDS patients.

Most of the outsiders were involved in selling, promoting, or producing supplements prior to the prevalence of HIV disease. Supplements had long been popular in the gay-AIDS community. That popularity made them gateway medicaments to alternative AIDS therapies. Many in the community already shared the outsider's libertarian bent along with their distrust of the Delaney-Corti underground and especially FDA with its well-known attempts to restrict supplements. Anyone who made covert deals with FDA was suspect in the eyes of the outsiders. They were libertarians ever watchful for government overreach. They found ready allies in the gay community where suspicion of government ran high during the AIDS epidemic. That suspicion was understandable given the government's history of open discrimination against gays and our pariah status in American society. A conspiracy theory that AIDS was a "Tuskegee experiment," a CIA developed genocide weapon for gay people, gained wide currency in those years.

The broader AIDS community wanted no part of knockoff versions of pharmaceutical drugs, they wanted FDA to approve the drugs expeditiously and leave their nutraceuticals alone. By the summer of 1991 the conflict over the underground had flared into a virtual civil war in the activist community. A lengthy front page story by *San Francisco Examiner* AIDS reporter Lisa Krieger on Sunday Sept 8, 1991 explained how things had come to a boil, at the same time as the article itself added fuel to the fire. The Sunday placement was significant since the *San Francisco Chronicle* and *Examiner* combined their Sunday editions which went out to more than half a million households in the Bay Area. Everybody saw it, everyone was talking about it. Krieger titled it, "Top AIDS Activist: Leader or Tyrant?" with the subhead, "Martin Delaney won't apologize for 'military tactics:'

> *Martin Delaney, San Francisco's most powerful figure in AIDS activism, was angry when he addressed a meeting of gay activists two weeks ago.*

"Somebody has complained to the FDA that people are exploiting the community by overcharging for the underground experimental AIDS drug DDC. If I should get my hands on the people who went and squealed to FDA about that, I'd have to beat their face in." Most of the audience laughed. But at least a few were uneasy. It was in their minds one more example of Delaney's attempts to intimidate.

The primary targets for intimidation were Barry Freehill and myself. In our letter to FDA several weeks after the Krieger expose, we compared the lawless situation that we faced personally, and that FDA had enabled, to the prohibition era:

Just as prohibition spawned racketeers who controlled the supply of liquor and offered political protection from the police, so our unconscionably slow AIDS drug approval system spawned racketeers who controlled the supply of underground drugs and offer political protection from FDA enforcement. Like common racketeers, the AIDS underground resorts to threats and physical intimidation when its business interests are jeopardized.

Delaney tried to inflame his followers with the charge that I was the culprit who "squealed to FDA" about overcharging. My articles, especially those in major newspapers, made me the most visible player in the sizeable cadre of activists and doctors complaining about underground DDC. However, my complaints centered on intimidation and the safety and efficacy of their product, not its price, as Delaney and Corti alleged. Opposed to FDA's allowing the sale of knockoff ddC at any price, I always argued for quick and full approval of ddC and ddI for marketing. Moreover, I knew that FDA lacked authorization to regulate the price of anything, least of all illicit knockoff drugs! However, no one in HHS or the White House, whether under Bush or Clinton, was willing to shoulder the political challenges involved in compelling FDA to abide by either the laws or its own regulations. In short, none were willing to spend political capital to protect or defend openly gay citizens let alone gay AIDS patients.

Contrary to Delaney, Barry Freehill and I did not operate in stealth. We spelled out our positions at public meetings, and in conversations with FDA officials including Commissioner Kessler himself. Here is my third person account, written contemporaneously, of one such meeting in May 1991:

> *Barry Freehill and Jim Driscoll warned Kessler personally that an even larger underground was certain to be established if ddC was not quickly approved. Freehill delivered the warnings publicly in a speech at the February 1991 FDA antivirals meeting at the Holiday Inn in Rockville Md. Though Freehill is not named, an account of his speech is given in <u>Acceptable Risks</u>. Kessler, Carl Peck, Randy Wykoff, and other FDA officials were in the room. At the same event, Driscoll and a small group of activists met with Kessler. He asked about the ddC underground and said that his concern was that "someone might be making a lot of money on an unapproved drug." Driscoll told him that so far it did not look especially profitable, but growth was inevitable and profit potential would increase if FDA failed to approve ddC. Driscoll added that his chief concern was manufacturing standards, whether the underground product was safe and effective.*

There were numerous angry complaints about pricing, though not from me. Jack Girard complained to FDA that Delaney and Corti were profiteering, and possibly Steven Fowkes and Paul Sergios may have complained also. At the time, I thought the price-profit issue a red herring. But I understood all too well why the complaints infuriated Delaney. His rationalization for promoting knockoff AIDS drugs was based on Larry Kramer's stock shibboleth that heartless drug company profiteers were the prime villains of the AIDS epidemic. For Delaney to turn around and profit off the underground drugs would make him the worst kind of fraud and hypocrite. And that is exactly how Girard, Freehill, Sergios, Dave Olson, and other patient advocates viewed Delaney, Corti, and their Manhattan accomplices.

Krieger was sufficiently taken with Girard to travel to Spokane to interview him in person and run a lengthy piece on him replete with photos.*12* Delaney was livid; and, the New Yorkers, who believed that they had been legitimatized by FDA, dismissed Girard and others, not anointed by FDA, as trash. However, activist-patients, like Girard, and their doctors' complaints about the underground drug syndicate had won over enough reporters like Lisa Krieger to create a serious image problem for Delaney and FDA itself. As Krieger had concluded in her Delaney "hit-piece" article a week before:

> *For the past six years of the AIDS epidemic Delaney's word has been gospel. He gave the floundering early AIDS movement direction and leadership, and continues to be the major link to the underground drug market . . .He is one of the few activists with real clout in Washington's inner circles, including Fauci and the US Food and Drug Administration.*
>
> *But Delaney's leadership style, described as dictatorial, now makes him difficult to work with. . .. 'Delaney is becoming less relevant nationwide,' said a prominent East Coast activist, "I can't work with him." Some say power has gone to Delaney's head. "Martin Delaney is to AIDS activism what Jimmy Hoffa was to the labor movement," said one activist.*

Comment: That Hoffa analogy, I recall, was Barry Freehill's brainchild. Like Girard, Freehill believed Delaney was desperate for power and grasping for recognition he had not earned. "Delaney is a legend in his own mind," Freehill often quipped.

> *Some worry that Project Inform has developed a cult like status with Delaney at its helm. "The danger is that you close off other options for activism," Said Jim Driscoll, a Shakespeare scholar who has become an activist. "it's like a dictatorship where you silence all other options."*

The danger of closing off other options for activism was indeed my over-riding concern. The most immediate option Delaney and the New Yorkers were trying to close off was legislative reform of FDA via the bill Rep. Tom Campbell had introduced in Congress earlier that year. And why did they want to close off that option? Because they had already reached an understanding with FDA wherein the agency would tolerate the underground if they relaxed pressure on FDA to speed AIDS drug approval and opposed legislative efforts for FDA reform.

But also because Delaney, the son of one of Chicago Mayor Daley's ward heelers, ruled out options that did not accord with the

Democrat party line or might create problems for its system of alliances, especially the alliances with FDA, rich trial lawyer contributors, and their friends in the consumer protection lobby. Unlike new Democrat and Arkansas country boy Bill Clinton who in 1997 signed an FDA reform bill which Delaney declined to support even at that late date, Delaney was at heart a big city machine Democrat. Jim Foster referred to him as a "yellow dog Democrat." Then as now, San Francisco had more such "yellow dogs" than it has rats, pigeons, and parking meters combined.

Though Lisa Krieger and *Chronicle* reporter Sabin Russell were the press critics who most upset Delaney, they were far from alone. He had alienated, a mild term here, the chief editors of the prestigious *New England Journal of Medicine*, Arnold Relman and Marcia Angell. "Mr. Delaney, you are really irresponsible," (*The Advocate,* "War over Compound Q," reported Relman as saying.) "Everybody wants to see a safe and effective treatment for AIDS, but we don't want to see people using an undocumented, untested drug that could kill."*13* Relman then accused Delaney of selling "black magic" by raising false hopes among AIDS patients. Angell was just as tough, "of most concern for people with AIDS, is Martin Delaney's appalling ignorance of the way science has to be done and evaluated to get effective treatments. This is grandstanding that doesn't do sick people any good whatsoever."

With such eminent critics calling foul, one has to wonder why Delaney's Washington allies, especially NIIAD Director Tony Fauci, maintained relations with him. (Delaney often boasted about his relationship with Fauci giving people the impression they were close friends.)*14* Fauci appears to have made a problematic political decision. As the head of NIAID and Federal AIDS research, congenial relations with activists who could be co-opted afforded Fauci an insurance policy against criticism from other activists, Congress, and the media. However, by legitimatizing Delaney, Fauci was legitimatizing the underground, thereby provoking criticism of himself. Fauci was nothing if not a political animal; more of a chameleon than ether Delaney or the New Yorkers, his coat sported many colors besides Democrat yellow. Over the decades Fauci, who will be 80 in December 2020 and still heads NIAID, has become one of the swamps most durable denizens. Nonetheless, since 1984 he has been

effective as Director of NIAID, his effectiveness a testament to his
political as well as scientific prowess. Fauci has a gift for making readily
understandable complex medical and scientific matters. It became evident
in the AIDS epidemic and proved to be, for better or worse, a major factor
in the Covid 19 epidemic.

The AIDS drug underground had been growing for years, along
with stories of its abuses. By mid 1991 cities with buyer's clubs included
New York, San Francisco, Los Angeles, San Diego, Palm Springs,
Denver, Boulder, Washington DC, Boston, Ft. Lauderdale, Phoenix,
Atlanta, Portland, Seattle, Tucson, Houston, and Dallas. The *Wall Street
Journal* and smaller papers had run limited pieces on the underground in
the summer and fall of 1991. But the underground did not enter the
national spotlight in a big way until Nov 4, 1991when a major *New York
Times* article by Gina Kolata outlined its scope and touched upon the
problems surrounding it. I will quote the relevant sections of her influential
piece rather than attempt to summarize:

> *Frustrated by the absence of drugs to treat their conditions,
> patients are turning to the buyers' clubs, as they are known,
> which sell drugs that are still being tested. The clubs also
> provide drugs approved in other countries but not in the United
> States, buying the drugs overseas and shipping them here.*

> *Some clubs also undercut the prices of an approved drug,
> aerosolized pentamadine, that is used to prevent a form of
> pneumonia that often strikes people with AIDS. To do this, they
> buy the drug from a European company at prices far below
> those charged by the American manufacturer. All of these
> activities violate, or at least skirt, Federal law. Until now, the
> Food and Drug Administration has left the clubs alone. But
> within the last few weeks, the agency has begun questioning the
> directors of the clubs. . .*

> *Advocates for people with AIDS readily admit that most of the
> clubs' activities are illegal. "Nobody disagrees with the fact
> that buyers' clubs are acting outside the law," said James
> Serafini, a member of the AIDS Coalition to Unleash Power.*

The clubs, he said, "operate in a sort of demilitarized zone." But he added that he and others who rely on the clubs were worried that the F.D.A. might cut off their supplies of drugs. . ..

"I think they're terrible," said Dr. Thomas Chalmers, an expert on drug testing who is Distinguished Physician at the Veterans Administration Hospital in Boston. He added that the clubs were "the most serious step backward I've seen in a long time."

The clubs began forming several years ago, when people with AIDS, frustrated by the lengthy Federal drug approval process, took things into their own hands. They began by smuggling in drugs from other countries and have progressed to a point at which they have some drugs manufactured expressly for them in the United States.

Fueled by the popularity of an experimental drug called ddC, the clubs exploded in scope and in number over the last year until, today, there are dozens of clubs around the country serving an estimated 10,000 or more patients . . .

The most popular drug is dideoxycytidine, or ddC, the AIDS drug being tested by Hoffmann-La Roche Inc. The drug, . . . is so popular that the clubs regularly run out of it. A call to Healing Alternatives, a San Francisco Buyers Club, was answered with a recorded message that began: "Hello. You have reached the Healing Alternatives Foundation. ddC is now in stock. I repeat, we have ddC in stock. For further information on how to obtain ddC, please keep listening."

James Driscoll, the vice president of DATA, said that the buyers' clubs usually mark up the ddC they buy from a middleman by only about 15 percent, charging about $60 for a month's worth of DDC. But since so many people are buying the drug "there is much more cash flow," he said. "This is allowing the clubs to grow and expand their product line and their inventory and for more buyers' clubs to open," he said.

Other patients say they have no choice but to use the clubs. Despite treatment with established AIDS drugs, John Dolan, a 35-year-old San Francisco man, has so many white blood cells infected with the AIDS virus that "I can't even participate in most clinical trials," Mr. Dolan said. In August, his doctor gave him a Los Angeles telephone number to call to order a drug, d4T, that is in a very early stage of development by Bristol Myers-Squibb. Without buyers' clubs, Mr. Dolan said, "I don't know what I'd do." . . .

But drug companies say there are dangers in buying bootlegged drugs. Dr. Paul Oestreicher, a spokesman for Hoffmann-La Roche . . . said he was concerned that some of the illicit DDC may be sold in dangerously imprecise doses. "ddC has a very narrow therapeutic range," Dr. Oestreicher said.

In addition, Dr. Oestreicher questioned whether buyers' clubs could ever properly test the drug's formulation. "The Roche compound undergoes 600 different quality control and quality assurance tests," he said.

After *The Time's* article, interest in the buyer's clubs really took off sparking stories in local press across the country and in electronic media. The publicity about them began to impact policy makers in the Administration and Congress who were wondering what their existence said about FDA's methods and the problems with its approval procedures. To understand the buyer's clubs themselves and the nature of FDA's relationships with them, we must bear in mind five critical factors.

1) The knockoff drugs violated Federal law: they infringed on the patents of legitimate companies because to be sold legally in the US pharmaceuticals must be approved by FDA and their manufacture must be monitored by FDA.

2) The buyers' clubs were commercial enterprises often making substantial profits re-importing drugs available abroad at lower prices, such as pentamadine, and from knockoff drugs not yet approved by FDA, and often sold at high prices and profits. Whether or how they paid taxes is an open question. Their books were closed which fed suspicion and resentment over the possibility that Corti, Delaney, and their local affiliates might be profiting off the desperation of people with AIDS. In place of a public accounting of their costs and profits, they resorted to distraction by blasting the high prices of available prescription drugs, particularly AZT.

Their strategy was to blame everything on the big, bad pharmaceutical companies and pose as heroic Robin Hood's whose motives it was treasonous to question. I doubt that Delaney himself profited inordinately, as he appeared to have accumulated no significant wealth in his years as an activist, and he lived modestly. But not profiting personally did not justify hawking dangerously defective products sold at high prices to desperate and often impoverished patients.

3) **More disturbing than concerns about illegitimate profits, the buyers' clubs' products lacked quality controls.** Their deficient controls posed a theoretical and actual threat to public health: theoretical because there was no manufacturing oversight; actual because the products that FDA and Roche eventually did test were miss measured and/or contaminated. ddC was a potentially dangerous drug with toxic side effects, the most common of these being debilitating neuropathy. If an underground version of ddC was mismeasured and the patient got too much, that would jump start peripheral neuropathy. If he got too little, then his virus could quickly develop resistance to the drug which would become useless to him.

4) The FDA's decision to turn a blind eye to Delaney & Corti's operation was selective non-enforcement to protect FDA practices regardless of consequences for public health. If a vitamin supplier were manufacturing unapproved products in facilities without oversight and selling them under false claims, FDA would have pounced to shut them down. They attempted, with far less justification than with the buyer's clubs, to close down Dr. Jonathan Wright and Saul Kent's Life Extension Foundation during this same timeframe. The FDA has been ever-ready to expand its regulation of the vitamin and supplements industry without presenting convincing evidence of need or of any specific health threats. Why then did they look the other way at the clearly dangerous and illegal underground ddC trade? Just as crackdown on supplements is selective enforcement, failure to police the ddC underground was selective non-enforcement in disregard of the rights of those patients the laws were enacted to protect. Either way FDA ignored equal protection of the law. Either way FDA valued safeguarding its institutional culture and methods over safeguarding the lives of patients, especially dispensable

homosexuals with AIDS. With FDA the Hippocratic oath always seemed to play second fiddle to the interests of the agency's bureaucracy.

5) The unavailability of ddC from legal sources and its value in combination with AZT were the chief spurs to the explosive growth of the buyer's clubs in the early 1990s. Patients benefiting from AZT were learning from trial results and their doctors that its efficacy could be increased and extended if combined with ddC. Had FDA honored their duty to protect public health, they would have made available through large scale expanded access safe ddC from the manufacturer, Hoffman La Roche, or best of all by approving the drug in a timely fashion.

Two months before the *Times* made the underground a national story, the *San Francisco Chronicle* reported that FDA had met with underground leaders in an effort to prevent profiteering on knockoff ddC. FDA's "concern" with profiteering was a blatant red herring. Omissions tell the real story. FDA's statutory responsibility is to protect public health. It has no authority to police anyone's profits, especially not on illegal knockoff drugs! By assuring patients that they found no evidence of profiteering, FDA protected the clubs against backlash, thus insuring their continuance. It was as if the DEA had twisted the arms of drug dealers to prevent price gouging on crack cocaine, lest they give narcotics pushers a bad name!

For those who wanted further proof of FDA's collusion with the underground, Jonathan Kwitney provided a detailed account written in cooperation with and sanctioned by Delaney and Corti:

> *Kessler said to Delaney he was worried about claims of selective prosecution. . . Selective prosecution was a valid legal defense; the FDA couldn't prosecute someone for violating a law that wasn't generally enforced.* [Of course they did prosecute selectively, they just wouldn't admit to doing so— JD] *Kessler **signaled** that he didn't want to close down Corti's operation if they could just find a rationale that didn't cause him problems elsewhere* [with FDA critics in the AIDS community, Congress, and the media--JD] *. . . Kessler engineered a conference call including his general counsel, Joseph Lovett, and regulatory affairs director Gary Dykstra . . . Delaney and Ponzi urged the need to distinguish what the*

clubs were doing from the kind of fraud FDA was in business to
stop . . . The signal to Delaney was that FDA would continue to
turn a blind eye to the ddC distribution [i.e. Corti's operation—
JD] *but that the agency felt it had to do something about the*
buyer's clubs violations. Delaney offered to go after the clubs
to stop impermissible advertising . . . That seemed to satisfy the
agency.15

In short, Delaney promised Kessler that the illegal operations
would keep a low profile so as to not embarrass FDA for failing to do its
job. Kwitney's account shows FDA colluding with a criminal operation
that violated the laws Congress had set up FDA to enforce along with the
rights of patients Congress was trying to protect. Indeed, the ddC
underground was exactly "the kind of fraud FDA was in business to stop."

Prefiguring and reinforcing Kwitney's account, a September 5,
1991 *San Francisco Chronicle* article stressed the agency's concerns
about profiteering. It does not, however, mention that the agency
expressed any concerns about the underground ddC being mismeasured or
contaminated. Both accounts show an FDA far more anxious about its
public image than about threats to the health of AIDS patients.

Concerned about possible profiteering in the black market for
experimental AIDS drugs, the FDA is preparing to tighten
controls on the network of "buyer's clubs" that procure and
sell the unapproved medicines. High level FDA representatives
plan to meet today in Napa in a closed door session with leaders
of the underground drug movement to define new ground rules
that will determine what practices will be permitted. . ..
Although it is illegal to make or sell unapproved medications,
the FDA has tolerated the underground network in the face of
criticism that the agency is dragging its feet on the approval of
AIDS drugs. . . Driscoll said that growth of the ddC
underground is evidence of what he calls "the FDA's failure to
approve a drug that is now accepted by most doctors on the
front lines of the AIDS epidemic"

Thus, in September 1991 FDA moved to curb overcharging for an
unsafe, illegal drug, but not until four months later did they actually test
for dosage accuracy. Despite their vaunted concern for public safety, either

FDA never tested the knockoff drugs for contamination or it declined to make their test results public. To say that FDA should have known better would be the understatement of the year. ddC was exceptionally difficult to measure or titrate because the amounts needed for a safe, effective dosage were miniscule. Accurate titration required a highly trained chemist with a professional laboratory. FDA knew that was unlikely to be available to any underground operation. Thus, FDA knew that allowing proliferation of underground ddC would expose sick patients to a dangerous product. Apparently FDA didn't care enough to act. I suspect it didn't even occur to them to care, after all the victims of their negligence were gay AIDS patients doomed to die anyway. Why modify for those pariahs FDA's approval procedures long ago made sacrosanct by their thalidomide myth?

However, Hoffmann La Roche did bother to test the underground knockoffs. They confided privately to local clinicians, and to me as well, that their tests confirmed contamination along with extensive mismeasurement—not at all surprising considering the primitive conditions of the products manufacture. Let it be noted that rigorous safety controls in compliance with strict FDA manufacturing standards are a significant factor in the high cost of legal pharmaceuticals. Our previously cited letter to FDA stated:

> Because of ddC's dangerous toxicities and narrow therapeutic window, mismeasured ddC poses a serious danger to people with AIDS. FDA, however, went out of its way not to protect people with AIDS but to protect the (underground) syndicate! FDA declined to seize bad batches, failed to actively publicize the dangers to public health or issue a cease and desist order. FDA did not even test for contamination. FDA's response was a transparent cover up. For more than one year in excess of 15,000 AIDS patients bought the syndicate's bootleg ddC; no one knows how much of the drug was bad or how many patients were harmed.

One morning in January 1992 Barry Freehill and I were surprised, to read in the *San Francisco Chronicle* that FDA had finally gotten around to testing samples of underground DDC, or at least admitting publicly that they had tested them. It was indeed news to us. However, in the myth promulgated by Delaney, Corti, and their New York cohorts Barry and I were not mere observers. We were highly paid operatives of Hoffmann-LaRoche. Some even speculated that we called the shots on that vast pharmaceutical giant's dealings with the AIDS Community! Here, without the conspiracy theories, is *The SF Chronicle's* version of FDA's actual seizure of the drugs:

> *Investigators from the US food and Drug Administration acting on warnings about potential safety problems with the black market AIDS treatment ddC, have seized samples of the drugs from underground buyers' clubs in San Francisco and New York. . .. FDA agents collected the bootleg DDC after the agency was told by drug maker Hoffmann-LaRoche that the potency of the pills from the buyers' clubs varied dramatically from the levels recommended by researchers.*
>
> *Potency in the Roche tested samples varied from as low as 50% to as high as 300% of the recommended levels according to one source familiar with company data. Neither Oestreicher nor the FDA would confirm the figures. Dr. Donald Abrams an AIDS researcher at the University of California said that such an extreme variation in drug potency, if confirmed, would raise serious safety concerns.*
>
> *"Buyer's clubs emerged as a cottage industry in an effort to get people as much access as possible. The potential downside is that there is no quality control." he said. . .. Although ddC has yet to win FDA approval, thousands of AIDS patients are taking the drug upon recommendation of their doctors. . .. Despite the illegality of bootleg ddC sales, the FDA has declined to shut down the buyer's clubs and in fact has been working with the community groups who operate them. (San Francisco Chronicle, January 29, 1992)*

A week after this story broke, FDA "recommended" that the buyer's clubs remove underground ddC from their shelves. Mild as the FDA move was, it sent shock waves through the AIDS community terrifying patients who realized they had exposed themselves to a drug that might have been dangerously miss measured or even contaminated. Here is the AP story about FDA's efforts to close the DDC underground:

SAN FRANCISCO (AP) _ The Food and Drug Administration has called for a stop to underground sales of the unapproved AIDS drug ddC, citing tests that show some capsules contain none of the drug and others potentially dangerous doses.

"These results indicate that underground ddC is produced under poor manufacturing conditions and that the overall safety and purity of underground ddC is suspect, " said an FDA memo sent to the agency's regional offices.

Capsules purchased at so-called buyer's clubs in New York and San Francisco were tested and held possibly dangerous variations. The FDA recommended an estimated 18 buyer's clubs nationwide take ddC off shelves and inform customers about the test results.

Tests showed some capsules contained none of the drug, while others contained more than twice the dosage recommended by researchers, the memo said. Large doses of DDC can cause nerve damage to the hands and feet. AIDS patients and a San Francisco buyer's club reacted angrily Thursday to the order. (February 5, 1992)

Commenting on FDA's dangerous and discriminatory selective enforcement, Steven Fowkes of *DATA* wrote:

According to Donald Pohl, Deputy AIDS Coordinator, the FDA 1) hasn't notified other buyer's clubs selling the same bad ddC, 2) hasn't checked to see if the notified buyer's clubs have stopped selling the affected ddC or 3) hasn't verified whether the buyer's clubs are indeed recalling product. . . . Dr. Wallace Sampson, Stanford University professor and physician stated: "HIV patients above all require protection from dosage errors and indeed recalling product. . . . FDA is apparently sacrificing consistent policies for unknown reasons, . . . It is hard to imagine a cogent reason why the FDA has not publicized this threat to public health nor ordered seizure of mismeasured ddC. "(DATA press release March 2, 1992.)

Actually FDA's reasons are not hard at all to fathom: they were the agency's indifference to the health and safety of the gay victims of the underground, and above all political considerations. Recognition of the problems with the underground would be tantamount to recognition of the flaws in FDA's approval procedures that created the underground in the first place. It would build the case for FDA reform.

In the postscript to *Acceptable Risks,* Jonathan Kwitney claims that by April 1992 ddC was again rolling out of Corti's underground labs on a larger scale than ever before and with the full knowledge and consent of David Kessler's Kafkaesque bureaucracy.*16* It became obvious to libertarian activists that FDA wouldn't enforce standard public health procedures when it came to protecting thousands of gay AIDS patients from defective knockoff ddC. Politics trumped public health, but of course the health of gay patients was a lower priority than that of the general public.

The leaders of the underground knew who to thank for their escape from prosecution and exactly how to thank him. On February 27, 1993, at the beginning of Bill Clinton's first term as President, the *New York Times* reported:

> *Dr. David A. Kessler will be reappointed Commissioner of the Food and Drug Administration, while Dr. Bernadine P. Healy has been asked to resign as director of the National Institutes of Health, officials of the Health and Human Services Department said today. Dr. Kessler is one of the few appointees of President George Bush who has been retained, (Another was NIIAD Director, and friend of Delaney and the New Yorkers, Anthony Fauci. JD) chiefly because of what department officials said is his nonpolitical approach to the job.*

Those who followed the agency agreed that David Kessler was the wiliest political animal ever to serve as FDA Commissioner. In the weeks prior to Kessler's re-appointment, Delaney sent pleas to his Treatment Activist Network imploring them to write to newly inaugurated President Clinton to urge retention of Kessler as FDA Chief. Other defenders of the underground, such as Derek Hodel, David Barr, and Mark Herrington also pushed for Kessler's retention. Was there a connection, many wary activists asked, between Kessler's kid gloves treatment of the underground and its leaders aggressive lobbying for his retention as FDA chief? Whatever their actual reason for pushing Kessler's retention, it certainly wasn't to reward him for speeding approval of ddC, ddI and other AIDS drugs.

Summary: The bureaucratic malfeasance of FDA's dealings with the ddC underground was monumental. Consider: to more exhaustively test the efficacy of ddC, a drug FDA knew to be safe only if manufactured under tightly controlled conditions, and only if its dosage was correctly measured, FDA delayed approval of the Roche product. Then, to reduce patient outrage over the drugs' unavailability, FDA allowed the proliferation of an underground knockoff with zero quality control. Thus, thousands of AIDS patients with severely depressed immune systems were exposed to a dangerous drug whose quality and safety was untested and unknown. After the defects of the knockoff were exposed, FDA delayed taking the illicit drug off the market to placate the underground's bosses and protect them from financial losses. As if to put a big red cherry atop their Kafka cake, FDA appointed a prominent defender of the underground, Mark Herrington, to their antivirals committee in charge of evaluating for FDA approval the legal Roche version of ddC!

The full backstory may never be known, at least if FDA can continue to cover up crucial details, and if no one in Congress or the White House cares to exercise their oversight responsibilities on FDA. The agency's AIDS activist critics knew that the backstory would be even more bizarre and deeply political than indicated by the newspaper accounts of FDA's closure of the buyer's clubs. Indeed, in that pre-internet era the general public learned more than it might today because newspapers were financially stronger then, and the professional and ethical standards of journalism were much higher. Reporters were expected to work to find the facts and then write the truth. The best of them refrained from pushing the talking points of interest groups. Among the best in AIDS were Gina Kolata of *NYT*, Marilyn Chase of *WSJ*, Sabin Russell of the *SF Chronicle* and Lisa Krieger of the *SF Examiner* along with many of the community reporters. Their work, largely unrecognized then and later, proved indispensable to pressuring the FDA to do its job, if only reluctantly in a spotty and erratic manner, of protecting people with AIDS from the dangers of knockoff ddC.

We now can say with some confidence that the FDA investigation was instigated by Hoffmann-LaRoche in response to reports from many doctors in the field about their patients' bad experiences with underground ddC. Why, one wonders, did Roche decide to set in motion in December 1991 an FDA investigation when FDA, along with everyone else, had known for months that the underground was breaking the law in ways that endangered public health? The most likely reason was that, since FDA was not doing its job of protecting patients, Roche decided to bite the bullet and do the job for the agency. Granted Roche wanted to protect the reputation of their drug and spur FDA to at long last approve it. However, in my discussions with the company's officials the genuineness of their concern that underground knockoffs of ddC would damage patient health became as apparent as FDA's habitual prioritizing of their bureaucratic powers over public health imperatives.

The battle over knockoff DDC taught FDA a lesson that they, or at least Kessler, did not entirely forget during the struggle to gain expeditious approval of the protease based anti-retroviral cocktails. FDA learned that there were conscientious AIDS doctors and treatment activists they could not buy off with a place at the table. They learned also that the San Francisco critics of the buyers' clubs enjoyed the support of many AIDS patients and their doctors throughout the country. As it turned out, our views also had support within New York ACT UP, and perhaps most important, within the Republican Party where FDA reform was a cause on the rise.

Chapter 3
Vigilante Activism

Laws are like cobwebs, which may catch small flies,
but let wasps and hornets break through.
Jonathan Swift

How did FDA's collusion with the AIDS drug underground damage community activists who opposed the underground's threat to AIDS patients? What violations of our rights did we suffer? Let me backtrack to the summer of 1991when stories of the dangers of underground DDC first broke in San Francisco. Opposition to the knockoff AIDS drugs was scattered across the nation, but had no formal organization. In San Francisco, though, Barry Freehill and I became the prime targets of Delaney, Corti, and their enforcers.

Jack Girard, Barry Freehill, Steven Fowkes, John Dolan, Ron Baker, and I had given Lisa Krieger, Sabin Russell, Marilyn Chase, Gina Kolata and reporters for community papers leads for articles that exposed the dangers of underground ddC. The articles upset some in the community, and the flames of their anger were energetically fanned by FDA's friends in New York ACT UP, and by Delaney, Corti, and their operatives.

But they did not stop at just stirring up the community against us. Jim Corti personally traveled to a Keystone Foundation meeting on FDA reform that I was attending at a Napa California hotel. Accosting me in the lobby with a fist raised to my face, he snarled: "You will not be safe to walk the streets of San Francisco, if you keep maligning the FDA and the underground to reporters."

I relayed his threats to one of the FDA people at the meeting, Randy Wykoff I think, and to John Petricianni of Pharma who was also attending. I did not at that point notify the police or the FBI. I feared that as soon as the authorities saw it as a dispute within the gay community, they would elect to do nothing. Remember, it was not until 2003 that the Supreme Court ruled sodomy laws unconstitutional. Until that time, gay men were all suspected of being uncaught criminals whose reliability was problematic and whose likely criminal conduct had undermined their moral claim to the protections due normal law-abiding citizens.

In the 1990's, I lived in the second floor flat of a typical Victorian building on the edge of the Haight Ashbury district near Buena Vista Park. It was a historic San Francisco location: a block down the hill across Haight St. were the Jimmy Hendrix Electric Church and the flats where Janis Joplin and Charles Mansion crashed during the Flower Children era. Up the hill two blocks was Buena Vista Park, an infamous gay cruising ground, and the old Spreckels Mansion, recently acquired and renovated by movie actor Danny Glover. The day after I returned home from the Napa conference, derogatory graffiti were spray painted on my building including a giant dollar sign on my front door. My roommates reported that my phone had rung constantly and there was loud banging on our door in the middle of the night. The downstairs neighbor said she heard a gunshot outside as a car drove by horn blaring late at night.

(My front door, decoration by Corti, Delaney & Assoc.)

The vigilantes' intimidation tactics were routine: threats of violence, hints at lawsuits, and of course spreading slanders. Barry Freehill suffered similar attempts at intimidation. Delaney told responsible people, like reporters and local doctors, that Freehill was "mentally disturbed." With me he went further claiming that I was "clinically insane." We assumed he repeated the slanders to his bosom buddies in NIIAD and FDA. It was an extremely disturbing time; we all lost sleep, peace of mind evaporated. However, in retrospect the bullies made fools of themselves while we gained sympathy from sensible people in the community.

They never succeeded in intimidating Barry: he had been battle hardened by his long combat with a more formidable adversary than Delaney or Corti: the AIDS virus. At a vulnerable age I had learned to weather a father's homophobic bullying. Our critics, I suspect, did not count on the toughening effects of our previous training, and they underestimated Barry. Nor did they count on my first lesson for activists taught me by Harvey Milk's word and example: "Never back down to bullies. Just remember when you stand up for yourself, you stand up for everyone like you."

Delaney, Corti, and their New York accomplices promulgated in ACT UP and other community circles the myth that I was the evil genius behind Hoffman La Roche's plot to shut down their underground. The only profit in underground drugs, they asserted, was the bounty Driscoll and Freehill get from Roche. Their charge was risible. No drug company would dare pay an activist to antagonize FDA. It was always those activists who attacked the drug companies and defended FDA whom the companies felt compelled to reward with big grants. That was how the game was played: the real money was in silence money, which didn't actually buy silence but only tuned down the volume. Our adversaries knew how to play it, and profited freely from playing it well. They also knew that Barry and I were far from being alone in opposing the underground, that we had many key allies in the medical profession and the patient communities. However, I had exposed myself by working with Republicans like Rep. Tom Campbell; and my op eds in the *Wall Street Journal* publicly identified me with a Republican de-regulatory approach. Our opponents didn't want de-regulation, they liked regulation where they could influence and profit thereby.

I also made myself a target by working closely with Roche which had become the bête-noire of the New York activists and Delaney. Since Roche held the patent to ddC, it was the prime competitor to the underground's most lucrative product. Given that, no one was surprised when Roche became the company the New York activists and Delaney most loved to hate.

By initiating the movement to get expanded access for ddC, I became the first AIDS activist to work closely with Roche. I took the initiative because no one else had and Dave and other friends wanted ddC. My work with Roche was facilitated by a Bay Area friend whose brother was on the Board of Roche in Basal Switzerland. So I developed a cordial relationship with the company, which aroused suspicions among those eager to be suspicious of any drug company, especially Roche. From my perspective, the activists' charges that Roche was worse than their competition in AIDS, Burroughs-Wellcome, Merck, Abbott, and Bristol-Myers, were groundless. Roche was a smart, ethical company. Like the others, it stayed in business by making profits.

Roche's US headquarters in New Jersey was hit by a number of vigilante style acts which were par for the course for an AIDS drug company that ran afoul of the New York activists and the underground. Not par for the course were the vigilante acts directed at myself and the individuals associated with me like Dave Olson, Barry Freehill, and even my downstairs neighbors. The three young women in the flat below mine, recent graduates of Bryn Marr College, were twice terrorized by the vigilantes while I was out. I explained to them what was happening and why: almost in tears, they backed me. One of them was struggling with Hodgkin's Lymphoma and later died. When they complained to the police, they got a callous brush off. "It's a dispute within your community, work it out yourselves," they were told. Since they did not have AIDS and weren't to my knowledge lesbians, I didn't see how they could be parties to our community disputes.

I complained to two members of the San Francisco Board of Supervisors who were from the community, but got the same answer: their policy was not to get involved in community disputes. These were typical of the many instances where the responses of San Francisco municipal authorities to LGBT community problems were remiss during the 1990s. It reminded me of the routine failures to enforce safety in African American communities. The gay male as N-word---?

Barry and I wrote to Mary Pendergast, Senior Advisor to the Commissioner of FDA, about the intimidation, threats, and vandalism. She finally responded in a November 20, 1992 letter, "your concerns about threats of violence must be addressed by local law enforcement officials." We did not buy Pendergast's buck passing. The ultimate source of our problem was not local, it lied in the politically motivated selective enforcement practices of FDA and their willingness to work deals with those running criminal enterprises to protect their own hardline drug approval policies. That in turn exposed us to the underground's felonious reprisals and all the stress and abuse that went with them. Of course FDA never acknowledged its responsibility, let alone apologized, for misdeeds and crimes against innocent gay citizens sparked by the agency's own negligence and politically motivated misconduct.

The derelict local authorities assumed Delaney and Corti held sway over an influential constituency and so it was not smart politics to reprimand them, law or no law. Politics again. Delaney had sold them a bill of goods on his putative influence over the gay-HIV constituency. TAG was selling the same thing, to FDA, to NIAID, and then to the drug companies. None of them realized that Delaney and TAG's claim to represent a broad constituency was as dubious as the claims for the safety and efficacy of their knockoff drugs.

To all of these authorities, the gay community was *Chinatown:* as in the 1970s Roman Polanski movie, it was a place where no one on the outside understood, or even wanted to know, what went on inside. The authorities steered clear of the outcast community leaving it to its own devices. Delaney and the Manhattan activists talked a good line posing as leaders the community had chosen. Knowing nothing about the extremely diverse and individualistic gay community, and not wanting to learn, federal and local authorities swallowed their claims no questions asked.

After all, FDA and Anthony Fauci was in effect vouching for Delaney, and didn't everybody trust them?

The young women's support moved me, as did the support of many other women and men in the AIDS movement. Most, although not all, of the women in AIDS activism were gay; they were fighting to save others, not themselves. The women gave emotional support that proved invaluable to countless gay male AIDS patients throughout the epidemic. Disinterested compassion made them especially strong, honest, and reasonable warriors for truth and justice. Many of the men survived despair, if not the virus itself, because of support from these women. At the turning point that laid ahead, support from women cancer activists would prove indispensable to me. One of my closest friends at that time was a prominent women's cancer activist, Beverly Zakarian.

My adversaries aimed their verbal fire principally at me though Barry Freehill did not escape their slanders. Their preference for me as a public target resulted from: 1) Barry had AIDS and they were reluctant to target people with AIDS, I did not enjoy that exemption; 2) my opinion pieces critical of FDA in *WSJ* etc. had made me the tall poppy they longed to whack down. Freehill might have ran for cover, but he never did. He remained a steadfast, loyal friend and a highly effective ally throughout this tortuous period. Dave Olson, John Dolan, his wife Linda, Jack Girard, Steve Fowkes and others on the West Coast also backed Freehill and myself without ever wavering.

On the underground, Jesse Dobson had thrown in his lot with Delaney creating a breach between us that never healed, despite my desires to the contrary, and I believe his as well. At the behest of Delaney, Jesse attacked Barry and me personally in a September 12, 1991 article in the *San Francisco Sentinel,* one of three widely read local gay community handout newspapers. His screed titled, "Bad Activists and Yellow Journalists," was the opening strike in Delaney and the New Yorkers inquisition against Barry and myself:

> *In the past week, the local papers published large articles on AIDS that have to rank with the worst, most journalistically unprofessional articles on the subject since Gina Kolata was replaced at the New York Times.*

Comment: The New York activists obsessively attacked Gina Kolata for not presenting them, and the facts, exactly the way they wanted them to be presented. Contrary to Dobson, Gina was not replaced as her previously quoted November 4 1991 *Times* article on the underground proves. Indeed, she is still with the *Times* as of this writing twenty-nine years later.

> *The articles were both more or less sleazy political attacks on Martin Delaney. And according to reliable, but unnamed, sources both were engineered by Jim Driscoll and Barry Freehill . . . The issue I wish to raise is not so much whether the articles were accurate, but whether it is OK for people to threaten the source of life sustaining drugs [e.g. the AIDS drug underground] . . . to gain personal power. . .*

Comment: A bizarre charge: what personal power could we gain this way? Moreover, if Jesse, Delaney and the New Yorkers believed ddC was life sustaining, why weren't they pressuring FDA to make it available to all by formally approving it?

> *Freehill has been an ally of Driscoll's on most issues and is a fierce critic of Martin Delaney, mostly because Delaney didn't listen to him either. . . Driscoll and Freehill have recently been pushing a bill in Congress sponsored by de-regulation minded Republican Tom Campbell and the first draft of which was written by Driscoll. The goal of the bill is to reduce the efficacy standard for drugs for life threatening conditions like AIDS. . . This sounds OK on the surface, but many AIDS activists the strongest of which is Martin Delaney feel the introduction of this bill will cause a backlash among consumer protectionists leaving us in a worse position than now.*

Comment: Jesse got his facts wrong. The core opposition to the Campbell bill was the FDA bureaucracy itself, not consumer protectionists, like Syd Wolfe, who bent over backwards to avoid being tainted as anti-gay by opposing access to AIDS medications. In objecting to the bill, Delaney joined his Manhattan buddies in their game of running interference for FDA.

An FDA official has told me that Driscoll personally alerted them to this alleged profiteering. In response, the FDA is now planning to regulate the Buyer's Clubs.

Jesse again got his facts wrong. I didn't target profiteering, although others like Jack Girard and Steven Fowkes who better understood the economics of the underground did. Barry and I focused on the safety risks of underground DDC. Our concerns were validated by FDA when they tested Corti's product. Moreover, FDA was breaking its own rules in discussing with Jesse our dealings with the agency. Though we asked FDA, mum was their word on their dealings with Delaney and the New Yorkers. But FDA's motives were transparent: Barry and I were the most visible AIDS community supporters of Tom Campbell's FDA reform bill which the agency bitterly opposed as a threat to their rigid efficacy standard. So FDA gave their Manhattan minions, along with Jesse and Delaney, information they had every reason to believe would inflame them against us and spur their attempts to discredit us as supporters of FDA reform legislation. Had we been violently assaulted, FDA would have been a moral accessory to the crime, and possibly a legal one as well.

Here is my response/complaint to Ray Chalker, publisher of the *Sentinel*:

With Jesse Dobson's "Bad Activists and Yellow Journalists" the Project Inform campaign of hate and harassment against Barry Freehill and myself intensified. My front door was defaced with a three-foot-high red, spray painted dollar sign. People have beat on my door at night and then disappeared. Freehill and I have received menacing phone calls and veiled death threats, and four "Project Inform volunteers," including Dobson, have attempted to expel us from ACT UP. [Chalker subsequently fired Dobson from the *Sentinel*.]

Jesse's relations with Barry and me had been souring for nearly a year. Months before he told me that Delaney and he "wished Dave Olson would just give up and croak" so that I'd "get the hell out of activism and go back to Jung or whatever." Dave, who fought his disease with incredible grit and resourcefulness, was infuriated; he forbade me to speak with Jesse and Delaney again. I never spoke again with either of them while Dave remained alive. In retrospect, I suspect Jesse's heart was not in this attack, that he was set up and used by Delaney and the New Yorkers. Jesse was very sick and no longer his old self. After Dave died and Jesse himself was dying, he expressed regret to me and wanted to get together. I did not respond, unsure how to handle this; but when he died I was sorry I had not responded.

At the time, Jesse's actions seemed a betrayal of the urgent needs of people with AIDS in order to gain favor with Delaney and the bureaucrats at FDA. By contrast, the support we got from rank and file AIDS patients in New York ACT UP itself surprised and moved me. I knew a few people in New York Act Up, like Kramer, Jim Eigo and David Gold, and had met Peter Staley, Mark Herrington, and David Barr at meetings. But I had never met any of the rank and file. The last time I had visited New York was in 1976, years before the epidemic began.

Delaney, Corti, and several New York friends of FDA, including the group that later formed TAG, concocted a hare-brained strategy to ostracize Freehill and myself from the AIDS activist movement and thereby end our "treachery." Treachery they defined as anyone's deviation from their agendas and talking points for dealing with FDA. We had traumatized them by working on FDA Reform with Republican Congressmen. I had even worked on FDA with the office of Vice President Dan Quayle. What could possibly be more treacherous than that!!

Delaney and the founders of TAG hoped to expel us from ACT UP Golden Gate in San Francisco, and have New York ACT UP, the mother ship, officially condemn us. They maintained that our influence with public and corporate officials arose from our affiliation with ACT UP, which they saw as their franchise. End that affiliation and we would shrivel up and vanish like the Wicked Witch of the West! What a delusion. Our influence depended not on ACT UP, but on support for our positions within the AIDS patient community, among doctors and researchers, and in our network of media and political contacts who believed our point of view worth hearing.

Their strategy relied on the General Bodies of ACT UP in both cities voting for our expulsion. In San Francisco Barry and I attended our "public trial" listening in silence while we were praised as heroes or damned as traitors. Despite the efforts of our detractors, the motion for our expulsion lost by more than 2 to 1, in part because it was seen as a free speech issue, and in part because of deep distrust of FDA in the community. The overwhelming majority believed that FDA delays on new AIDS drugs made no sense medically and were immoral to boot because they violated individual free choice. Moreover, by that time the city governments of San Francisco and New York had made noticeable if incomplete progress integrating gays and lesbians into their policing, fire, and other authorities. That made the almost entirely straight white male FDA officialdom seem by comparison like an occupying alien power.

Our critics charged that we instigated FDA's investigation of the underground. Their allegation should have been dismissed outright by any who thought it through. FDA doubtless knew far more about the underground than we did. Indeed, they had discussed it with its principals, Delaney, Corti, and their New York allies, perhaps extensively given the close relationships between FDA officials and some underground players. FDA's investigation was sparked by complaints from doctors in the field and new reports from Roche that their tests showed the knockoffs to be dangerously defective.

Most of those who attended our "trial" in ACT UP Golden Gate felt they were not given all the facts, and refused to condemn us on the basis of incomplete knowledge. I was very moved by the impassioned speeches in our defense from community people who praised our courage, effectiveness, and commitment. Linda Dolan, John's wife, stood out as a powerful defender, whose testimony I will always recall with deep gratitude, affection, and respect.

New York ACT UP was a huge surprise. Barry and I expected the general body to follow its putative leaders, the friends of FDA. But those "leaders" were male, and we had not counted on the power and conviction of the women activists. Previously we had worked with the budding breast cancer movements, giving the women tips on dealing with FDA. I recall my many interesting talks with their founder Eleanor Pred before her death. I also worked closely with the wise and wonderful Beverly Zakarian, who started the ovarian cancer movement in New York. As with Eleanor, I spoke regularly with Beverly by phone, and we met numerous times in Washington DC to do joint Congressional meetings urging FDA reforms.

Without my asking her to do anything, I just told her what was going on, Beverly and five other women battling advanced cancer went to the ACT UP New York meeting. Their powerful defense of me and, more important the cause of FDA reform and its crucial importance to women with cancer, rallied the ACT UP women who swayed the entire group. Nearly 300 attended. The ACT UP general body rejected overwhelmingly the motion to expel and ostracize Barry Freehill and myself.

Angered by rejection, Delaney's New York allies began to pull back quietly. They soon formed an exclusive membership only group whose ideology and agenda they could control and FDA could rely on. They named their tight little elite TAG for the Treatment Action Guerillas which was later changed to Treatment Action Group. The new name, they realized, better positioned them to rake in largess from liberal foundations whose great wealth exceeded their good sense.

****

I hold FDA, not Jesse and not even Delaney or TAG, primarily responsible for what Barry, myself and many others, including the hapless patients, suffered at the hands of the AIDS drug underground. It was FDA's obligation to protect the public, instead, they colluded with a criminal syndicate to protect their arbitrary enforcement of the efficacy standard. The "corporate culture" of the agency, more than Kessler who at times seemed its captive, was the underground's prime enabler and bore ultimate responsibility for the bad drugs it hawked. Free to go rogue in the absence of effective Presidential and Congressional oversight, FDA's culture acquired a refractory "deep state" autonomy long before that term became current.

The agency was so distant from the gay AIDS community that commercialization of a ddC knockoff it knew was ineffectual and dangerous did not trouble its official conscience, if such there were. Individual FDA officials must have known that earlier approval of AZT/ddC and AZT/ddI combinations would have endangered no one and might have bought many patients more time. Making no concessions to the emergency conditions of an epidemic, they continued to demand efficacy data up to FDA tough standards. We will never know how many AIDS patients were damaged by the defective underground ddC, or how many might have been saved but for FDA's refusal to give the patients timely access to safe versions of ddC and ddI to use in combination with AZT and with 3TC, another early drug that proved effective in combinations. Delaney, Jesse, and their comrades behaved badly, but they were aided and abetted, and in some instances may have been recruited, by FDA officials. In their own deeply misguided ways, most of these activists were nonetheless struggling to make a desperate situation better. FDA has no claim to that defense.

As we have seen, on January 24, 1992 FDA officially began to collect ddC samples from the buyer's clubs. On February 5, 1992 FDA notified the clubs that they found significant variations in dosage. Shortly thereafter Roche and FDA worked out a plan to expand the Roche ddC access program. On June 22 1992 FDA approved Roche's ddC for sale. It had already approved ddI on October 9, 1991.

Had complaints from HIV community patients and doctors not forced FDA to test the underground product, the safe ethical drug from Roche would likely have languished another year or more in FDA's regulatory morass. The thousands who appeared to derive some benefit from combining ddC with AZT would have been denied that benefit. Some who lived long enough to be saved by the protease cocktails may owe their lives to ddC's earlier than expected approval. Those who made sacrifices to speed ddC's approval and give patients a safe alternative to the defective underground product have never received recognition or thanks from the broader AIDS and LGBT communities.

Neither FDA nor anyone in the federal government has ever apologized to the gay and other victims of FDA's many unnecessary delays. The World War II Japanese Americans were generously compensated for Roosevelt's internment. Oppressed racial minorities have affirmative action. The first time our government ever apologized to LGBTs for anything was in 2017 when John Kerry, Secretary of State for the outgoing Obama Administration, apologized for the State Department's decades of blatant discrimination against their LGBT employees. It was a moral advance that does great credit to Kerry and the

Obama Administration. The struggle for just recognition of the long and terrible history of injustices against LGBTs has only begun. So far under the Trump-Pence Administration it is not a work in progress.

****

The approval of ddC, the failure of Compound Q and collapse of the market for underground drugs triggered a crisis of confidence and finances that took Project Inform to the brink of insolvency by the fall of 1992. Lisa Krieger wrote in the Nov 2,1992 Examiner:

> *Project Inform, the nation's first and most prominent informational network for sick HIV patients is now struggling for its own survival and is perilously close to closure. Insiders say the controversial AIDS organization cannot pay creditors, failed to meet payroll this week. . ... No other AIDS organization has suffered a comparable drop in donations in the last six months. Audit reports obtained by the Examiner . . . confirm a pattern of overspending. . . . Its resources were strained by the early trials of the experimental Compound Q.*

Delaney's activist critics speculated that loss of income from underground drug profits coupled with reduced support from disenchanted donors caused the crisis. These speculations were never substantiated.

Nonetheless, the consequences of the wars over the AIDS drug underground and ddC were momentous. Delaney and Project Inform had suffered a major setback and serious reputation damage. Out of the chaos a loose coalition of activists arose that was solidly committed to FDA reform and opposed to any compromises that saved FDA's face at the cost of the lives of people with AIDS. On the other hand, TAG and its allies ingratiated themselves more deeply with FDA officials: these activists' commitments to hardline FDA policies had crystalized. Lacking significant grassroots community support, the alliance with FDA was all TAG had left, but that proved more than enough to sustain them and increase their influence. Project Inform recovered soon, in part due to FDA and Tony Fauci's NIAID whose continued "friendship" legitimized the group which in turn inspired the beneficence of the pharmas and other deep pockets. By 1994 Delaney was again where he liked to be, in the middle where the deals are made. His flexibility and resourcefulness would be put to surprising good use in the climatic struggle with FDA and TAG over their budding scheme to thwart accelerated approval of the protease based cocktails.

Chapter 4
Regulation without Representation

"You seem to know an awful lot about what transpires inside the belly of the beast," I told Barry Freehill on one of our late night phone calls. "I have a secret source," he said in his teasing voice. After his little cat and mouse routine, he told me about Duane Dugger a friend with AIDS who worked as AIDS Coordinator for the San Francisco FDA office. Duane understood from both sides the conflicts between gay activists and FDA over AIDS drug approvals. He was loyal to his fellow AIDS sufferers. He was also loyal to FDA, but had his own ideas on what should constitute loyalty. Duane believed that loyalty to FDA required not blindly following the FDA party line, but instead guiding the agency toward sound public health policy.

Duane's position resembled that of a conscientious official trying to operate in an unscrupulous authoritarian state. He regularly provided us with information on what FDA planned and who and what was influencing them. They knew about his relationship with us, and to my knowledge did not try to prevent or hinder him. But they did let him know they were watching him. He was an astute observer, and lot smarter than his bosses at FDA gave him credit for. Like many other terminal AIDS patients, Duane was exceptionally courageous, and nothing would stop him from doing what he believed needed to be done to save others.

I began to admire Duane and value his commitment to our cause as well as his friendship. I thought he deserved better of FDA, a promotion maybe, and they certainly could benefit by listening to him carefully to learn from one of their own what it meant to be battling AIDS without effective help from medical science. Bill Clinton had recently been elected President promising to make his administration "look like America." I looked at the FDA family photos and saw whole segments of America missing. There were lots of white Masons, almost no Blacks, few women, fewer Hispanics, and Duane was the only openly gay person in sight. So I wrote a censorious piece in the *San Francisco Sentinel* that was intended for Washington eyes:

> *Kessler has hired no minorities or gays for any key job in the FDA AIDS division (antivirals). The top 20 jobs at FDA remain similarly free of diversity. Kessler has not lacked opportunities to diversify his staff since he has reorganized the FDA and created and filled many positions. . ..*
>
> *1.Of 31 FDA regional AIDS coordinators, only one or 3% is gay, 3 or 9% are minority, 27 or 88% are white heterosexuals.*
>
> *2. The one gay regional AIDS coordinator [Duane]is the only openly gay person working on AIDS in all of FDA. He may be the only openly gay person of any rank anywhere in the FDA!*
>
> *3. The Director of AIDS Coordination in Washington is a heterosexual white male, as are all members of his staff.*
>
> *4. However, approximately 70% of people with AIDS are gay or bisexual,35% are minority, and less than 10% are white heterosexuals. . ..*
>
> *Hiring in Kessler's FDA reveals a narrow elitism that disenfranchises minorities, gays and lesbians. . .. Because FDA jobs are a training ground for researchers, drug company officials, and lawyers, exclusion from FDA means exclusion from the wider drug development process. (San Francisco Sentinel, January 7, 1993)*

For an agency that *de facto* excluded gays and minorities to make life and death decisions on a disease whose sufferers were overwhelmingly gays and minorities was a travesty. America was founded by revolutionaries fighting taxation without representation. AIDS brought a new tyranny: regulation without representation and, worse, without accountability. I faxed David Kessler a copy, and soon Duane's colleagues at FDA began to show more respect for his peculiar expertise.

Then I directly pressured them to send Duane to the 1993 International AIDS Conference in Berlin that summer, because I was sure they could benefit from the perspectives of AIDS patients other than their predictable Manhattan minions. But also because Duane was dying and had never seen Europe. I wanted to show him the nearby and glorious city of Prague and we traveled there together after the conference. FDA went along with the idea, but groused to me about seeking special privileges for my friends---as if FDA officials were above such doings.

Before writing the *Sentinel* article, Duane and Barry instructed me on how FDA's revolving doors operated. In Washington, Barry asserted, revolving doors are as common as toilets, and can be just as fetid. The regulatory and compliance departments of the pharmas and biotechs are heavily staffed by former FDA officials. It is an incestuous relationship that functions as a stealth restraint of competition and trade. The established companies hire those with the strongest relationships inside FDA, and then use them to lobby for regulatory barriers against competitors trying to enter their markets or for faster approval and broader labeling for their own products.

One high level FDA official told us that he had four children all of whom would be in college about the same time; and he wanted them to attend Ivy League quality colleges. It was very reassuring, he confided, to know he could leave FDA and take a job at Merck or Pfizer at three times his salary whenever the need arose. FDA's are not the only or the smelliest revolving doors in Washington, every agency, every government department, and of course Congress itself, has them aplenty. The Defense Department probably has the biggest and the most mephitic. But all the revolving doors have the stench of discrimination because they open only for those individuals from groups that are already well represented inside.

Since gays were banned until the 1990s as security risks by the State and Defense departments as well as other parts of the government, few gays got near those "open Sesame" revolving doors to automatic advancement into Federal positions and their wealth and power.[17] Gays were at risk in many other areas of government employment and we suffered loss of opportunity accordingly. Moreover, because of stigma and bias many gays that succeeded stayed in the closet and were often afraid to help their friends. Congress has yet to pass non-discrimination laws that would insure LGBTs protection and opportunity on an equal footing with other abused minorities.

FDA heard us out, but they listened to and appeared to confide in their Manhattan minions. Their minions were saying what FDA wanted to hear, and we were saying what they didn't want anyone to hear. Useful info on FDA came our way from Duane or friendly pharma employees. So I cultivated sources within the pharmas who kept me in the loop about backstage actions in FDA, Congress, and the White House. Sometimes these sources took significant risks giving confidential information their companies and FDA did not want known.

Chapter 5
Activists, Media,
and Scientists

Activists can turn the media into sources by becoming a source for them. You must refrain from public criticism of them--something that proved difficult for Delaney and FDA's Manhattan minions, as Gina Kolata and Lisa Krieger discovered. The media prefer low maintenance sources that can be trusted to provide reliable leads to information they cannot get on their own. I fit that bill. Reporters often can be the first to know and have excellent general knowledge of their fields, at least this was so in AIDS in the 1990s. Since I had worked as a free-lance journalist with my opinion pieces for *The Wall Street Journal,* other papers, and stories for the *B.A.R* and the *Sentinel,* I learned how to handle reporters and what they and their editors wanted. I knew it was bootless to attack the media, because no one, other than their employers, had power over them---a lesson for Donald Trump, perhaps.

Often the best sources for information that could be traded to the media were the doctors and research scientists, and they tended to be willing to talk to any knowledgeable community activist with standing. Again Delaney and the New Yorkers sometimes failed to grasp that little could be gained and much might be lost by attacking researchers. People who are quick to make enemies render themselves vulnerable to opponents who understand the power of networking their foe's adversaries with each other. I learned this technique early, and used it to link, doctors, researchers, industry reps, bureaucrats, and media in opposition to my opponents. Delaney and his allies accused me of personally ratting on the underground to FDA. That was not only false, it was completely unnecessary. A better way was to set up a network among those who opposed the underground and leave them alone to do the work in their own fashion.

In school I was proficient at science when I needed to be. I even won my High School science contest, and had friends in science or math. But I did not pursue science for its own sake, only as a means to solving practical problems. There's a danger science can become a game of multiplying hypotheses to be tested and retested for the fun of it, rather than for solutions to real problems. Yet it was clear that the most essential solutions to the challenges of AIDS were through science. So I relied on friends, especially Barry and Steven Wright, who knew that area much better than I did.

In the early stages of my activism key scientists, like Sam Broder Director of the National Cancer Institute, would take calls from informed activists. I had science conversations with Broder, Tom Merigan, and many others including industry researchers and local doctors like Marcus Conant. I came to admire their abilities, integrity, and commitment, but they were not celebrities to me, as they were to others. Unlike Delaney and TAG, I never criticized them in public. It became obvious that what the scientists valued most from activists was the political support they needed to secure research funding and improve regulatory speed, not our scientific acumen.

As Barry showed in our ddI-ddC petition, a crucial scientific question for AIDS drug research was which indices, T cells or viral load, accurately measured disease progression. If accurate, the indices could quickly tell us whether the drugs were working and how well. However, FDA wanted to run trials to test the accuracy of viral load counts as indices of disease progression; such trials would delay approval and thereby restrict access to life saving drugs to those in the trials. They sought slow, pains taking scientific documentation with no shortcuts, not to protect patients but to maintain their dilatory procedures. FDA did not smile upon shortcuts through their regulatory song and dance, which given the emergency of the AIDS epidemic, they should have welcomed. Like many libertarian activists, I feared that FDA assumed it was morally acceptable to sacrifice human lives to secure their policies, something unaccountable bureaucracies have done from the Pharaohs on.

The New York activists were all too eager to trust and defend their friends at FDA. The drug company people also defended FDA in public, though speaking one on one with activists they told a different story. For all his flaws, Delaney was reluctant to sacrifice patients to pander to FDA's desire to defend turf. Marty was ambitious and could play fast and loose with the truth, but I saw early on when he first visited me at my house that he had a streak of genuine compassion contending with his ambition. To many people of the generation of Delaney and myself, including the doctors, FDA rigidity was disturbingly reminiscent of the Vietnam era, government officials sacrificing lives just to save face and protect their power. Moreover, the best scientists were loath to sacrifice science on the altar of FDA's risk adverse consumer protectionist ideology. Their loyalty to science proved to be a critical factor in saving great numbers of patient lives. Like the activists, many of the scientists realized that the vaunted cautions of FDA and other agencies were just the hubris of overweening bureaucracies.

Chapter 6
Racing Against the Clock
(1992: 38,333 deaths from AIDS)

Why fear death? Who knows what that undiscovered country holds? I fear losing the sun's golden rays breaking suddenly through afternoon rain, the sounds and scents of a forest waking to life at dawn, the warmth and smooth, sinewy strength of another man, the glorious exhilaration and sheer agony of just being conscious, all so full of surprising beauty. Even from the pits of despair, life can fill magically with so much to know, love, understand, and give. I fear losing this ever challenging, terrible, and unspeakably marvelous world before I can drink it to the dregs.

AIDS patient before his death at age 27

The 1991-1995 period was a race against the clock for knowledgeable AIDS patients, especially the treatment activists. Early in 1991 Dr. Tom Merigan invited an ACT UP Golden Gate group of about a dozen including Jesse Dobson, Barry Freehill, Dave Olson, Bill Thorn, John Dolan, Hank Wilson, and myself to Stanford to discuss treatment development prospects. As mentioned before, Merigan, Doug Richman, and Margaret Fischl, were deemed the most influential researchers running ACTG trials. They were prominent among those vilified by the New York activists at the San Francisco International AIDS Conference the previous year.

Where was their research likely to go, we wondered? Did Merigan see a light at the end of the tunnel for those battling AIDS, and how dim and far away was the light? Merigan, a leading cancer expert, brought to AIDS his methods and special insights from cancer research. His experience with cancer made him wary of the FDA's preferred monotherapy model, then relied on by conservative infectious disease doctors. While single drugs were easier to run through FDA testing routines, that approach deprived doctors of a diverse arsenal to combat the wily virus. HIV, Merigan stressed, was a virus that readily mutated against a single agent and eventually developed resistance to it.

Some patients held on for years with AZT, a few lived long enough to benefit from the cocktails in 1996. Far more often, however, patients developed resistances quickly or had to drop AZT because of its toxicity. Others, like *POZ* magazine founder Sean Straub, attributed their survival to avoiding AZT's toxicity.*18* The side effects and efficacy of the available drugs varied greatly among individuals. Those who failed AZT usually tried to go on to ddI, ddC, or D4T and often failed or developed resistance to all of them. Dave Olson tried all of the nukes. Each time he enjoyed brief respites of a few weeks where he rebounded to something near normal until the toxicities prevailed forcing him to drop each drug.

The 1993 Concorde study would reinforce already widespread doubts about the value of AZT in extending life. Even so, the virus like cancer, Merigan explained, would have greater difficulty developing resistance to an assault by multiple drugs. This would be especially true if those drugs were more powerful than AZT and had lower toxicities that patients could tolerate. The most promising of the new drugs appeared to be the protease inhibitors, but in 1992 their development was still early stage.

Merigan's hopes made sense to me. I refused to believe in the omnipotence of the AIDS virus. That notion came from the despicable idea that AIDS was God's punishment for sinful homosexuals. Although science had never before vanquished a retrovirus, I believed science could bring the terrible virus to its knees, it was only a matter of time. However, many patients along with some activists who worked in AIDS services thought we'd never find effective medicines. Treatment activism attracted the fighters, the optimists, and, as it would turn out, the realists. An ominous cloud hung over our hopes: FDA. Could we drag its sclerotic bureaucracy kicking and screaming into the reality we all faced, or would their regulation without representation succeed in protecting us to death? The answer might depend as much on politics as on science, but in the end it depended most crucially on the grit of activist patients.

The take away for those at the Merigan meeting was: live long enough to benefit from the protease inhibitors and you might well live to collect social security and make progress on your 'bucket list.'

We didn't use that term then, but we had the concept. Dave Olson, for example, had an ambitious bucket list, but was able to complete little of it. He did learn to scuba dive and even picked up a little Spanish for when he went to the Yucatan to explore and dive. He wanted to travel and often fantasized about places to visit across the world, should he live. I've traveled often since that time, exploring every continent except Antarctica. When I see extraordinary sights like Iguassu falls or Uluru or inside the Sagrada Familia I sometimes invite the spirit of Dave and other lost friends to see them through my eyes.

Steve Wright did the grand tour rounds of European cities in a great hurry. He wanted to take in everything while he could. I was able to postpone what I did not have time for then until I was actually collecting social security. Dave and Steve, like most who had AIDS in 1991, didn't have that luxury. Some, Barry and Jesse Dobson for example, chose to stay home and devote their best energies to activism. Yet all were racing against the clock because the clock had different strokes for different folks. AIDS progressions and deaths had a strikingly individual character, more so, it seemed, than other killers like cancer or cirrhosis. HIV was an especially unpredictable monster.

Over all, 1990 to 1995 for San Francisco HIV activists resembled a warzone; like soldiers, the patients never knew when their time was up. For HIV negative friends, these were years of living dangerously. The terror, despair, and deep frustration of the epidemic's first decade was still very much evident, and every year more patients got sick and more died. Repeatedly we'd learn that someone who in recent memory was the picture of health now had weeks to live, or had lost 40 pounds and much of his hair, was suffering dementia, or simply passed suddenly. Every week we'd gaze at the obituaries in the *Bay Area Reporter* and usually find someone we'd known, someone with whom we'd talked and laughed, or shared our newfound sexual freedom with. It is terrible to recall, but worse to experience. AIDS was a veritable holocaust, not inflicted by human intent, but aggravated by bigotry, neglect, and stigma. Yet there was great challenge, struggle, and heroism that brought out the real strengths of many.

There were wonderful patient activists I got close to in both AIDS and cancer, sometimes talking to them often, only to see them pass suddenly with almost no notice. Unless you were very close to someone, like a near relative or a longtime friend, they were not likely to call you up to say 'better hurry over, I'm going to croak soon.' Despair can reflect off friends in amplified form. Most patients wanted to shield from their personal despair all but those closest to them. They had been in the places of their current friends when their own friends had passed. Everyone feared saying goodbye for the last time.

Steve Wright called me one Saturday afternoon. "I think you better come over," he said, "KS is going crazy in my lungs, at best I have a week." He had recently returned from a trip to Rome with his companion, and showed me their pictures. I remember we laughed and joked a lot that afternoon. His mother had brought him a twelve-pack of pork chops. "I won't live long enough to eat all of them, besides I had enough pork chops for two lifetimes from Mom back home in Oklahoma—why don't you take them?" I told him, "No thanks, my mother in Oregon is the same as yours." Steve was never one to let Churchill's black dog take up residence in his psyche. His death a few days later was especially terrible, Kaposi sarcoma had eaten up his lungs and he died of asphyxiation desperately struggling for breath.

1991 was an exceptionally dark, traumatic year. Steve died along with several other friends. Barry and I suffered continuous slanderous and libelous attacks for our attempts to warn the community about the dangers of underground drugs and the mortal need for FDA reform. On August 5 my mother died unexpectedly. She had an operation that appeared to go well. I called her once she'd recovered enough to speak on the phone. After a few minutes talking she said, "you know, I feel just terrible, I better hang up now." Twenty minutes later I got a call informing me that she had succumbed to a massive heart attack. I was the last person she ever spoke to, fitting I suppose since she and others said I was her favorite and she was of course my favorite parent.

My mother was an exceptionally loyal and stable person, grounded in common sense, and tough in her own ways from having struggled through the great depression in South Dakota. She accepted my gay friends and welcomed my companions. Though she was always urging me to pick one and settle down with him. She strongly supported my AIDS work; had she lived longer she would have favored gay marriage. She and her mother, my grandmother, were the only members of my family who always treated me unconditionally as family. When my book *The Unfolding God of Jung and Milton* came out in 1993, I dedicated it to her and to Dave Olson.

Dave had gone up and down through 1988 into early 1991, yet always seemed to bound back with a new drug leveraged by his undaunted will to live. He re-tried AZT repeatedly but always had to drop it because of toxicities, he could not tolerate ddC or ddI. By pressuring Bristol Myers with bad publicity, I managed to get him D4T three years before FDA finally approved it on June 27th 1994. D4T gave him a respite of about 6 weeks, then the toxicities set in. During that brief vacation from dying, he was able to return home to Nebraska to visit relatives and friends one last time. He failed D4T, and I failed in my renewed efforts to get him on passive immunotherapy. My last ditch attempt to get him AZDU, a low toxicity experimental nuke that was never developed, also failed. In October 1991 he was diagnosed with lymphoma and soon began to go blind from CMV retinitis. Then he was hospitalized: it was so serious this time that his parents drove out from Nebraska.

Judging his case hopeless, Dave's doctor wanted to pull him off his meds to let him die. But Dave needed more time for reconciliation with his mother. I could see that it was crucial for both of them. The doctor had to get his mother's permission. She refused to give it unless I advised her to do so. Our confrontation with the doctor over whether to pull Dave's meds ended with a memorable scene in the office of the hospital's head doctor. Barry Freehill was there with us. Barry had watched several friends die including a former lover. He did not believe Dave's time had yet come.

The head doctor glanced at some charts and then addressed Dave's doctor like a professor upbraiding a misguided student. Pointing at me he said, "he and his friends are the most powerful activists in this city. If I go against them this hospital may not be able to move a single shrub on its grounds without being blocked by the city." He pulled out some more charts, studied them, then looked Dave's doctor straight in the eyes, "Besides they're right medically, and you're wrong, look at these charts, Dave's still got two or three months." Such confrontations were not unusual, often the doctors could not tell how long a patient might have. Some who seemed OK were dead in a fortnight, other desperate cases hung on for months or even years.

People who know their time is short, have a different relationship to time and the big questions of life than do those who believe death lies years or decades away. For the dying, death can dominate consciousness as a supreme existential fact. To others death is usually a theoretical concept. The dying often feel a peculiar urgency to do and say what is important to them while they still have time and coherence. A few weeks prior to the confrontation with his doctor, knowing death was near, Dave felt this urge. He called me to come into the hospital saying he wanted "a serious talk."

Dave disliked sentimentality even though he occasionally indulged it, but he hated it in weighty matters and grave situations. For him, it let phony emotion hustle out truth and authentic feeling. "I don't want no talk about any maudlin stuff," he declared the moment I entered the room. "You know I love you, if you don't you'd be blind and a fool, and you're not that. And I know you love me. Enough said." Then, to my surprise, he confided that he'd been thinking about God. Shortly after his diagnosis four years before, he told me he'd come to believe in God and an afterlife. Again he reminded me of that earlier conversation, saying he'd given it more thought. Now he was convinced after death there was nothing. "You will remember me, my family will, and a few friends. But when all of you are gone, like my ashes scattered into the cold Pacific, it will be as if I never existed."

He confided with faint self-disapproval that he had believed in a deity when he was a boy, though he didn't know what it meant, and later also with people who wanted him to believe. But he withdrew from them to discover his own truths. "There may be a supreme being or universal ordering force, like in *Star Wars*" he mused, with a weary smile. "But there cannot be a God Who thinks or cares about individual people or even about mankind itself. I've known too much senseless suffering, too many cut down, their lives extinguished before that had really begun. As for the Christians, I've seen too much of their cruel discrimination, and mindless hatred of gay people ever to believe a just, humane God inspires them."

Dave's arguments did not win me. It was the loss of the one who succeeded Dave in my life that most moved me toward his opinion. Real experiences are ever more powerful arguments than arguments themselves.

Dave Olson died at age 33 in the late afternoon of January 10, 1992. I was holding his hand as he took his last breath. His mother from Nebraska was staying with him in his small basement apartment. They had achieved reconciliation and were at peace with each other at last. That week I came by every afternoon and brought him a red rose. Two days before he died Dave sat up in bed, took the rose and said "Hello Jim," He hadn't spoken for three days, his mother told me that was the last thing he ever said.

After they came for his body, I drove home. A cyclone whirled in my head, I accidentally ran a red light and nearly collided with a pickup in a busy intersection on Oak Street. I felt numb and disoriented. At home I sat for an hour, maybe two, staring in silent despair out my window at the evening San Francisco skyline. Finally, I realized that somehow I needed to find ballast for my soul. On impulse, I called Beverly Zakarian, the ovarian cancer activist from New York whose testimony rescued Barry and me from being ostracized by ACT UP. We spoke for a long time, but I never mentioned my loss, I couldn't. We just talked about other things, her trip to Ayer's Rock in Australia, her daughter getting married, Shakespeare, our distrust of FDA and the drug companies and activists who pandered to FDA. After talking with Beverly, I felt better, felt it was OK to be in this world. Beverly died about a year later, as did another courageous and brilliant cancer activist we were both close to, Dr. Eugene Schoenfeld.

Beverly's daughter asked me to write a remembrance for her service: Beverly had told her I was the activist she felt closest to. I cite it because it says a lot about the struggles of AIDS and cancer activists in those years, and shows through Beverly how activism often brought out the finest in people:

In Remembrance of Beverly Zakarian

In her ten years as a cancer fighter, Beverly Zakarian became a touchstone for integrity. Beverly never did anything or took any position because it was politically smart or correct or because it would put her name in the lights. Beverly did what she did because she believed it was right, period. Ignoring expediency and self-interest, she was nonetheless highly effective. Her very integrity was the secret ingredient of her effectiveness: because you could always trust Beverly's sincerity and intelligence, she could be very persuasive.

I first got to know Beverly in the late eighties when many in the media and politics were trying to pit cancer patients against AIDS patients. AIDS was getting too much research money, and too much attention they asserted. Beverly stepped forward to defend AIDS research pointing out that most of it had significant implications for cancer. As for the attention given to AIDS activism, she said the cancer activists should take notes from the AIDS activists to get more attention for their own cause. Beverly was a pioneer in applying AIDS activist practices to cancer. She focused especially on FDA where she worked harder than any other cancer activist to awaken that somnolent agency.

For the integrity and courage of her activism, Beverly sometimes paid the price of exclusion. Exclusion hurt her, the hurt never tempted her to compromise her principles and integrity.

Beyond being a heroic activist, she was also a heroic cancer patient who showed others how to confront cancer with courage, resourcefulness, and indomitable spirit. What I came to value most about Beverly, however, was something different. She was great fun to be with and a wonderful, caring friend. We conducted joint AIDS-cancer meetings in Washington with FDA, the Administration, and Congress always working to speed drug approval and research. We believed that the AIDS and cancer causes were related and best served when each group supported the other.

I remember particularly that January day in 1992 when my very close friend Dave died. After returning home I realized it might help to talk to someone, but I didn't want to go out. The phone sat before me, but who to call? Suddenly it seemed obvious that the one person to call was Beverly. I called her, we talked for more than an hour, and once again I felt connected to humanity and my life.

Dave had many of Beverly's best qualities, her unflinching integrity, sincerity, intelligence, and a highly focused sense of purpose that gave clarity about priorities. Like her he was a lot of fun and a wonderfully loyal friend. He enjoyed life enormously and loved to give enjoyment to others. He longed to experience all the riches of life, a miserly fate denied him that. I never wrote a memorial to Dave, it would have been too difficult to say what he was to me. But Dave had left me with a duty. He honestly believed that I was the most effective activist working then, and he had known many of the others. Twice when visitors in his hospital room criticized me, he told them to get out and not come back. He believed that FDA was the key to saving more lives and I was the activist most determined and best able to hold FDA's feet to the fire. So I continued with activism. At times I did not want to, but a sense of duty, and the hope that I might prove Dave's belief in me justified, held me on the course he had set for me.

Dave also left me with a suggestion that I definitely did not want to pursue. "You should find," he told me, "another young AIDS patient to help, so that you will think less about me." The last thing I wanted to go through again was losing someone like Dave. So I became careful not to get too close to or involved with any new AIDS patient. You don't always get what you want. Whether you get what you need is another question.

A little over a year after Dave died, I began noticing a young guy in his mid-twenties who worked out at my gym. Ironically, his name was David. His sad beauty, like a sorrowing angel or Nordic Christ, moved me, and it took an effort to keep my eyes off him. But he was out of my league, young enough to be my son, and rather reserved; so I did not want to approach him. Moreover, I knew he was HIV positive. Once he entered the sauna finding me alone, he seemed a bit disoriented and dropped his towel in a bucket of water. On the spur of the moment, I handed him my extra towel with a smile. At first, he looked like he was going to cry. He had misinterpreted my interest in him as judgmental; seeing his error, he was eager to talk. David knew who I was, read my articles in the papers, and attended the ACT UP meeting where they tried to censure and expel

Barry Freehill and myself. He'd actually spoken on our behalf because of his bad experiences with underground ddC. Indeed, to him I was a hero.

He told me he'd wanted to talk to me, but was afraid because he got emotional discussing his medical condition. Inhibition was a problem among AIDS patients then, especially the younger ones. We left together as he confided that he'd just learned his T cells were dropping again. David had been an English major at a small college, continued to a Master's degree, and had taught high school English. He was shy, sweet, and modest, the last trait was a little surprising since his physical appeal far exceeded modest. We loved many of the same writers, like Milton, Shakespeare, Melville, Dostoevsky, and Flannery O'Connor. Jung was also a favorite. He was currently reading O'Connor's letters. He loved jazz too, along with Bach, Verdi, Hieronymus Bosch, and El Greco.

Religion fascinated him, Christianity in particular where he drew sharp differentiation between Christians and Churchians. Christians worship a God of Love and Truth and strive to live by the golden rule. Churchians worship outdated conventions and live by social conformity and unexamined biases. They are the modern Pharisees who deify their group's ideas and customs and blaspheme God by attributing to Him hatred of and lies about gay people. He particularly despised the Evangelicals' hypocrisy in glibly condoning divorce for straight people while they cherry pick scriptures to find ways to harshly condemn same sex love. "The Churchians turn a God of love and truth into a devil of hate and bigotry," he would complain.

An artist's temperament and a way with words made David a kind of poet. As a writer his main subjects were himself, his inner world and immediate experience, as well as the gods and God. His relationship with his father had been close, complex and deeply dysfunctional. Strict "Churchians," his parents brutally rejected him when he revealed he was gay and HIV positive. He characterized his mother as "an Anita Bryant who can't carry a tune in a bucket," and believed his father was a repressed version of himself. Another refugee, he fled to San Francisco where he came out as what was often called a "daddy's boy," in that he preferred men old enough to be his father.

Although he had rejected intellectually the guilt and sense of sin for being gay, he remained a divided soul with a grey cloud of indeterminate guilt always hanging over him. In compensation he, like many individualistic gay men in that place and time, was attracted to the symbolism of the leather S & M world whose acts for him were rituals defying conventional notions of sin in order to purge guilt. Yet part of him still saw AIDS as a punishment for sin. Like many AIDS patients, he couldn't avoid the gnawing question, why me? Expiatory punishment offered him a way to fend off his inescapable temptation to give in to the disease. Patient activists like Jesse Dobson and Dave Olson had an opposite response to the same problem, they purged through rebellion the guilt society imputed to them. We quickly became close and he confessed that he longed for intimacy, but feared infecting others. He sought, as an act of expiation, to be ritualistically punished with humiliation by a benevolent father figure. Altogether, David seemed like a character out of Flannery O'Connor, had she known the San Francisco S & M scene. He once remarked that no other writer could have done it justice as well as she.

Deeply sorry for him, I became powerfully attracted as well. His vulnerability seemed to amplify all his attractions. Searching for ways and ideas to make him happy and get him laughing became a favorite pastime. No one had a more beautiful laugh. He asked me if I thought I would be safe with him if I wore double condoms. I told him yes, knowing the odds of getting infected that way were low, and doubting that I could deny him anything. This was the only case where I had risky sex with someone I knew to be HIV positive, although I was tempted before. In the long years prior to PrEP, sex between HIV positive and negative gay men was a sensitive and sometimes a taboo matter. After a couple of weeks, he complained about losing hair. He asked me to give him a buzzcut so no one would notice. I didn't want to, liked his long wavy blonde-reddish hair and didn't believe he was losing it anyway, yet I couldn't refuse. As his hair fell before the clippers he started to cry, but we laughed at the mirror when it was done. It seemed his rite of expiation. We had sex then using condoms and often thereafter; I remained HIV negative. I thought he was too young for me, but he thought I was just right for him: he won that debate.

A few of months passed. We would ride our bicycles through Golden Gate Park to the ocean, taking a different route each way. We'd take off our shoes, run in the sand on the beach, then dash into the water; usually no one but us was there. Or we'd stroll along the Land's End cliffs talking about all manner of different things, or simply listen to the waves crashing against the rocks. At home we'd read poetry aloud together, something I never did with any other lover. Absorbed in him, I had time or thought for little else. In memory, it seems as if he filled that entire brief period, for I remember almost nothing but him.

He lost some weight and his T cell decline continued. But he appeared to be in much better physical shape than Dave ever was during the four years before he died. I hoped he'd last to benefit from Merigan's new cocktails. At times contemplating his fate, an immense, impenetrable sadness would settle over him. By nature, he was pessimistic; part of him wanted to die to expiate his amorphous guilt and nagging sense of sin. Not a fighter like Dave, he was more of a submitter. In late autumn he decided to make a last effort to reconcile with his parents. I was against it, but not strongly enough feeling we both could use a small break from this intense relationship. In any event he was determined to go come what may. I might have forbidden him and he might have obeyed me, but I had great difficulty saying no to him.

After several days when I didn't hear from him, he called to say he'd gotten sick and had checked into a hospital. His parents had again brutally rejected him, plunging him into a vortex of despair and guilt. We talked for a long time, and I offered to come to Colorado, but couldn't get away until two weeks from then. We spoke again the next day, and the day after, then he didn't call for two days. When he did, that call left me with an awful foreboding that I might not see him again. Rejected once more by his parents, whom he loved despite all, I suspected he might be in danger of losing his will to live; that was a risk for some AIDS patients.

In his last call he sounded weak, and wavered into incoherence. Always disliking discussion of medical details, he revealed only that the doctors were not hopeful. With a shock I realized he'd been sparing me the worst. I saw that denial had been blinding me. Fully awake at last, I made arrangements to leave the next day. The morning before my flight, a nurse from the hospital called to tell me he had passed in the night. Gay lives are precious; like too many others his ended alone, unvalued, in an alien place. He'd left the nurse a package with a few things he wanted me to have in case I didn't arrive in time. The package had a brief note in trembling handwriting: "I'm so sorry for the terrible pain I know this will cause you. Most of all, I regret that we did not meet years before, yet feel deep gratitude for our few short months together. My spirit will wait for you amidst the mystery of things. Take your time, there is much left for you to do."

He seemed the most thoughtful and vulnerable person I knew then, his combination of qualities profoundly touched and attracted me. I was inconsolable upon learning of his death. Fate had toyed with both of us, like the proverbial cruel boy torturing flies for sport. Today I remain grateful for the all too brief times we shared, yet some losses can never be repaired. He was not the first patient friend who seemed all right, got sick, and never left the hospital. It tore the survivors' hearts in pieces. One of the worst things about the AIDS epidemic was that so often you never got to tell them what they meant to you.

If only I had insisted he'd stay in San Francisco with me where his doctors and support system were, if only I, if only . . . Guilt seemed illogical because I had no idea he would suddenly get sick, but feelings have their own sovereignty that refuses to bow to mere logic. No one can help thinking of what might have been if those they loved had lived, of the experiences and lives they would have shared, of the happiness lost to them and to all. Like many survivors of a war, I felt cursed to have survived comrades who had become the dearest parts of my life. As a defense mechanism, I became more resistant to allowing those under an AIDS death sentence, or anyone else, to get close. Yet that generated more feelings of guilt and of cowardice for somehow betraying them. Though most would consider my withdrawal excusable, I never did fully excuse myself. People you love die, but grief and love for them can live as long as you do.

My story may be more the rule than the exception. Nearly everyone who survived that time has sorrowful tales of dear ones who did not make it. Did those left behind after the deaths of friends and lovers get an AIDS version of PTSD? Of course we did! But like so many others, I already had PTSD. Mine began with the homophobic abuses at UW-Madison that drove me to became a refugee in San Francisco. A great deal has been said and written about survivor guilt. The term in my situation seems a misnomer. I did not feel guilty about surviving, but did experience a range of painful emotions: exasperation with myself over my failure to do enough; frustration with the boneheaded, intolerant politics of AIDS, outrage at the smug indifference of society and the prevalent notion that gays deserved AIDS. Above all David fired my fury over the perversion of religion that allows crass, opportunistic bigots to claim their prejudices and abuses are sanctioned, indeed demanded, by their "loving God."

Chapter 7
The Moral
Challenges of Partisan Politics

The deaths of the two Davids, my mother, Steve, Beverly, and many other friends in the short space of two and a half years left an abyss in my life. I was still busy with real estate, an aggravation that nonetheless kept up a reasonable flow of money, but my second book *The Unfolding God of Jung and Milton* had just been published and I had no ideas then for another. By late 1994 I was looking for new activities to keep at bay grief and depression. That year Newt Gingrich's Contract with America turned US politics upside down, creating thereby possibilities for real FDA reform. To pursue that opening, would require more extensive involvement with the Republicans.

Other than the duty to do what was necessary to save lives, my most powerful motive for working with Republicans on FDA was intellectual integrity. The Republican position of balancing the risks of drug approval against the benefits, made sense. The Democrats giving free reign to the FDA bureaucracy to enforce an arbitrary efficacy standard at the cost of lives and avoidable suffering made no sense morally or medically. It was just plain wrong to put politics above human lives and suffering, wrong and oh so typical of FDA and most bureaucracies.

However, working with Republican officials was rarely a path strewn with roses for me or any of the Log Cabin Republicans, and it often became a crown of thorns when dealing with the gay community. Yet there seemed to be no selling the Democrats on FDA reform. At least no one any place in the political spectrum thought this feasible, and none of the gay Democrats were willing to spend chits trying. Of course there were a few admirable conscientious objectors among the Democrats, like Tom Harkin and John Kerry, but they were a tiny offshoot from the vast, blind herd. I remember that John Kerry once said if he were on the ledge atop a skyscraper with Ted Kennedy and said join me in reforming FDA or I will jump, Kennedy would say, "Jump!" In other words, real FDA reform would be political suicide for any Democrat. No fan of suicide myself, Democrats like Kerry and Harkin had my sympathy.

Thus, our very limited leverage against FDA remained with the Republicans, so I became Log Cabin's AIDS Advisor in late 1994. Even when individual Republicans were ready to work with us, they did not want to risk making it known to media or their rank and file. Too many Republicans expected us to be grateful to them whenever they tolerated us, which wasn't all that often, while most liberals expected total loyalty in gratitude for their more frequent toleration. In retrospect, I realize neither party saw it that way, but that's how most of us perceived it.

Then as now, most gay liberals were in denial about the devaluation of our humanity implicit in expecting gratitude let alone blind loyalty for being tolerated. Those who strayed from the plantation must be punished with *ad hominin* abuse, and ostracism, as is the case today for some blacks who stray, like famed rapper Kanye West. The Democrats wanted LGBTs and blacks to support them as an indivisible block to pressure apolitical people in these groups to get out and vote with their friends for the party. Although the Republicans welcomed first Jews then began to welcome blacks and Hispanics who left the Democrat reservation, they have never yet welcomed LGBTs. Exceptional grit, or at least steadfast masochism, is required of LGBTs who consistently stick with the Republican party.

Most Republicans still fail to recognize their political need for securing support among LGBTs. Denial on the party's LGBT problems runs deep. Orrin Hatch, a man who understood the Christian ethic better than most of his fellow Republicans wrote early on that no major party and no major church (including his own LDS) could afford to write off permanently any substantial subgroup of the population. Outreach to us was essential. Still openness, let alone outreach, was rare then and remains the exception rather than the rule today. Although public attitudes on LGBTs have improved over the last fifteen years, too little of that improvement spilled into the ranks of GOP leaders. As a result, while the number of voters who self-identify as LGBT has risen to 6%, the number of LGBTs who support Republicans has fallen in every presidential election since 2000 reaching a low of 14% under Donald Trump in 2016. If Trump keeps the amiable bigot Mike Pence on the ticket, LGBT support will likely fall lower in 2020. If Mr. Pence heads the ticket in 2024, LGBTs may overtake blacks as the most solidly Democrat voting bloc. That will bode ill for LGBTs, the Republican Party, and America itself.

It will also create perturbation and conflict within the considerable section of the LGBT community who, except for social issues, tend to either align with Republicans or remain independent thinkers. Our minds may be with the Republicans on most issues. But since too many in that party stigmatize us for who we love and who we are, our hearts will remain alienated. Conflicts of heart against mind are profoundly frustrating, ever painful, and never easy to resolve. Yet the heart remains the default setting for most of humanity, so in the voting booth most LGBTs will continue to pull the lever for Democrats until there is a change of heart within the GOP.

Republican pandering to homophobic wolves posing as righteous sheep deserves sharp condemnation. It genuflects to crude bigotry posturing as religion. It ignores LGBTs' constitutional rights to equal protection, and it besmirches the religions it purports to champion. Homophobic bias, discrimination, and oppression is never sanctioned in the New Testament. Discrimination is an offense against the very spirit of Jesus's teachings. Homophobic bias does as much damage as racial bias and is just as wrong. Since racial bias has been repudiated by the churches, homophobia has become the last refuge of bigotry. Attributing such an abuse, such a deficiency of love and indulgence of hate, to a God Who is defined as Love is, as David stressed, sheer blasphemy.

In centuries past Christians in our Southern slave states used scriptures from the Old Testament and St Paul to condone and even defend slavery. After emancipation they used the Bible to justify racial segregation and prohibiting inter-racial marriage. The Afrikaners used the Bible to support Apartheid. Until the Mormon Church's leader was enlightened by a "vision," the Mormons believed that the Old Testament sanctioned denigration of Black people. For centuries religion was a rationale for persecuting Jews as "the murderers of Christ." The Catholic

Church only began apologizing for Christian antisemitism in the 1960s. Even human sacrifice and genocide have been championed in the name of religions.

Using religion to sanctify perpetuation of stigma and anti-LGBT discrimination is as heinous as any of the above moral crimes. Those who attribute to deity the evils in human nature ultimately promote atheism. To sanction bias against LGBTs on the basis of religious freedom is as much an abuse of religious freedom as is using the same rationale to sanction slavery, segregation, apartheid, or anti-Semitism. In America human rights should trump any claim of religious freedom to violate those rights, and it does even for the Republican party except when it comes to the rights of LGBTs!

Yet the Democrats are no angels. Few batted an eye about sacrificing countless LGBTs and African Americans with AIDS to the rigidity of FDA drug approval policies. On LGBTs they follow the curve of public support, but are never ahead of it. That's not surprising in view of the party's past defense of slavery and promotion of Jim Crowe laws and segregation. Democrat Andrew Jackson pursued genocidal policies against native Americans. President Wilson pushed segregation and encouraged the Ku Klux Klan. Even Franklin Roosevelt, proponent of the Four Freedoms, interred our Japanese citizens to placate racist paranoia. Democrats today court champions of Sharia law with all its ingrained misogyny, homophobia, and rank violations of human dignity, not to mention sometimes embracing anti-Semites like Louis Farrakhan, Ilhan Omar, and Linda Sarsour. Every bit as bad considering her position, Karen Pence, second lady of the United States teaches in a school whose biased policies on LGBTs are illegal in the twenty-nine states. To their shame, no prominent Republicans have spoken out against Mrs. Pence's affiliation. Our two parties remain a lose-lose proposition for LGBTs, it's just a question of what you lose and how big you lose.

To those who criticize me for working with Republicans, I say anyway you get involved in politics you make compromises that dirty your hands. The all-important question is whether by dirtying your hands you can save and improve people's lives. Mother Theresa worked the dirtiest slums of Calcutta: she became a saint for it.

Chapter 8
FDA Reform Gathers Steam
(1993: 39,779 AIDS deaths)

As previously mentioned, the first persons to encourage me to start advocating for AIDS with Republicans were themselves prominent gay Democrats, notably Jim Foster and Tim Westmoreland. When I met with Tim in 1989 he asked me to visit Senator Pete Wilson's health aide Kim Belshe and called her on my behalf. That was the beginning of a productive relationship with Kim, a distinguished public servant, that continued when she became Head of the California Health Department during Wilson's terms as governor. It brought significant benefits to people with AIDS: for example, under Wilson California established an AIDS Drug Assistance Program that became a model for the nation.

In the early Clinton years, I worked with Diane Abbitt and David Mixner of MECLA and the Human Rights Campaign (HRC). Their groups had tried legal action to get FDA to move the drugs but got nowhere. They noticed, however, that street activists, particularly Martin Delaney and myself, seemed to be making a dent. HRC did not want to engage in ACT UP tactics against FDA because that might bring confrontations with key Democrats, like Waxman and possibly Kennedy. Such confrontations, they believed, would threaten hard won and fragile backing for gay rights; and that would spook their donors. Still, at one point it was suggested that I come to Washington to represent HRC on AIDS.

During that period, I formed four key friendships with pharmaceutical industry people, John Petricianni and Linda Nersessian at Pharma, Lisa Raines at BIO and then Genzyme, and Marty Rose at Genentech. Moderate Republicans, they were all fine people, honest, loyal, and compassionate, who belied the leftist stereotypes of pharma executives as greed driven villains. John was gay and Linda, Lisa and Marty were gay friendly. But it was the op eds in the *Wall Street Journal* that really opened the door to Vice President Quayle's office and that of Palo Alto Congressman Tom Campbell. Despite President Bush's failure to fire FDA Commissioner David Kessler, a loss of political nerve much lamented by key Republicans Orrin Hatch and Newt Gingrich, the Bush Administration was decidedly interested in FDA reform.

Because its decisions affect a vast swathe of the economy and the lives of everyone, FDA was, is, and always will be a political body. That point was made to me in a memorable way by Louis Lasagna, an expert on FDA at Yale University who had developed reform recommendations that became popular in the AIDS community. Professor Lasagna told me that President Nixon once called him for advice on a new FDA Commissioner. Lasagna offered Nixon three names, listing the merits of each. He then added, almost as an afterthought, "all three are Democrats, but that won't matter, I suppose." There was a long pause at the other end, then Nixon rejoined, voiced lowered, "You suppose wrong." Nixon was of course right, and no one illustrated better how right he was than Bush's new FDA Commissioner. David Kessler was chosen in order to win Ted Kennedy's support for confirmation. Kessler promised reform, but was not delivering the types of reforms Republicans and most AIDS activists wanted. His "reforms" made the FDA bureaucracy more powerful and efficient, and thus better able to resist pressure for change from the public and patients.

The arena for FDA reform under Bush 41 was not the White House itself, but next door in Vice President Quayle's office where I worked with his FDA expert John Corrhson. Quayle headed the Council on Competitiveness, whose prime focus was the impact of regulation on US competitiveness. Like Senator Hatch, Quayle and his staff were quick to grasp the value of AIDS activists as motivators for FDA reform. The activists had mounted aggressive demonstrations against the agency at its Rockville headquarters. Film clips of hundreds of demonstrators confronting mounted police were broadcast on the nightly network news. The country hadn't seen anything like it since the Vietnam war. Everyone interested in FDA was fascinated, including the Vice President.

I had several meetings with Quayle staffers. In an especially memorable one they asked high FDA officials to come to the Vice

President's office to meet with me and two AIDS patients. I chose Jack Girard, a figure in the AIDS drug underground, and his wife Cindy. Also with them was their infant daughter Jackie who would be orphaned when her parents died: they both succumbed before the cocktails arrived. We berated the FDA officials in front of their bosses. I compared them to apparatchiks for mindlessly following FDA procedures regardless of the impact on public health and human lives. The Girards, who seemed typical flyover country Americans, but weren't of course, laid out their dilemma powerfully. Jackie boosted her parents by crying almost on cue. It was good theater, and it left the FDA officials decidedly uncomfortable. Their discomfort peaked when Girard explained how FDA, in order to relieve pressure to approve drugs, had colluded with the AIDS drug underground to overlook its sale of unsafe, illegal knockoffs of AIDS drugs stalled in FDA. Most important, the meeting drove home a valuable point FDA would not easily forget: at least one activist was able to bring AIDS complaints against FDA to the highest levels of government where the patients' cause found very receptive ears.

George H. W. Bush, his re-election campaign tainted by the rank homophobia in the 1992 Republican national convention, lost to Bill Clinton. Clinton was, unlike Ted Kennedy, Ted Weiss, and Henry Waxman, a pragmatist on many things including FDA. Moreover, he was concerned about the impact of FDA delays on the gay vote. To his credit, Clinton was the first President to give a fig about the gay vote. His concern was illumined by his friendship with David Mixner who helped him do the numbers on the impact of gay issues at the ballot box—an area of chronic denial for Republicans.

Rudy Giuliani's political star was on the rise. In his 1994 run for New York Mayor he secured nearly half the gay vote. But a worse threat than Giuliani took the Democrats by surprise in late 1994. Hillary Clinton's healthcare reforms failed, the Republicans swept the House and Senate in the midterm election making Newt Gingrich the Speaker of the House in 1995.

Gingrich was a tireless proponent of sweeping FDA reforms. His privatization proposals made sense to me then, as they still do today. Remembering Nixon's words, I knew that being a government agency did not guarantee freedom from political influence. In reality, it made influence peddling easier and more likely. Like Gingrich, I had reached the conclusion that FDA's massive regulation of drug development was far from being cost effective. Overall it often was and remains an impediment to innovation. It neither adequately protects public health, nor respects the rights of individual patients, largely because it fails to properly assess policies and approval decisions on a basis of risk/benefit to patients and public health. Similarly, it tends to ignore or discount the importance of inevitable tradeoffs. Too much of FDA is bureaucracy for bureaucracy's sake, a problem endemic to the DC swamp. Peter Barton Hutt, a leading Washington lawyer on FDA matters who taught the FDA law course at Harvard, had guided my research which led me toward these conclusions. Peter's knowledge of FDA was encyclopedic. Always ready to answer my questions, he was ever generous with his time and sage counsel.

Gingrich had established the Progress and Freedom Foundation to promote his ideas; its flagship project was FDA reform. They asked me to join their Advisory Board headed by the estimable Louis Sullivan, former Secretary of HHS under the first President Bush. Gingrich, a classic disrupter, was the Donald Trump of his time, though more of an intellectual. The liberal press routinely blasted him for a litany of charges, high among them was "trying to gut" FDA. "Beware Thalidomide! Ohhhh, Beware, beware, Thalidomide!" FDA's camp followers cried, like the proverbial broken record. The Human Rights Campaign (HRC), at the urging of the Democrats, recruited Newt's lesbian sister Candace to travel the country rallying the gay community against Gingrich and his government reform policies. But Newt proved wily and impervious, I knew those qualities would be needed to get anywhere with FDA. And I saw he could be our ace in the hole in the inevitable showdown with FDA when the researchers finally found breakthrough drugs where speed of FDA approval would become a life or death matter for tens of thousands of AIDS patients.

Unfortunately for the Republicans, in the 1990's they lacked the imagination to grasp and the will to seize the political opportunities that FDA delays were opening for them with gays and with AIDS as well as cancer patients. In the wake of the Republicans' 1992 "Pat Buchanan convention" they got only 27% of the national gay vote, but in 1994 their share rose to 40%. Had they capitalized on this rise with a more aggressive effort to gain gay support on the issues of AIDS and FDA, they might have done even better in subsequent elections, and people with AIDS might have gotten life-saving access to the breakthrough cocktails precious months earlier.

Through the San Francisco ACT UP demonstrations, my op eds castigating FDA abuses, and the connections with Quayle, Tom Campbell, and Gingrich, I had become the most visible AIDS activist dealing with Republicans. FDA's patsies in the activist community targeted me as if I were a miniature Gingrich. A September 5, 1995 article in *The San Francisco Chronicle* discussed my positions on FDA reform and pinpointed my key place in the movement:

> *Driscoll, as national AIDS policy advisor to Log Cabin Republicans, is at the forefront of the push for speeding up the FDA's drug approval system...." On FDA reform the Republicans are the only game in town," Driscoll said. "Luddites are in control of the Democrats." The combination of conservative ideology and direct experience with AIDS gives the gay Republican group a unique slant---and considerable credibility on the highly complex FDA reform proposals. . . Most AIDS advocacy groups are deeply suspicious of Republican "reform" efforts at the FDA, seeing instead a thinly veiled industry push to advance its own interests. . .. Driscoll, however, accused the established drug companies of trying to slow down the proposed speed up at FDA---because slow approvals keep competitor's new products at bay.*

FDA's Manhattan minions already hated me for exposing their underground drug hustle; the Gingrich connection only intensified their animosity. At the 1996 International AIDS Conference in Vancouver Canada, I asked Gary Rose, a notably reasonable Democrat AIDS activist from New York, to explain their animosity. He paused, then said delicately, "you're, well Jim, to them you are Satan."

Their animosity was worth enduring because the connection with Gingrich would become indispensable for a new activist alliance fighting to save tens of thousands of our people's lives. It was essential for FDA to know that delays in approving AIDS drugs could bring serious reprisals from the party that controlled the US Congress and from the Speaker of the House whom they regarded as a holy terror. They already realized that Bill Clinton could not be relied upon to defend FDA if the agency delayed AIDS drugs. Clinton knew that the media was sympathetic to the plight of the patients, and he was ever attentive to the potential power of gay voters and especially wealthy gay campaign contributors.

In 1990 the most gay-friendly Republican in the California congressional delegation was Tom Campbell, from Palo Alto. Tom, a rare intellectual in Congress who later joined the Stanford Law School faculty, readily understood the dilemmas FDA had created for AIDS patients. As mentioned previously, in 1991 I wrote the rough draft for his limited FDA reform bill to speed approval of drugs for life threatening conditions. Most Republicans signed on to the bill. The June 20 1991 *Wall Street Journal* ran my op ed supporting his bill: "Drugs that Could Save and a Bill that Could Help." It summarizes the dilemma of the patients and their urgent need for FDA reforms:

> *Rep. Tom Campbell's . . . legislative proposal would expedite approval for drugs for life threatening conditions: approval would depend on risk benefit judgments. . . This would be a radical departure from traditional FDA policies which stress the danger of mistakenly approving a harmful or worthless drug and disregard the benefits of rapidly approving drugs with unique advantages. The rationale for FDA's unbalanced approach is easy to understand: People hurt by bad drugs know it and complain to the media and Congress while those denied the benefits of valuable unapproved drugs seldom recognize their loss.*
>
> *The FDA's approval policies have spawned an imbalance in pharmaceutical development. . . the firms too often concentrate their resources on sure bet mass-market drugs and carefully limit their commitments to breakthrough drugs for smaller markets. . ... For the one million Americans with the AIDS virus, expedited approval has become a life and death issue. Many experts believe that we already have in development drugs that used in combination can make HIV a manageable illness. But those drugs will not reach the people who need them anytime*

soon. While the FDA pedantically measures the exact efficacy of new AIDS drugs, tens of thousands of lives could be needlessly lost.

Under Mr. Campbell's expedited approval approach, new drugs for life threatening diseases such as AIDS, Alzheimer's and cancer, could be approved as soon as we have credible evidence that their benefits are likely to outweigh their risks. . . The shortcomings of our present Band-Aid system of "expanded access" has failed to provide early or ready access . . . Because it is utilized only by well-educated, affluent patients "expanded access" discriminates against minorities, the poor and people outside major cities. . ..

Moral outrage joins with common sense and fiscal sanity to call for faster approval based on risk-benefit analysis. AIDS, Alzheimer's and cancer patients have a human right to attempt to save or improve their lives with promising new treatments whose efficacy has not been fully tested.

The Campbell bill was the first and only bill to address the dilemma of people with AIDS, cancer, and other killers. So why didn't Project Inform, TAG, HRC, and other AIDS groups rally to it? Because the Democrat establishment thought Campbell's reform bill conflicted with obligatory obeisance to thalidomide FDA's great totem to excess caution and rationale for regulatory feather bedding. When push came to shove on FDA, the gay groups loyalty to the Democrats trumped their loyalty to AIDS patients. Consequently, the AIDS community itself was divided. FDA's shills zealously attacked the bill, Tom Campbell, and myself. They resembled today's "resistance" a quarter of a century early, demonizing all Republicans and those who worked with them. All things of Republican provenance were verboten, even if they could save countless lives.

But the Campbell bill was basically "an idea bill," and many, including reasonable Democrats, like Rep. Tom Lantos and Sen. Tom Harkin, thought it was a good idea. Still, the Democrats who liked the ideas in the Campbell bill wanted to see them in a bill written by Democrats—not that Tom Campbell did not try for Democrat co-sponsors. Given the influence of FDA's bootlickers in Congress, waiting for such a bill would be tantamount to waiting for Godot. However, had the mainstream AIDS activist groups supported the Campbell bill, it could have become a game changer by putting intense pressure on the Democrats to develop a compromise bill.

The cases for and against the Campbell bill were judiciously laid out by John James in "Expedited Access: the "Campbell Bill" Controversy." The main contention of the bill's opponents,' voiced by Delaney, the New Yorkers, and other gay democrats, was that we could trust FDA to reform itself. A Republican bill they argued, without a shred of real evidence, would stir up the consumer protectors to demand tightening of the efficacy standard for approving AIDS drugs. FDA knew, Delaney contended, that testing efficacy precisely was difficult in a raging epidemic and so Kessler was working on ways to solve the problems. As John James put Delaney's position:

> *FDA Commissioner **Kessler very much wants to speed critical drug approvals and is already preparing a plan to do so**---a plan based on new regulations (or on a policy statement) under existing law, not new legislation from Congress. Most experts believe that the FDA already has the power to do what the Campbell bill would ask it to do. Why then, is new legislation necessary? (AIDS Treatment News, Oct 11, 1991)*

The answer should have been obvious. As our 1990 petition of FDA had demonstrated, the agency did indeed already have the power to speed AIDS drugs approvals under existing accelerated approval policies. But years into the AIDS epidemic they continued to stubbornly resist relaxing their efficacy standards to allow for regular use of accelerated approval. Compulsion from outside was necessary, and it would be up to the AIDS community to provide that compulsion.

(John James at FDA demo before SF Federal Building)

As stressed previously, FDA's rigid enforcement of the efficacy standard was not dictated by either the letter or spirit of the law. Congress left efficacy up to the FDA's discretion, it was arbitrary and that's exactly the way the agency wanted it. Being arbitrary, as we have seen, gave them great discretionary power. When does a bureaucracy voluntarily roll back its power? Delaney and his community allies should have known better than to expect FDA to limit the arbitrary power their undefined efficacy standard afforded. Some of FDA's Manhattan minions may actually have been taken in by all of FDA's statistician legerdemain. The shrewder among them should have known better, they liked FDA's arbitrary power too because it left the agency free to favor their friends in the AIDS community who thereby gained legitimacy and influence with the researchers, the drug companies, and rich liberal foundations.

Everything that I learned about FDA told me Delaney's assertion that Kessler would formulate new regulations to speed AIDS drug approval was either a dangerous delusion or a deliberate hoax to hide Kessler's inaction. In the following years we saw zero evidence that Kessler's FDA was working on new regulations to speed drugs for AIDS or other killers. Why make new rules? Kessler knew the obstacles were not their rules; they were in the FDA culture that administered those rules. By 1994-1995 when approval of the new protease based cocktails became a life and death issue, Kessler had not presented any new plan to speed AIDS drug approvals and Delaney apparently had forgotten his earlier assurances that Kessler was working on one. Amazingly, no one in the community followed up with Delaney or Kessler on their promised internal FDA reforms to speed drug approval. As we shall see, Kessler, FDA, and TAG were instead scheming to discontinue accelerated approval and return to snail paced full approval for AIDS drugs.

Chapter 9
Log Cabin Republicans
and other Republicans
(1994: 42,645 AIDS deaths)

With the Campbell bill, which Log Cabin Republicans alone among gay community groups supported, LCR became a major player in AIDS treatment activism. Let me quote a summary of LCR's FDA related activities written by the Georgia chapter upon belated passage of a successor to the Campbell bill, the FDA reform bill of 1997:

> *Beginning with legislation first introduced by Rep.* **Tom** **Campbell** *(R-CA) in 1991 to speed the approval process for life-saving drug therapies, Log Cabin activists have been key players in the FDA reform movement. Since early in the epidemic, pro-treatment activists have complained bitterly about the FDA's erratic, politicized and slow approval process for each new drug treatment, leading to thousands of needless deaths of people with life-threatening diseases. . . . LCR was the only gay or AIDS organization to support FDA reform. Most gay and AIDS organizations joined with . . . consumer protectionists on the left to form "the Patient Coalition," which mounted a major attack on the bill. Many of these same AIDS groups opposed fast-track approval of the protease inhibitor drugs, which since their approval in 1996 have shown to be extremely effective at improving the health and extending the lives of people with HIV/AIDS....*
>
> *In July 1997,* [when another FDA reform bill] *moved onto the Senate floor and Sen. Ted Kennedy (D-MA) made clear his intention to stop it, Log Cabin wrote a detailed letter to Sen. Jim Jeffords(R-VT), chief Senate sponsor, refuting the Patient Coalition's attacks on the bill. In the letter, Log Cabin's national AIDS policy advisor Jim Driscoll reminded Congress*

that the majority of patients and people with AIDS were on the side of reform, despite the efforts by national gay and AIDS organizations to stop FDA reform. Driscoll, who has helped in drafting FDA reform bills since 1991, dubbed the opponents "ideologues" who preferred price controls and nationalized health care over regulatory reform....

Kennedy mounted lonely opposition on the Senate floor, holding up the bill for several days. But in the end he voted for it and the FDA reform passed 98-2 in the Senate and by unanimous consent in the House, dealing a crushing blow to the opposition. [The TAG controlled New York based Patient Coalition fired an unprecedented attack on Kennedy for caving.] *Driscoll joined Republican supporters of FDA reform as the sole representative of a gay or AIDS group at the White House signing ceremony on November 21."FDA reform will save countless lives in the future," said Richard Tafel, executive director of Log Cabin Republicans. "We have a duty to remember all those who didn't survive the long drug approval processes that kept life-saving treatments out of their reach. The invitation to attend the White House ceremony demonstrates the wide recognition of Jim's leadership on this issue."*

My link with Log Cabin began when Jim Foster asked me to contact Chris Bowman, head of the San Francisco chapter of LCR. Chris introduced me to others including Marty Keller, a key member of the California LCR, and soon to be an appointee of Governor Pete Wilson. Marty introduced me to the shrewd and resourceful founder of Log Cabin, the redoubtable Frank Ricchiazzi, aka "the Godfather." It was Frank's idea for the national office headed by Rich Tafel to hire me as their National AIDS Policy Advisor, a post I assumed in late 1994.

A myth perpetrated by Log Cabin's detractors held that its members were a privileged elite untouched by AIDS. They claimed we just used AIDS as a stratagem for getting a toe in the doors of Republican officials. The reality was starkly different. Frank Ricchiazzi recalled that in a single year in the early 1990s almost the entire Board of California LCR was wiped out by AIDS. The group then found a dynamic leader in Ron Kershaw, a handsome Mormon who seemed strong and healthy.

Everyone was shocked when he died unexpectedly from an AIDS complication. Incomplete records indicate that at least a dozen LCR California officers died of AIDS, plus nearly three dozen other active members. Frank, as "Godfather," served as executor of the estates of fourteen AIDS casualties.

LCR has many survivors too. Chris Bowman, long a mainstay of Log Cabin San Francisco told me his T cells were plunging in 1995, and he would have died but for the early approval of the antiretroviral cocktails. He is still active in Republican politics. Eddie Hamilton, a gay Ohio Republican received a similar stay of execution. He has gone on to become one of America's most vocal grassroots activists with a reputation for speaking out for the urgent needs of people fighting AIDS. Eddie's the one who won't be shut up.

It was extremely valuable to be able to put the crusade for FDA reform under the aegis of a respected national gay organization, headed by a loyal and persuasive supporter of the cause, as Rich Tafel became. The media savvy Tafel, aided by his indefatigable man Friday, Kevin Ivers, rapidly brought Log Cabin to national prominence. Because of Log Cabin, and Tafel and Ivers' efforts, everyone in the gay-AIDS community, and most important FDA itself, knew there were Republicans gays who had connections with clout in Washington and who commanded attention in the media.

(Rich Tafel, Executive Director of Log Cabin Republicans)

This recognition was not attained without struggle and willingness to endure abuse. Pat Buchanan had partially based his challenge to Bush in 1992 on homophobic demagoguery. Like George W. Bush in 2004 with gay marriage, Bush senior caved to the homophobes letting them write a nasty anti-gay plank into the party platform. Many gay independents and Republicans, including myself, voted for Clinton. Buchanan and Jesse Helms, the leading homophobic demagogue in Congress, were able to intimidate much of their party. The Log Cabin struggle for tolerance and acceptance in the Republican party has been particularly lengthy, painful, and heroic.

Notwithstanding, the 1994 Republicans victory, under the leadership of Newt Gingrich with his Contract with America, brought in dozens of new conservative congressmen committed to fundamental reforms throughout the federal government, including FDA. One of the most interesting and able of them was Dr. Tom Coburn of Oklahoma. Tom Coburn took seriously the promises that got him elected. What his voters saw was what they got. He was the only Republican congressman elected in the 1994 wave that kept his word on term limits.

Coburn was a religious conservative who opposed all abortion and was viewed as anti-gay. But Coburn was also a doctor with AIDS patients, a strong interest in HIV disease, and a professional and religious commitment to saving lives. One of a handful of doctors in the lawyer filled halls of Congress, he quickly became the GOP's in house AIDS expert. This alarmed gay Democrats, or so they pretended secretly hoping to turn Coburn into a fund raising icon like Jesse Helms. Coburn disappointed them by becoming our most effective advocate in Congress and later the Senate on several key AIDS issues. Coburn interested Rich Tafel, himself an ordained minister and one of the most resourceful gay leaders of that era. He saw in Coburn's commitment to AIDS an opportunity to make an unusual alliance, and unusual alliances were one of Rich's specialties. Tafel was quick to grasp that Coburn's religious conservatism could be an asset dealing with AIDS because it shielded him from attacks by the professional homophobes.

Together Tafel and I visited Coburn's green new health aide, Roland Foster, early in 1995. Roland seemed fascinated by us, yet wary.

His boss evidently shared his fascination with the possibility of working with Log Cabin Republicans on AIDS. Thus began a long and fruitful relationship between Coburn, Log Cabin, myself, and later my other close allies like Bill Arnold co-founder of the ADAP Working Group, Jules Levin of NATAP, and the AIDS Healthcare Foundation and its President, the indefatigably ambitious Michael Weinstein. Perhaps to the surprise of both sides, we found wide areas of agreement on HIV, and common ground in other areas. Areas of difference were on making abstinence the primary preventative strategy for HIV, and Coburn's opposition to condom and needle exchange, programs the entire community favored. But this did not preclude an otherwise mutually advantageous working relationship. Coburn was a strong supporter of the Ryan White Care act, expedited FDA drug approval, and especially rapid HIV testing. These commitments again proved valuable to us after he entered the Senate in 2005.

Many in the gay-AIDS community saw the vital role LCR was playing in the struggles for gay rights and access to life-saving medicines, though few were willing to credit us publicly. Many were also intrigued by our working relationships with Gingrich, Coburn, Hatch, and other conservatives, relationships which pragmatic gay democrats privately encouraged. We were, nevertheless, labeled uncle Toms by kneejerk liberals who felt that ostracism was the only acceptable stance toward even moderate Republicans. More astute eyes saw it was crucial to insure that FDA knew there was a widely recognized gay organization that it could not easily co-opt, an organization that was ready and able to marshal powerful Republican opposition to any FDA delays that would cost lives among our people.

Why were so many gay Democrats so quick to be co-opted? Nearly everyone values acceptance and seeks respect, but some need them more than others. The need for respect usually rises in proportion to how much one feels disrespected. In my experience gay men strive for respect more desperately than just about anyone else. Gay women are more likely to hold the realistic attitude that respect from those that refuse to respect you for who you are is not worth the seeking, let alone agonizing over. Some gay men were so desperate for respect that they were willing to trade their fellow gays welfare and even survival for a place at the Democrat table, or at the table of some liberal interest, such as FDA, offering them legitimacy.

Many Republican gays did the same, but their compromises came at higher personal cost because they gained their places only by retreating into the closet. It's understandable why people who had experienced rejection and discrimination because of an essential and unalterable aspect of their identities should put a high premium on acceptance, or should be desperate for legitimacy. What is understandable is not necessarily morally admirable in all situations. What was admirable, if not always prudent, was to follow Harvey Milk's dictum: "Never back down to bullies. Just remember when you stand up for yourself, you stand up for everyone like you."

Log Cabin Republicans were also eager for acceptance, but in some respects they were made of sterner stuff than either the gay Democrats or the closeted gay Republicans. Being a Log Cabin Republican was tough road to hoe. In many cases Log Cabin people chose this arduous course because of deeply rooted conservative principles and values. But some, like Rich Tafel, were practical moderates who realized that in our two party system gays had to work with Republicans wherever they could to leverage movement among the Democrats.

To an extent that was the case with me. Although I am conservative on some issues, like immigration, taxes, and big government, I am radical on others. I support women's unabridged right to abortion in the first 20 weeks, and think more effective regulation is needed in many areas, such as to protect free speech and intellectual diversity in education, and to protect small investors rights and curb fraud. Hard experience has taught me to be hard-nosed on gay rights. But I try to evaluate each issue on its merits and flaws. My readiness to work with Republicans stems from my refusal to support policies I believe are irrational or unethical simply to go with the herd. It was and remains a matter of intellectual integrity.

The gay Democrats failure to get effective help from their own party on FDA's delays illustrates a crucial fact: ***when you are willing to give anything to get a place at the table, you will get nothing else.*** While the gay democrats longed for acceptance, what they really needed was power to negotiate concessions and the indisputable respect power brings. They called LCR people "Uncle Toms," but on FDA reforms, they were the real "Uncle Toms," willing to give up almost anything, even the lives of their fellows, to placate the "massas" in FDA and the Democrat establishment. With FDA, Log Cabiners were the true trailblazers for gay rights, we alone were ready to sacrifice popularity and break with the herd to save our people.

I've always held the unconventional opinion that the Human Rights Campaign made a mistake when in exchange for Democrat support for gay rights they agreed not to ask for affirmative action for gay people or for any recognition, let alone apology, for the abuses and denial of our rights we have too long suffered. Those compromises impeded our entry into areas dominated by our adversaries. Denying recognition of the systematic wrongs we suffered was a rank injustice because in the 1980s and 90s LGBT people were experiencing far more direct discrimination than any other major group.

We could not marry, we had great difficulty adopting or retaining custody of children, we were denied justice and reparations for past crimes against us, we were banned from openly serving the military (don't ask, don't tell) and most federal employment, we still faced widespread discrimination in jobs and, as I learned the hard way, the professions.*19* Even hospital visitations to dying companions could be in jeopardy. All LGBTs were stigmatized by the bullying of Pharisaical hypocrites, and we remain so today. Truth and reconciliation for LGBTs has yet to find a place on the Democrats' agenda even though they are in some respects leagues ahead of the GOP. Yet LGBTs will never gain true equality without recognition of and justice for past wrongs. The truth alone can make us free. Woke liberals have yet to wake up to this challenge.

My own career as a scholar and teacher of Shakespeare suffered a brutal partial birth abortion due to homophobic discrimination. Today our young still suffer bullying and esteem deprivation that result in exceptionally high LGBT suicide rates. Openly LGBT people still hold disproportionately fewer positions of political power, even in the Democratic party. There are only two openly LGBT persons in the US Senate and ten LGBTs in Congress, all of them Democrats. If represented proportionally to the numbers of our voters, we would have six senators and twenty-six Congresspersons.

Among elected Republicans, open LGBTs are almost as rare as hens' teeth. No current Republican members of Congress or any cabinet or sub-cabinet level appointees in the Trump Administration are openly LGBT. Yet self-identified LGBT voters are as numerous as Mormon and Jewish voters combined and nearly as numerous as Asians: compare our numbers in high government posts with theirs and you get indisputable statistical evidence for blatant discrimination. The only openly LGBT high official of note in the Trump Administration is Rick Grennell, US Ambassador to Germany. Imagine if Jews, or Mormons, or Asians only high appointment was a single ambassadorship: I'd be seen as proof indisputable of systematic discrimination.

There is but one trustworthy guarantee of a people's rights: their power to defend them. The Blacks and Jews have come to understand this. Harvey Milk and Jim Foster grasped it back in the seventies. But most LGBT people lag, and our current leadership is not leading. We are still struggling for mere tolerance, rather than demanding the proportional power our numbers, contributions, and abilities should command.

PART III: Climax

Chapter 1
Celebrity Deaths and
Non-Gay AIDS Activists

Throughout the 1988-1996 period celebrity deaths from and involvement in AIDS fueled momentum and gave cache` to AIDS activism. The initial first magnitude celebrities to die of AIDS were Rock Hudson (1985), Roy Cohn and Perry Ellis (1986), Liberace (1987), Amanda Blake and Bruce Chatwin (1989). These were followed by a rash of high profile celebrity deaths in the early 90s: Keith Herring and Ryan White (1990); Freddie Mercury and Brad Davis (1991); Anthony Perkins, Alan Bloom, and Isaac Asimov (1992); Arthur Ashe and Rudolf Nureyev (1993); and Elizabeth Glazer, Pedro Zamora, John Boswell, Randy Shilts, Marlon Riggs, and Derek Jarman (1994). In 1991 one of the most celebrated athletes on the planet, Magic Johnson, announced in that he had been infected with HIV.

Celebrity deaths and celebrities embracing the AIDS cause profoundly shifted public attitudes toward AIDS patients. The most famous AIDS activist of all was already one of the most famous women in the world, Elizabeth Taylor who became an activist upon the death in 1985 of her old friend and co-star Rock Hudson. Taylor taught the world that the true moral defect associated with AIDS was indifference to human suffering and blaming the sufferers. She transformed AIDS patients from ghoulish victims to normal human beings who deserved compassion, care, and our commitment to finding remedies and ultimately a cure. If there was a woman as famous as Taylor, it was Princess Diana. She began her influential career as an AIDS activist in 1987, and did in Britain what Taylor did for AIDS in America.

A critically important activist with a far more powerful story was an obscure schoolboy from Kokomo Indiana named Ryan White. A hemophiliac who became infected with HIV from a blood transfusion,

White was first excluded from his school and then taunted and shunned after a court ordered his return. Vandals broke windows in his house, and his family suffered harassment and discrimination that shocked a nation. In his own words:

> *Because of the lack of education on AIDS, discrimination, fear, panic, and lies surrounded me. . . I was labeled a troublemaker, my mom an unfit mother, and I was not welcome anywhere. . . We had great faith that with patience, understanding, and education, my family and I could be helpful in changing their minds and attitudes around AIDS.*

Ryan and Jeanie White, his heroic mother, became crusaders for the rights of people with AIDS. Together they made an immeasurable contribution to teaching the country to understand his disease and accept the afflicted. In 1990, the year of White's death, Congress enacted the Ryan White Care Act to fill in the gaps and improve the quality of AIDS care in America.

AIDS also made a celebrity of C. Everett Koop, the Surgeon General under Reagan. After being long silenced by his superiors, in 1988 Koop gained wide respect by finally initiating credible US AIDS policies. Celebrity activists like Taylor, Diana, Elton John, Koop, Magic Johnson and the Irish singer Bono educated the public on HIV-AIDS and strengthened public and political support for fighting the disease. As the new millennium approached, defeating AIDS became a popular cause for America and for Western society itself.

Among the AIDS patients, non-gay activists, led by Ryan White, emerged to have important impact. After John James introduced us at a conference in early 1995, Jules Levin became a key ally in the building coalition for accelerated FDA approval of the protease cocktails. Jules had worked in a Manhattan stock brokerage before becoming sick with AIDS. He contracted the virus through injection drug use. From the same cause he also contracted HCV or hepatitis C. In the first decade of the new millennium, he became the most visible advocate for HIV-HCV co-infected people. I served for several years as his consultant for Congressional affairs under the auspices of his group, National Treatment Advocacy Project (NATAP.)

By 1995 the AIDS epidemic was moving in a big way out of its original center in the white gay male community, into injection drug users, women, and the Black and Hispanic communities. Through dirty needles, drug users often became co-infected with HCV which accelerated the progress of HIV. While many of the new patients from these groups were men who have sex with men, some of the men and most of the women were heterosexual. The heterosexual men had wives or lady friends, whereby HIV began to infect significant numbers of women. The problems facing single mothers were severe, especially when their children were also infected.

People in the newly impacted groups, seeing that treatment activism was getting results, took up activism themselves. Jules was possibly the most effective and long lasting of these new activists. He combined ability in medical science with a "won't take no for an answer" attitude backed by relentless energy. He was not, however, an intuitive politician or a careful diplomat. For years I played this role for him, as best I could. When we first met in 1995 his T cells, the then common measure of the immune system against HIV, had fallen to an ominous level of 70. Without the new drugs he probably would not have survived 1996. Jules was extremely passionate and never one to be intimidated. He was fighting for something he valued dearly, his own life.

Jules was particularly effective in dealing with the HIV and HCV researchers and in reaching outside the gay AIDS community to the broader population of HIV and HCV co-infected. This was valuable because FDA had co-opted most of the leading New York activists, and it entertained hopes of co-opting Delaney who liked to play hard to get but had his price, or so they thought. Gay male activists, ever desperate for acceptance, sometimes seemed willing to trade precious parts of their bodies just for a place at the table. FDA, for its part, was ready to trade support for a seat in a government issue plastic chair: it was a tremendous bargain for them! As a New Yorker who refused to sell out for a spot to rest his derriere, Jules became a key player in my strategy of forming a broad, if loose, coalition ready to challenge FDA's complex bureaucratic maneuvers to delay HIV therapies.

First and foremost that coalition consisted of patients, treatment activists, and their friends, families, and doctors whose bottom line was their survival. Then came silent partners in Republican circles who wanted to cut FDA down a notch or three and who knew from personal experience with relatives and friends the suffering AIDS caused. The media was often an effective exponent of sensible public policy in those days. Many of them who had seen what AIDS could do to people they respected, liked, or loved were reluctant to mince words or withhold embarrassing truths.

Finally, the pharmaceutical companies were important behind the scenes allies whose motives were never exclusively selfless compassion. They were in AIDS for the money. They knew they could ill afford to call FDA to task; FDA had a thousand ways to hurt or help their businesses. So they were glad to quietly help activists doing the hard and dirty work that benefited their companies. Seldom, however, did the companies gratitude to the activists who helped them match their eagerness to court and buy off the FDA shills who noisily attacked their pricing and vilified their reputations. Virtue is its own reward, but time and again vice is what really brings home the bacon.

Chapter 2
The Great Commissioner

David Aaron Kessler served as FDA Commissioner from November 8, 1990 to February 28 1997, the crucial period for AIDS drug development and approval. He was probably the most effective and certainly the most controversial and consequential of the FDA Commissioners so far. During that period, I was FDA's and his prime critic and adversary among HIV treatment activists. But I was not alone, far from it. Kessler's critics in other disease areas and in research, industry and Congress were legion. Alone among AIDS activists, I criticized him where it hurt him most—in the press, particularly in one of the two papers he could not ignore, with my opinion pieces in the *Wall Street Journal*.

But the disputes weren't personal on my part, nor it seemed on his. My strategy required marshaling a tacit alliance against FDA in case they tried to delay any breakthrough AIDS drugs the way they delayed ddI, ddC, D4T, and combination therapies.

(FDA Commissioner David Kessler)

Enlisting FDA critics from other diseases groups, particularly cancer and Alzheimer's, was helpful in getting Republican support. We raised patient complaints against the agency under Kessler, and there was fodder aplenty. An example of our criticisms was the piece in the February 10, 1993 *Los Angeles Times,* "We Need an FDA Leader Not a Regulatory Czar" which I co-authored with Beverly Zakarian and William Summers, an Alzheimer's doctor who had tangled frequently with FDA:

> *Kessler is not a team player. He follows his own agenda with a headline grabbing style. . . Kessler's slow, overly cautious philosophy ---with moments of inappropriate regulatory zeal— restricts access to life saving therapies while it increases the costs of medications and healthcare.*
>
> *Kessler claims to champion faster AIDS drug approval. But ignoring the advice of AIDS activists and clinicians he delayed approval of ddC/AZT combination therapy for one year, waiting for data that never arrived. During that year he sanctioned an illegal underground drug market to silence AIDS activists demanding ddC. If Kessler had no new data, what made him finally approve ddC last April? First, California AIDS activists and Vice President Quayle's office criticized Kessler's delay. Second the ddC underground collapsed because of defective quality control. The FDA was facing the scandal of sanctioning a dangerous bootleg product for political reasons. Rather than expediting scientific procedures, Kessler merely caved to pressure.*

Despite his disregarding criminal violations of public health laws, working with, and thereby legitimizing, the violators, David Kessler had accomplishments that I supported, though many Republicans saw them as regulatory overreach. Chief among these were the regulation of tobacco to weaken the tobacco industry and curb tobacco addiction by raising the costs and reducing the appeal of cigarettes. He also initiated food nutritional labeling, which seemed a no brainer (how can people make prudent nutritional choices unless they know the ingredients?), and modernization of the FDA bureaucracy. Perhaps Kessler came too soon, the country might be better off today if we had an over-reaching activist Commissioner like Kessler when the opioid epidemic began taking hold.

As I said before, I think the culture of FDA was primarily responsible for the AIDS drug delays. Kessler, whose greatest faults were lack of imagination and love of bureaucratic power, gave in too soon and too much to that culture.

Kessler's critics among the regulated industries, especially nutritive supplements, were myriad. Senator Hatch was their political leader, his engagement in part due to the supplements industry in Utah. Then, as now, I believed more regulation of supplements would be a wasteful and unnecessary intrusion. My opposition to supplement regulation had broad support in the gay and HIV communities where supplements were widely used and where harsh personal experience taught people to be wary of government interference with individual choices.

When Kessler first became Commissioner, all the AIDS treatment activists, including my group DATA, curried his favor. Everyone knew he would have to make key decisions that might mean life or death for themselves or their friends. Various activists had several initial meetings both on the phone and in person with him and FDA's top brass, such as Carl Peck, Director of Drug Evaluation and Research for FDA. Initially, Kessler was very open. He even gave some of us, myself included, his phone number at home in Bethesda and for his condo in Florida. He told us he would work to balance our concerns with those of the staff of FDA. While his intentions seemed good, it soon became apparent to me that the views of his FDA staff would weigh more heavily with him. No surprise, FDA was a bureaucracy after all, and Kessler felt at home in a bureaucracy.

Soon activist alliances settled into their accustomed patterns. The dyed in the wool New York consumer protectionists strengthened their bonds with FDA hardliners and Kessler himself. FDA welcomed their Manhattan minions as a kind of "beard" to help them maintain their pretense of openness toward the gay community. My allies and I worked hard to form an effective opposition, and Martin Delaney stood in the middle looking for ways to make deals that everyone would have to accept and for which he could take the credit.

Kessler lost no time making himself unpopular with Republicans in Congress, especially those with ties to the pharmaceutical, biotech, medical devices, and nutritional supplements industries. The *Wall Street Journal* kept up a drumbeat of criticism from patient activists, clinicians, and industry. Speaker Gingrich and Senator Hatch were his leading Congressional critics. Senator Tom Harkin, a strong believer in supplements and the need to test alternative therapies, shared their concerns. Harkin, however, muted his criticisms out of deference to his fellow Democrats, an old story. Fed by Kessler's aggressive expansion of FDA activity and turf, the impetus for FDA reform legislation with teeth burgeoned among Republicans, in the media, and with the public.

But it was the AIDS activists with their repeated, highly visible public demonstrations and heart rending personal dilemmas that became the most prominent and powerful drivers of reform, especially in securing media publicity and public support. To move Congress, you always need an outrage with sympathetic victims and, thanks to activists like Ryan White, patients were gaining sympathy. The treatment activists called FDA's competence and ethics into question as never before. They gave the agency's longstanding critics a powerful narrative to tarnish its claims of scrupulous public health protection. We reminded all who would listen of our frustration with FDA's delays in approving vital AIDS drugs, along with our outrage at the agency's turning a blind eye to useless and sometimes toxic underground knockoffs of these drugs.

By the year 1995, the great divide separating the cocktails from the preceding era of death and despair, Kessler had solidified his alliance with FDA hardliners. FDA's Manhattan minions supported him, with overweening gusto it seemed, repeatedly running interference with the community to give FDA cover. From late 1992 onward we heard nothing more of Kessler's once vaunted plans to reform FDA approval procedures internally. Among the San Francisco activists not even Kessler's erstwhile defender Martin Delaney was willing to trust FDA to expedite approval of the crucial protease based cocktails rolling down the pipeline.

Chapter 3
The Axis of Obstruction
(1995: 48,979 AIDS Deaths)

It is useless to attempt to reason a man
out of a thing he was never reasoned into

Jonathan Swift

Betrayal, a powerful word, conveys intense condemnation. Neither my allies nor I ever used it publicly to characterize TAG's apparent collusion with FDA in the agency's attempt to derail accelerated approval for the protease inhibitor cocktails, though the word quisling did recur in private. Yet the collusion was no surprise to anyone who didn't wear blinders. Indeed, FDA's continued attempts at delay, were exactly what we expected. From the onset, we pushed the Campbell bill and put no stock in Kessler's promises of reform because we knew FDA would to try to delay the new AIDS drugs by any means they thought they could get away with. As Dave Olson always put it, "can a zebra change its stripes?" Not if the zebra works for a sclerotic regulatory bureaucracy, it seemed.

Delay was FDA's *modus operandi* hardwired into their culture and institutional DNA. Delay was their most effective weapon and the ultimate source of their power. We had long before fingered TAG as FDA's de facto gay community "go guys" and expected them to be FDA's Trojan horse when the agency made its move to delay a new class of drugs to test more exhaustively their efficacy. Others who trusted FDA or believed that TAG shared the community's goals of faster drug approval were surprised, even shocked, but they did not use the word betrayal either. They were either too polite, too cautious, or just intimidated by TAG which could be as ruthless toward fellow activists as they were to drug companies like Hoffman-La Roche. During the July 1996 Vancouver AIDS Conference Jules and I asked Delaney about TAG's betrayal. "You guys can use that term, I won't." Then he added with a sly grin, "But I certainly won't say you're wrong either."

We need not rely on journalistic accounts or the blurred memories of aging activists to substantiate FDA-TAG's cooperative efforts to delay approval of the protease inhibitors. They can be readily and conclusively documented using their own official papers from the time. TAG first detailed its dilatory objectives and strategy in a June 10, 1994 letter to David Kessler wherein they unequivocally opposed accelerated approval for the first protease drug, Roche's Saquinavir.

> *As has been stated both in meetings with you and your staff, and in FDA Advisory Committee hearings many of us are very concerned about the level of data that will be required for the marketing approval of new classes of antiviral treatments. As people with HIV-AIDS, advocates and physicians we believe that people with AIDS are entitled to information about new therapies that is sufficient to make necessary risk/benefit analysis regarding their treatments. In regulating the first generation of antiviral drugs many felt that a reduced evidential standard was appropriate; now, however, we believe that the development of protease inhibitors offers a new opportunity to rethink the regulatory process in ways that will ensure reasonable access to the drugs, while producing clinically relevant information about their use.*

Comment: Under community pressure, and due to the absence of effective treatments, FDA had reduced the level of data for efficacy required for approval of the first generation of HIV antiretrovirals, the nucleoside analogues. As the Concorde Study indicated back in 1993, AZT, ddI, ddC, and D4T, when tolerated, seldom extended life more than few months and did not significantly reduce the overall AIDS death rate. Because of the inadequacy of the nukes, the same argument (no effective treatments available) used to justify reduced levels of efficacy for the earlier drugs held for the new protease drugs. But TAG and FDA forgot or more likely ignored that, along with their previous public commitments to accelerated AIDS drug approval. The TAG letter continues:

> *We are concerned that Hoffmann-LaRoche, Inc. intends to apply for Accelerated Approval based on changes in CD4 levels*

*and virological markers observed in ACTG study #229. We feel
that such an approval would penalize people with AIDS/HIV by
setting an inappropriately low standard of evidential
requirements that would govern the regulation of this entire
class of therapies. We urge you not to invite Hoffmann-LaRoche
to apply for Accelerated Approval of Saquinavir until we can
complete further discussion between FDA, its Advisory
Committee, the company and people with AIDS/HIV. . . The use
of surrogate markers to evaluate potential efficacy in ACTG
229 is completely untested in this class of therapies.*

The words "penalize" and "invite" stand out like Falstaff's red
nose. How could people with AIDS be penalized by *failing to deny them
access* to therapies that might save their lives? TAG was getting this bass-
ackward, as Dave Olson or Jesse Dobson might have said. Urging Kessler
"not to 'invite' Roche to apply" references the regulatory real world where
companies dare not apply unless invited, again underlining the obstructive
practices of FDA. The TAG letter questions the validity of surrogate
markers (CD4 count and viral load) in a new class of drugs. Because the
markers were used in every clinic, this seemed grasping at straws to
everyone outside of TAG and FDA.

To replace expanded access, TAG proposed large simple trials
(LSTs). But trial size would be up to the company and FDA. While trials
might be large enough to include most activists, especially those with
friends in FDA and NIIAD, cost restraints meant they would include only
a small elite from the vast number of patients desperate for a new
treatment. Everyone who understood the pharmaceutical industry knew it
was wildly unrealistic to expect Roche, or any other drug company, to
conduct and provide free drug and care for an 18,000-patient trial lasting
several years with no compensating revenue and no guarantee of approval
at the end.

Two months after their letter to FDA, TAG finally laid out in
detail to the entire community its rationale for formally asking Roche and
the FDA to launch large simple trials in place of accelerated approval for
the new AIDS drugs. *Poz* magazine, a community publication usually
friendly to TAG, reported:

But in August, 1994, the New York-based Treatment Action Group (TAG), shocked the AIDS community by asking the company and the FDA to hold off. TAG sought Roche's agreement to an 18,000-person long-term trial to insure collection of in-depth data. TAG founder Peter Staley wrote in POZ: "If you accept the premise that our goal with antiretroviral research is to prolong life for as many people as possible, then our desire for early access to a promising treatment must be balanced with a desire for reliable information on the treatment's ability to prolong life. "Start Making Sense," POZ No. 9 April 1995. (X)

Staley's "reliable information" means further efficacy testing: the safety of Saquinivir was never an issue. Staley's conclusion is a *non sequitur* because there is no necessary conflict between giving accelerated approval and getting "reliable information." If more data was desired, post marketing studies and clinical experience would provide it. TAG's intent was transparent, if unstated: they wanted rock solid proof that the drugs did in fact prolong life before allowing people with AIDS to use them for any purpose. Statistician pedantry would take precedence over saving human life.

FDA sought exhaustively tested efficacy data prior to approval because since thalidomide that was their *modus operandi*. But why would TAG, which claimed to represent desperate AIDS patients, want that? *POZ* did not probe TAG's motives. Much more serious, it failed to mention an absolutely critical factor that Staley ignores: a drug's ability to ***improve quality of life***. Evidence of improvement in quality of life comes in quickly within weeks or sometimes even days. Prolonging life itself takes much longer to document. For dying patients both factors are crucial: ask anyone with cancer.

TAG's initiative with FDA sparked intense community consternation along with vigorous objections. Other community activists indignantly demanded to know who authorized TAG to conduct discussions with FDA's Antivirals Advisory Committee and Hoffmann-LaRoche on behalf of people with AIDS/HIV? Clearly, TAG was the AIDS group with whom FDA preferred to collude, they were comrades in collusion from the days of the underground. Since then FDA had even appointed TAG leaders to its antivirals committee which was otherwise composed of highly credentialed researchers. FDA had almost no gay people on its staff, by what right did it presume to select spokespersons for the gay-HIV community? This was arrogant paternalism at its most offensive. TAG, a small membership by invitation elite, lacked popular support from either the wider HIV community or from broader based advocacy groups like Project Inform, the San Francisco AIDS Foundation, AIDS Atlanta, AIDS Action, AIDS Project Los Angeles, the National Association of People with AIDS, the National Minority AIDS Council, AIDS Healthcare Foundation, AmFAR, the Human Rights Campaign, or Log Cabin Republicans, to cite some of the more prominent groups who declined to endorse TAG's LST proposal.

When things settled down, almost the entirety of ACT UP nationwide came out categorically opposed to TAG's plans to abort accelerated approval for protease based drug cocktails, as did most of the major advocacy groups, and the overwhelming majority of AIDS clinicians and researchers. Yet FDA continued to treat TAG as if it were the official, legitimate voice for the national gay-AIDS community. It seemed yet another instance of a Federal bureaucracy treating minorities like colonies who could not be trusted or lacked the maturity to choose their own leaders, let alone make their own decisions. FDA's regulation without representation, fraught with offensive paternalism, showed its overbearing face yet once more.

John James in the July 23, 1994 issue of *AIDS Treatment News* gave a sober assessment of the widening dispute over TAG's letter:

> *What is the dispute about? As I see it, over the last few years a tight group has come into possession of much of the inside track in Washington on AIDS treatment issues. They have the ear at FDA . . . FDA listens to them not as several individuals, but as representing the AIDS community in treatment issues. . . The dispute is not about the merits of a large simple trial, however, but about the use of special access to powerful institutions. This special role is a community resource, a community trust, not one organization's asset. Those who speak for the community, explicitly or implicitly, must consult with the community and seek consensus first, before going to government or industry.*

A question none of the community people asked but should have was: Where was TAG's concern for "proof of efficacy and full data before marketing" when their principals, including Derek Hodel head of the New York Buyer's club, were defending the underground sale of Compound Q, dextran sulfate, ribavirin, and miss measured knockoff ddC? Not only did they lack evidence for efficacy, their products safety was problematic. Their past involvement with underground drug sales raised questions about their motives for seeking to preempt accelerated approval of the protease cocktails. Indeed, some anxious patients wondered if they were planning another underground in knockoff protease drugs for the tens of thousands who failed to get into their FDA sanctioned large simple trials.

TAG put out a more detailed exposition in September (*Rescuing Accelerated Approval: Moving Beyond the Status Quo*, A Report to the FDA Antiviral Drugs Advisory Committee, Sept 12-13, 1994). Despite the misleading title, "rescue" and "terminate" are not synonyms except in Orwellian newspeak, it was a carefully written primer covering the major issues from TAG's peculiar perspective. It overlooked, however, their plan's most serious drawbacks.

In the midst of TAG-FDA's strategy room, stood an African bull elephant seething with musth: *if the protease drugs worked well, waiting for the large simple trials to be set up, enrolled, and show scientifically acceptable results would delay full approval at least three years, a delay that would cost the lives of the countless patients excluded from the trials.* Few knowledgeable patients with advanced AIDS were willing to accept the risk of exclusion from a viable treatment. For that reason, TAG's plan was flatly rejected by the AIDS community at large.

Another glaring problem was TAG's and FDA's skepticism about HIV viral load as a measure of HIV disease. "Do the minutes that pass in an hour measure the hour's passage?" Barry Freehill asked, not without sarcasm. In a twist oddly similar to the HIV denialist theories promulgated by the infamous Professor Peter Duesberg, TAG, and FDA were demanding evidence for the predictive value of HIV viral load. It seemed almost as if they, like Duesberg, wanted proof that HIV caused AIDS! Scientific minded advocates along with leading scientists like David Ho, insisted, moreover, that it made no sense to accept viral load as a standard yardstick in one class of drugs but not another. Delaney compared it to demanding for each new class of drugs new studies to validate the use of a thermometer as a measure of fever reduction.

Nine months after TAG's June letter to FDA, the agency laid out its own homologous strategy for delay in a March 1995 *Scientific American* article by Commissioner David Kessler and Karen Feiden. This complex review of FDA evaluation procedures for AIDS drugs purports to set forth a balanced picture of the agency's rationale for delaying approval of a drug along with the reasons for speed. The article never addresses the moral crux--whether the patients or the government should have the final say about patients with fatal illnesses taking a risk to save or improve the quality of their lives. The medical crux is ignored as well--does the risk lie in the drug's safety or merely its efficacy? If acceptable safety is already established, as it was with Roche's Saquinivir, patient risk in taking a drug of uncalibrated efficacy is minimal, especially when the patients have no effective alternatives.

Kessler, like TAG, blithely assumes the moral acceptability of FDA's paternalistic regulation without fair representation. The assumption revolves around a fundamental question in political philosophy: does the citizenry own the government, are they sovereign, or does the government own the people? In a democracy the citizens theoretically own the government whose duty is to protect and serve the citizens' interests. In a totalitarian state, the government is pre-eminent and owns the people *de facto. A* citizen's final duty is to serve the state by obeying the king, the party, or the dictator. In ancient Egypt, there were two veritable classes of slaves: slaves who were owned by individual citizens and the citizens themselves all of whom were in effect owned by the Pharaoh.

Under democratic theory, where citizens own the government, for FDA to forbid patients to try experimental therapies the agency must show that individual patient choice would damage the interests of society, or hurt other people; the purpose of government in a democracy being to protect individuals from each other, not from themselves. To gay AIDS patients, haunted by the specter of criminalization of consensual sex, preventing dying patients from trying experimental treatments that were safe but might not work reeked of the stench of victimless crime laws. Gay

AIDS patients were quick to rebel against FDA because they had a lifetime of violations of their individual rights. That went with the territory of being gay in America in the 1970's, 80's and 90's.

Kessler presents his potentially disastrous LST proposal as FDA's response to pressures from the AIDS community. Yet neither Kessler nor anyone else in FDA had bothered to listen to a representative spectrum of our exceptionally diverse community. Indeed, Kessler refused the many requests to meet to hear community objections to TAG's proposal, including repeated requests from Delaney and myself.

> *In the spring of 1994 a group of AIDS activists gathered in the third floor of the Parklawn Building, headquarters of the Food and Drug Administration in Rockville, Md. The activists made an extraordinary plea to top agency officials: don't approve drugs to treat disease caused by the human immuno- deficiency virus (HIV) too quickly. No one familiar with events of the previous decade could have predicted this turnabout.*

Comment: As noted previously, anyone who understood the dynamics of AIDS treatment activism, particularly FDA's hand in glove relationship with its Manhattan minions, could and likely would have predicted the turnabout.

> *Only a few years earlier angry activists had besieged Parklawn, demanding access to compounds that had barely moved out of the test tube. Faced with imminent death, people with AIDS clamored for the right to take therapeutic risks. Experimental drugs were a ray of hope on a bleak treatment landscape, and many patients were unwilling to accept any restraint on access.*

> *Promising drugs generally take several years to test; an additional 18 months or more may elapse from the time a sponsor requests product approval until a compound is widely available.*

Comment: It usually takes years to test efficacy exhaustively since efficacy varies with dosage, subject population, and concomitant therapies, but safety testing is faster and always precedes efficacy testing. Efficacy specific trials are not started until we have established an acceptable safety profile.

In response to concerns about the length of time needed to develop and evaluate new drugs, the FDA made some dramatic changes in the way it conducts business. In the late 1980s it introduced rules that expand access to unapproved but promising therapies. In 1992 the agency adopted a regulation that allows it to approve drugs before complete data on their safety and efficacy have been collected. These initiatives, which apply only to drugs for serious and life- threatening diseases, attempt to balance the urgent needs of desperately ill patients with the FDA's responsibility to determine whether the drugs work.

Comment: As Kessler indicates, the 1992 regulations set up FDA to approve new AIDS drugs quickly. However, the agency already had this power, the new regulations simply formalized its implementation. Whether and how they would use it remained at FDA's discretion, since neither Congress nor the President had done anything to require FDA to move quickly. Kessler's article lays out the agency's reluctance to do so.

Have these policies been too successful in speeding up the availability of new drugs? AIDS activists at the FDA last spring feared that answers had begun to take a back seat to access. They were concerned that patients and their physicians did not know how to make optimal use of the existing antiviral AIDS drugs. They wanted to discuss ways to learn more about the value of experimental therapies and to learn it sooner—when each drug should be administered, to whom and in what dose. Without such information, novel drugs might be of little use.

Comment: Post approval, clinicians continually learn more about when to administer the drugs, to whom, and at what dose; such information is passed on to the drug companies and usually FDA which may incorporate it in the drug's labeling. For example, the optimal dosage of AZT was not clear until we learned it from doctors in the field nearly three years after that drug's approval. Had FDA waited until further efficacy trials established that dose, as TAG sought to do with the protease cocktails, many of those helped by AZT would have died earlier than they did. Kessler continues:

*Although **these activists' caution** reflected only one perspective within the AIDS communities,*

Comment: As we have seen, "these activists' caution" was indeed representative of only of a small elite in the AIDS community, an elite with a history of working closely with FDA itself---a critical fact Kessler fails to disclose. David Kessler was a lawyer as well as a doctor. He knew full well that a hard and fast rule for lawyers requires checking for conflict of interests for everyone in a case, including the lawyer's own personal conflicts. He continues:

*there is no doubt that making a drug widely available early means that it will initially be used without **full understanding** of its characteristics.*

Comment: "Full understanding" of a drug's characteristics is an impossible goal because that would include all its interactions in diverse human subjects under varying conditions. Drawing the line on how much understanding is needed is as much an ethical and political as a scientific decision.

Kessler's article deceptively, one might say shamelessly, touts the putative advantages of TAG-FDA's proposed "large, simple trial" while glossing over the adverse consequences of denying or delaying approval. Like TAG, he ignores the earth-shattering possibility that the drugs might immediately start saving large numbers of lives (that is exactly what happened!). If so, would FDA still withhold approval of the drugs for three or more years until the trials were set up, enrolled, and all their efficacy data was in and fully evaluated? Would FDA keep the patients in the standard treatment arm after it became evident that the protease cocktail treatment arm patients were healthier and living longer? What about the more than 90% of all patients left behind? To benefit from the new drug cocktails, they would have to wait for approval, then most of them would wait again while our cumbersome healthcare system geared up to treat them! What if the drugs showed *decided improvements in quality of life* before prolongation of life could be documented? From the patients' point of view, quality of life can be as important as prolongation of life.

Oblivious to these glaring objections, Kessler persists in his push for "large simple trials:"

One approach to speeding data collection is the "large, simple trial." Such trials have relaxed criteria for eligibility, enroll patients in a variety of care settings and collect considerably less extensive baseline and outcome data than do traditional trials. As a result, more patients with a broader range of characteristics can participate, and researchers can conduct very large studies in a remarkably short time.

Such trials are generally most feasible when a drug's toxicity profile and mechanism of action are already well understood.

Comment: In other words, such trials are most feasible when the drug's safety (toxicity) has already been tested! If we know the new drug's safety parameters, why wait when we have nothing else that works well? Moreover, conducting "very large studies in a remarkably short time" is problematic since large, multisite trials will take longer to set up, enroll, and collate their data.

*They can identify effects of moderate size that could not have been discovered in small populations. Large, simple trials can also be used to collect important data about how a drug is best administered in clinical settings and can be a tool for making promising experimental therapies available while research is completed. Recently **some observers** have proposed that the FDA consider requiring such trials either before granting accelerated approval or afterward, as a means of completing post marketing studies.*

Comment: "Some observers" refers to TAG alone, since no other prominent patient or clinician group supported requiring the LSTs as a prerequisite for granting approval. Kessler's failure to identify TAG as the source and the only community advocates of LSTs encourages the false impression that the LSTs had broad support.

The criteria for entry into a study are another area where investigators may be more flexible. Historically, researchers have defined entry criteria narrowly and excluded, as far as possible, patients who use concomitant therapy. These restrictions have some merits, because they decrease variability and make it easier to show an effect of the study drug. Nevertheless, they also have scientific downsides. For example,

> *it may be **ethically difficult** to deny seriously ill patients potentially beneficial treatments as a condition of trial participation.*

Comment: *"ethically difficult"* is a weasel phrase Kessler employs to avoid acknowledging the inconvenient truth that denial of treatment is **ethically abhorrent**.

> *Moreover, these restrictions may slow enrollment, encourage the unrecorded use of other therapies and result in trials that do not mirror the actual conditions under which a drug may eventually be used. With acceptable increases in sample size, it is possible to apply much broader entry criteria and allow patients access to other treatments. This relaxation of entry criteria has been especially important in trials of AIDS drugs.*

Like TAG, Kessler ignores the near impossibility of getting drug companies to finance large, costly multi-year trials with no guarantee of approval at the end. (Maybe he's relying on TAG to show up at midnight outside the CEO's estates blasting car horns and igniting firecrackers!) Kessler ignores, furthermore, the potent disincentive the cost of LSTs would create for other companies weighing development of new AIDS drugs. Particularly shocking is TAG and FDA's obliviousness to the racial and economic discrimination inherent in restricting access to life-saving medications to the privileged few who know about and understand how to enroll in trials.

Although FDA's case is carefully presented, it is full of omissions, deeply misleading, and hopelessly imbalanced. As a result, the article sparked carefully reasoned objections along with powerful emotional resistance from doctors, researchers, treatment activists, and patients across the nation. Too little attention and weight, they objected, is given to the consequences of delay. Careful and objective risk/benefit assessment is slighted along with the inevitability of difficult tradeoffs. No attention is paid to patient needs for access to drugs that enhance quality of life but have not yet been proven to prolong life. Ignored are the greater difficulties black, Hispanic, female, and rural patients would face in enrolling in the trials. Disregarded is the sheer cruelty and injustice of denying any patient a chance to save his/her life. Utterly spurned is the moral imperative for regulators themselves to show flexibility and sometimes take risks for the greater good of public health, or simply to save human lives. **What would we gain for creating all of these appalling problems? — pedantically precise assessments of the efficacy of drugs we already knew were safe and effective!**

The article ends by repeating FDA boilerplate cautions about early approval:

> *Although the FDA has not yet had to revoke an accelerated approval, it is likely that we will eventually allow widespread access to a drug that does not work. Patients will have wasted precious time taking an ineffective product; they may even be harmed.*

Comment: Since 1995 FDA has approved all AIDS drugs on accelerated approval; none of these approvals have been revoked. Moreover, patients will not have wasted time on an ineffective product if they have exhausted the alternative treatments, which was the case for many AIDS patents then, and still is for many with terminal cancer, Alzheimer's, and other killers. The ineffective alternative may have a placebo effect, but more importantly it will allow patients the dignity of fighting for their lives when that is what they are determined to do.

> *This risk underscores the need for clinical trials to continue after accelerated approval has been granted. Incomplete or misleading data serve neither patients nor the cause of knowledge. For all the mechanisms that may be put in place to speed access to new therapies, the FDA's commitment to safety and efficacy remains unchanged—all approved drugs, even those for potentially fatal diseases, must ultimately meet the same rigorous standards.*

As I have said, the rigor of FDA efficacy standards is not set by statute; Congress left it up to FDA's policies, practices, and ultimately its discretion. Repetition is necessary because FDA is ever reluctant to acknowledge this crucial fact. Moreover, the agency has never been called before Congress for approving drugs with deficient efficacy, only for safety defects.

To appreciate the brazen incongruity of Kessler's position we must reiterate how much was at stake. It bears repeating because so few now remember, and FDA would like us to forget, that the agency tried and almost succeeded in delaying for several years the amazing advance in drug treatment that in a matter of weeks turned AIDS from a death sentence to a medically manageable condition. Indeed, soon after the HIV cocktails approval, tens of thousands would experience "the Lazarus effect." In a few short years, the cocktails would save millions of lives and rein in the HIV epidemic. Holding up their approval to complete the large simple trials would have been the equivalent of delaying penicillin or the polio vaccine several years in order to conduct more exhaustive efficacy testing.

****

Five months after Kessler's preliminary endorsement of the TAG proposal, a front page article in *Barron's* titled, "Do We Have Too Many AIDS Drugs?" hit like a grenade in a crowded marketplace. Activists and patients who remained asleep to the threat to access to the cocktails awoke with a start. In the August 15, 1995 article *Barron's* reporter Edward Wyatt related how New York AIDS activists were calling on FDA to slow the approval of AIDS drugs. Wyatt did not bother to interview Martin Delaney, Ron Baker, Barry Freehill, John James, Jules Levin, myself or any activists outside of TAG, or any outside AIDS clinicians or researchers. Evidently trusting FDA to tell him who the legitimate activists were, Wyatt gave his readers the misleading impression that TAG spoke for the entire National AIDS community, including all of us!

Wyatt went so far as to predict that FDA would be approving fewer AIDS drugs. Fewer approvals would surely discourage companies from funding new AIDS drug research, something every thinking person with HIV disease feared. Predictably, the article sent a chill through all the companies involved in AIDS research, and through all the patients whose lives depended on that research. Wyatt writes:

> The complaint is that AIDS drugs are coming to market in confusing profusion. . .." The kind of data that have come out of these trials is uninterpretable and ambiguous," charges Link. (Derek Link of TAG and the New York Buyer's Club-JD)

*"No one knows when to take them, or if the toxicities outweigh the benefit." An especially blunt assessment comes from **Joseph L. Fleiss**, an FDA consultant . . . After reviewing the data supplied in one fast track application he growled, "**I think the accelerated approval process is a horror. The person who thought of it and saw it to acceptance should be shot.**" . . . Such charges by their nature can be expected to slow the fast-track approval program, affecting companies working on a variety of life threatening diseases including cancer and multiple sclerosis. But the most resounding impact by far will be on the host of companies preparing to submit new AIDS drugs for FDA approval. . . . Treatment Activist Group, a New York based activist group recently met with officials from Merck and Hoffmann La Roche as well as Feigel and other FDA officials, to discuss a proposal for tests of protease inhibitors that included patients being assigned to either get the drug or a placebo.*

AIDS researchers and clinicians everywhere were appalled by the potential dampening effect of the *Barron's* article on continued AIDS drug research and development. Treatment activists widely denounced the article as irresponsible journalism, and it inflamed opposition to TAG's and FDA's LST proposals, across the country, and above all in San Francisco. Here is Martin Delaney's take on the alarming prospects for AIDS drug research after the article in *Barron's* reinforced Kessler's piece in *Scientific American*:

*It is hard to say what effect this fractured picture had on company decisions to commit to full scale production of the protease drugs. But many acknowledged that they were losing confidence that the prize of accelerated approval would still be there when the drugs were ready. **Kessler at FDA ran around the country for the next six months** [after his March 1995* <u>Scientific American</u> *article—JD] **repeatedly telling a dramatic tale of how "the AIDS activists," as if he meant everyone, had, ironically, stormed his office demanding that he slow down the approval of new AIDS drugs.***

Comment: The *Scientific American* article was cautious and measured, which was appropriate for the standards of that respected publication. However, as Delaney indicates below, Kessler's dramatic public statements for the next six months more resembled a no holds barred political campaign to sell the LSTs any which way FDA and TAG could:

> *At every public meeting, the complaints about "too little is known,' 'we need longer and larger studies,' 'surrogate markers don't work' 'all current studies are inadequate,'" rang from the same few voices. Their proposed solution was always a "large simple trial." What chilling effect did this have on the mood at FDA or the senior management of companies trying to make hundred million dollar decisions about new drugs?"*
> "Protease Development: A Real World View," October 8, 1995.

While Delaney no longer entertained illusions about Kessler's objectivity, he always liked to cover his posterior and knew the value of a plan B. So he went on to claim that the drug companies were not ready to manufacture the protease drugs on a scale required for full approval. He failed to mention that the major reasons for not getting ready were TAG's opposition to approval followed by Kessler's inhibiting article in the *Scientific American,* FDA's discouraging private communications with the companies, and the chilling August 15 piece in *Barron's.* Delaney's claim would give cover to FDA if they delayed approval, but only among those ignorant of how FDA works and only for a delay of a few months.

The drug companies, ever fearful of offending FDA, did not comment publicly on Delaney's assertions about their scale ups. The three protease drugs that were in testing then were, Roche's Saquinivir, Abbott's Norvir, and Merck's Crixivan. However, from my discussions with Roche and Abbott, I inferred that they, though not Merck, could have been ready to manufacture several months before their drugs were approved. Certainly, Kessler's article, TAG's stance, and the Barron's piece gave them no incentive to rush scaling up their factories. TAG was correct in assuming that Roche intended to apply in early 1995, but TAG's meeting with Roche and their June 10, 1994 letter to FDA put a damper on that. Delaney wanted Kessler to approve the drugs ASAP, but if they delayed he did not want to be blamed for giving Newt Gingrich and the *Wall Street Journal* the rope to hang Kessler.

The case for the San Franciscan community's opposition to TAG's plans and Barron's claims was laid out definitively by Ron Baker, Ph.D., in the September 1994 *Beta*, the SF AIDS Foundation treatment publication:

> *A small but influential treatment activist organization has ignited a firestorm of controversy in the AIDS community by asking FDA to raise standards for accelerated approval of promising new AIDS drugs. Specifically, TAG has lobbied FDA intensely to deny accelerated approval to Saquinavir, the protease inhibitor drug from Hoffmann-LaRoche. Roche had been expected to apply before the end of 1994 for accelerated approval of Saquinivir in combination with AZT and DDC, based primarily on promising results from ACTG 229.*

Saquinivir approval was delayed almost a year, if the expected late 1994 approval date was correct. Approval did not actually occur until Dec. 6, 1995. More lives could have been saved had FDA given Saquinivir accelerated approval earlier in 1995. Just how many of the 48,979 who died of AIDS that year is difficult to estimate. Saquinivir was the safest, but also the weakest of the new protease inhibitor drugs, and it was costly and difficult to produce. Yet its earlier approval might have saved at least a few hundred lives. Baker continues:

> *It appears that FDA wants additional . . . data from the Phase III trials of the drug . . . before the agency will consider an application for early approval.*

> *TAG opposition to accelerated approval of Saquinivir clearly played a major role in FDA's decision. TAG asked FDA not to invite Roche to apply for early approval of its protease inhibitor. The TAG letter argues that in order to receive accelerated approval, the protease inhibitor must first demonstrate clinical benefits (e.g. significantly delayed disease progression.)*

> *To evaluate the protease inhibitors as candidates for accelerated approval, TAG has proposed implementing a Large Simple Trial (LST) that would attempt to enroll 18,000 participants taking a protease inhibitor or a placebo for 3-5 years. Apart from widespread community opposition to placebo*

controlled studies among people with AIDS, LSTs represent the dinosaurs of clinical trials . . . to many researchers who say that the cost effective test for AIDS drugs is smaller studies enrolling fewer people for less time.

In discussions with FDA and others, TAG has argued that Saquinivir is not a suitable candidate for accelerated approval because the drug has been studied in too few patients for too short a time. . . In addition, TAG argues, the use of surrogate markers (e.g. CD4 counts and viral load). . is untested and therefore suspect,)

Many AIDS advocates, including this writer, regard the TAG proposals as well-intentioned, [Here Baker is tactful to a fault. --JD] *but unfortunately outdated, unworkable, . . . Implementation of these proposals would be devastating to the medical needs of people with AIDS who require the earliest possible access to new therapies. . . . Thousands of people with AIDS may die waiting 3 years for access to a protease inhibitor that might help improve the quality of their lives and extend their survival.*

For the vast majority of people with AIDS, accelerated approval is the only hope for access to these promising drugs. A recent front-page article in the financial magazine Barron's entitled "Do We Have Too Many Drugs for AIDS?" (August 15,1994) strongly suggests that FDA intends to revise significantly its accelerated approval policies, making it far more difficult for new AIDS drugs to get to the market. Many AIDS activists are appalled and angry that the article presents only the TAG point of view and implies that TAG speaks for the entire treatment activist community.

Baker precedes to echo John James on the opposition of the AIDS communities to FDA's designating TAG the sole or primary representatives of the HIV communities.

It is inappropriate and unacceptable for FDA (or any other government agency, organization, or company) to regard members of TAG as the sole or primary spokespersons on treatment issues for the HIV/AIDS community at large. While TAG may have the ear of FDA and other government health

officials, they do not appear to have a constituency beyond their own relatively small membership. There is absolutely no evidence of broad support in the AIDS community for TAG's effort to gut accelerated approval. On the contrary, there is growing opposition, even outrage at the Tag initiative. **20**

We were alarmed that not only did Barron's buy FDA's scam that TAG legitimately represented the AIDS community, so also did some of the drug companies along with many funders in the liberal establishment. Merck bought into it sufficiently that it told Delaney and myself in mid 1995 that FDA informed Merck it was not open to accelerated approval for the protease drugs, and therefore Merck should not plan to bring their drug Crixivan to market for at least three more years. Relying on FDA's projections, Merck was unprepared at the time the agency approved their drug in March 1996.

The community was rife with speculation over whether TAG's leaders were manipulated by FDA, or did TAG instead take the initiative with the FDA telling them and the world what they knew hard-liners at FDA wanted to hear? TAG and FDA appeared to be locked in a secret marriage of convenient collusion or at least collaboration. Clearly, FDA was using TAG to manipulate the community and give the public the impression of community support FDA did not actually have. Many TAG members seemed to believe they were doing the right thing, but self-deception makes us quick to equate our own interests with the right thing. Delaney, like most other treatment activists, had become cynical about TAG-FDA collusion, as he put it, "TAG's link with FDA is the cornerstone of its business plan. Without FDA, TAG is chopped liver. "

Why did TAG do it?**21** Were they deceived by FDA, drunk with the power they thought alliance with FDA gave them, or were they just not nearly as smart as they pretended to be? Like Delaney, Ron Baker, John James, Barry, Jules, and many others in the broader community, I was struck by TAG's parochialism and hubris, the way their spokespersons always seemed to focus on their own personal situations, frustrations, and opinions. They were out of touch with common patients who lacked their access to medical resources. AIDS always seemed to be about them. Their top guys seemed would-be celebrities—1990s versions of Andy Warhol superstars. Never original thinkers, they bought into the "woke" groupthink of the day. With the benefit of hindsight, I have concluded that they must have been easily manipulated by hardliners at FDA and by their statistics guru Columbia University Biostatistics Professor Joseph Fleiss whose influence on them appears to have been excessive.

I once remarked to Delaney that they were like spoiled children. "Remember," he said, "they average at lot younger than us. We're the Vietnam War generation, we question, we're gadflies, rebels. The TAG boys are the 'me generation,' they expect to be pampered, gratified, and admired." It amused me that whenever we discussed TAG, Delaney always referred to them as the TAG boys. Ron Baker, also of our Vietnam War, generation was harsher when he later remarked, "for people who try to sell themselves as the smartest guys in the room, TAG's LSTs were a really, really dumb idea."

Intellectuals and would-be intellectuals, like the TAG boys and the FDA hard liners, have a fatal attraction to ideologies and bureaucracies. Ideology provides the security of a default position one can rely on to avoid the uncertainties involved in critically examining real life situations in order to make authentic decisions. When facing a difficult decision, just apply the formula, that makes it so easy. Bureaucrats are like house cats, they love ease and fixed routines and expect them as their right. Authentic decisions require the hard work of studying all aspects of the situation and scrutinizing all options. They demand the resourcefulness to find new solutions outside the box and the courage to pursue them. Shakespeare grasped the moral side of authentic decision: *"Who chooseth me must give and hazard all he hath."* Authenticity is much too much to ask of bureaucrats and ideologues. Easier to just follow the rules and "think" according to their formulas: that intellectual sloth, perhaps, was the fundamental problem with TAG and FDA.

Chapter 4
The Grand Patient Alliance of 1995

"Thus the whirligig of time brings in his revenges."
Shakespeare, Twelfth Night

The crucial roles of TAG's activist opponents in enlisting the media and researchers in their victorious alliance against TAG-FDA remains as yet an untold story as are the political backstories. What transpired inside San Francisco's warring gay and AIDS treatment activist factions, how did we quickly come together to thwart the TAG-FDA plans to delay the protease antiretroviral cocktails? The answers are an essential part of AIDS history and LGBT heritage. Too long ignored, the activists story needs to be detailed and its implications understood. Fear that it might be lost in oblivion, moved me to undertake this work in hopes of spurring further re-assessment of a critical chapter in America's AIDS epidemic.

At the start of 1995 there were three separate factions of AIDS treatment activism in sharp contention with each other. Soon after Kessler's March 1995 *Scientific American* article there were only two. The San Francisco based factions, the first headed by Martin Delaney and Project Inform, the second by myself, Log Cabin Republicans, and our libertarian allies, had quarreled bitterly for years over underground drugs and the need for FDA reform legislation. To the astonishment of everyone, we joined forces in unified opposition to the FDA-TAG plan for large simple trials for the cocktails, and we worked together to recruit an array of allies from across the country.

The relationship between Delaney-Project Inform and the Treatment Action Group had long been a simmering distrust, though they had joined forces to protect their underground drug operations. The two factions made sporadic attempts to cooperate because they thought the appearance of a united front would strengthen them in dealing with

Washington. Indeed, Washington officials, whether in the agencies like FDA, NIH and CDC, or on Capitol Hill, or in the Administration, or in the drug companies and their lobbyists on K Street, always resisted dealing with rival AIDS factions. This reflected their discomfort with the gay community and LGBT people in general.

The more libertarian West Coast faction, nominally led by myself, loosely included the San Francisco AIDS Foundation and the Los Angeles based AIDS Healthcare Foundation. Both Foundations dismissed TAG as not representative of people with AIDS. Both represented many patients desperate for the new drugs. Our people recognized that Martin Delaney was far more willing than the TAG boys to stand up to FDA, and we knew he would be more ready to compromise with FDA than we were. We also knew he would never support FDA reform initiatives to forestall the agency's deadly delays in the future. But FDA itself had not been our main bone of contention with Delaney—that was the AIDS drug underground. Like us, both foundations had also opposed the underground for safety reasons.

Before the libertarians' support widened to include the two foundations and others around the country, our main organizations were Direct Action for Treatment Action, DATA, founded by Jack Girard and Steven Fowkes, and the Log Cabin Republicans. I was on the Board of DATA and being AIDS Policy Advisor to LCR opened up valuable connections to powerful Republicans, chief among them, Newt Gingrich. Additionally, the doors of top researchers were open to us, and we had reliable media connections, especially with the papers important for our issues, the *SF Chronicle*, *SF Examiner*, the *Bay Area Reporter*, the *LA Times*, the *Washington Times*, the *Wall Street Journal*, and even the *New York Times*. We also had relationships with some of the pharmaceutical companies, but the other two factions had these as well. It seemed that everyone had some friends in the pharmaceutical industry, they were the rich uncles on the scene.

From September 1994 to February 1995 TAG's LST plan kept the activist community in a state of nervous agitation. Increasingly, people were conferring and ruminating on what might happen next. Still the TAG threat was only theoretical, FDA had not yet endorsed their plan. When

David Kessler signaled an implicit endorsement in his *Scientific American* article that, along with the delays on Saquinavir, elevated the LST plan to a real and present danger. Activists were alarmed because we knew FDA hardliners had long supported the positions TAG was pushing. I suspected the hard liners and Professor Fleiss had goaded TAG, though Kessler was eager to present LSTs as TAG's initiative. Once Kessler's article was out, activists across the country, realized that FDA was not neutral, they were deep in collusion with TAG.

Most observers assumed the plan for LSTs in lieu of accelerated approval for the cocktails was TAG's brainchild that FDA had adopted. I suspected just the opposite: FDA and allies like Fleiss had conned TAG into shilling for FDA's decades old practice of delaying drugs until they demonstrated the agency's power to get the last scintilla of data. But it didn't matter who was parent to this terrible idea, FDA and TAG worked hand in glove. What did matter was that if their LST scheme succeeded, tens of thousands would die unnecessarily.

Despite differences in politics and methods, Delaney and I both were deeply bound into the LGBT and HIV communities. Each of us stood to lose more precious friends. However, distasteful it might seem, the need for us to ally was a no brainer practically as well as ethically. It resembled the allies teaming up with Stalin to defeat Hitler, as Barry Freehill joked. We all had our own rationales. Par for the course in our individualistic community where tall poppies are aggressively mowed down and leading can be an exercise in herding cats: something Delaney and many others found out the hard way. I avoided leading in a conspicuous manner, and tried to work by suggestion more than by directive. The Obama era's term "lead from behind" usually seemed the most prudent option given the open hostility to anything Republican.

To his credit, Delaney first breached the idea of truce and alliance. Barry had attended a Project Inform meeting, an update on drug development. Afterwards Delaney approached him to say that our group needed to work with his or else TAG and FDA would likely block accelerated approval of the cocktails, substituting instead full approval waiting upon their flawed LSTs.

Never before had I agreed with Delaney so whole heartedly. Barry, however, had personal reasons for holding back. Delaney and his people had slandered and libeled both of us, but Barry had taken bad drugs from Corti that put him in the emergency room. His *animus* was understandable, almost killed is worse than slandered. But having watched close friends die, I knew death from AIDS was far worse than slandered or even almost killed. I saw Delaney as overly ambitious, and deeply misguided in his political priorities. Certainly, he had behaved badly on the underground. Notwithstanding, I didn't see him as evil. He seemed an exceptionally able person who had made regrettable compromises, not unlike many of our leading politicians. Barry and I argued. I asked him to get back to Delaney, he refused. Instead, I asked John James. John was hesitant. He wasn't exactly a neutral party, he seemed closer to us than to Project Inform and he was no friend of TAG on FDA issues. Moreover, he was an almost Olympian figure in the community; his *AIDS Treatment News* was widely read, so Delaney would listen to him. After weighing the stakes, John called Delaney.

Our meeting occurred in a quiet restaurant on Franklin Street behind the San Francisco Opera House. John attended along with Barry, Delaney, his lawyer Curtis Ponzi, and myself. Considering past disputes, it was surprisingly cordial, without recriminations, or even visible suspicions. Delaney and I, along with everyone present, had a powerful sense of where our ethical duties lay. For each of us saving huge numbers of lives far outweighed our troubled history and even personal pride.

We agreed to join forces to marshal an *ad hoc* national activist coalition to challenge FDA, TAG, and their dangerous LST plans. Instead of LSTs, we would demand accelerated approval of the protease drugs for as soon as their makers could supply them. Delaney brought to the deal Project Inform's mailing list and data base of patient supporters. I brought my ace in the hole: high level Republican political opposition to FDA. We both had critical contacts with researchers. Thanks to Ron Baker, we had a determined ally in the most respected AIDS organization in California, the San Francisco AIDS Foundation.

The reaction of the national AIDS treatment activist community to our alliance was sheer astonishment. Theo Smart of New York ACT

UP told people he literally fell off his chair. Disbelief was widespread. I got a number of calls asking me to confirm that it was actually true. The irony of it amused both Delaney and myself, and our past bitterness faded quickly. Why be bitter against someone who was helping save the lives of your friends? The rarer action is to save life.

The pharmaceutical sponsors had told us FDA advised them to be prepared to deliver their drugs large scale in three years. When I informed Linda Distalrath of Merck in September of our goal to have the first three protease drugs, including Merck's, on the market within six months, she laughed. "FDA won't move that fast," she declared, "a snail can't sprint! Besides Merck, has relied on FDA's timeframe. We can't scale up our production fast enough to have adequate Crixivan ready that soon."

"The broader community stands united on saving as many lives as we can," I declared, "that requires approval of the protease cocktails by early 1996, whether Merck is ready or not." Though Merck was unprepared when approval came, they rose to the challenge pulling out all the stops to get Crixivan to the patients. Speed was essential. Since the protease drugs had different toxicity and efficacy profiles, Crixivan was an indispensable alternative for those who did not respond well to the other two drugs.

The researcher community did not laugh at our goal, but they were skeptical about its realism. The patients were a different story, their lives depended upon early approval. They had all lost friends and lovers, and knew what unpredictable monster the disease was. Recruiting patients to our cause was about as hard as giving away US gold double eagles. All across the country people who did not work with us, those who distrusted my group because of our Libertarian-Republican associations or Delaney because of his tactics and history with the underground, put aside past distrust and joined our burgeoning alliance against FDA's deadly LST strategy.

The biggest challenge was New York, the seat of the Treatment Action Group. TAG was used to getting its way with FDA and with NIAID as well. TAG was known for its aggressive actions against the pharmaceutical companies. The pharmas feared them, but respected them because they were educated (or so it seemed), resourceful, and above all well connected with FDA which gave TAG legitimacy in the pharmas eyes that ordinary gay community people lacked.

We had plenty of able allies inside New York's large, diverse activist community. Jules Levin became particularly active at this time even though his disease was advancing rapidly, which gave him urgency on steroids. Another with advanced HIV was Bree Salzman, whose wife was an AIDS doctor. There were several phone conference calls with other New York activists not affiliated with TAG who were devoting full time to the cause. Activists and patients from around the country became fully involved.

FDA was likely to make a decision on accelerated approval for the protease inhibitors after the FDA Antiviral Drug Committee made its recommendations at the meeting on November 6-8. The preceding weeks were a season of angry rhetoric and internet mudslinging unprecedented for even AIDS activism. A typical foray was Spencer Cox's attack on Jules Levin. Jules had sent Kessler a carefully reasoned analysis of TAG's letter of June 16, 1994 opposing accelerated approval for Saquinivir. Rather than responding to Jules' points with argument, Cox hit back with insults: *"Not only are you a blazing idiot Jules, but you are a bald liar as well. You are beneath contempt. And I would add you are the first to jump when Hoffman La Roche says to, like the industry lapdog you are. I am not even going to dignify your idiocy with a response."* Cox's attitude might be dismissed if he were speaking for himself, but he was TAG's top public relations officer. Despite such extremes, TAG people were not wackos. I suspected that they over-reacted because they were egged on by the deep dyed wacko ideologues inside the FDA bureaucracy.

Jules Levin

Unused to criticism, TAG went berserk over the avalanche of censure of their LSTs. In November 1995 when FDA approved a new drug, 3TC, faster than they liked, some TAG members went off the rails by shouting and stomping their protest in the back of the room. They sensed 3TC's accelerated approval was handwriting on the wall for their plans to sidetrack the protease cocktails into their LSTs. Anyone, including reporters and researchers, who disagreed openly with them was likely to suffer demonization or be dismissed as an ignorant nobody, or a pharma lapdog. Still officials at FDA, NIIAD, and TAG's funders continued to treat them as the legitimate voice of the AIDS community. After all these straight officials surely were entitled to decide who would represent gays and people with HIV. The choice could never be entrusted to those outcast communities themselves, that would be unthinkable!

TAG people excoriated the San Francisco AIDS Foundation as an organ of Hoffmann-La Roche for running Ron Baker's *BETA* articles critical of their LST proposal. Other TAG inspired contentions presented Delaney as a relentless FDA basher, champion of Republican deregulation, and closet fan of Newt Gingrich; odd behavior for a dyed in the wool Democrat with a history of congenial collusion with Kessler and others in FDA. There was an activist who did fit the FDA bashing label TAG tried to pin on Delaney. Despite my recent Log Cabin petition demanding accelerated approval for Glaxo's new drug 3TC, TAG blasted me for, guess what? — "maligning Glaxo!" Seems an inside the beltway newsletter, the *FDA Insider,* ran an article castigating Glaxo for a $1M contribution to AmFAR whose board two TAG members graced with their presence. TAG couldn't easily scapegoat the actual culprits, Ron Baker and Martin Delaney, since their organizations, like AmFAR, also got munificent contributions from Glaxo; the abhorrent Jules was disqualified for terminal idiocy. So the only prominent "industry lapdog" left to target was yours truly. Being the lapdog that bit Glaxo wasn't enough however. Rumors soon fingered me for a card carrying member of the John Birch Society, as if that group would welcome an in-your-face gay AIDS activist from Baghdad by the Bay!

Throughout, Delaney, Jules, Ron Baker, and I, were more amused than disturbed by the battery of misfiring personal attacks. If TAG wanted to make fools of themselves, more power to them. We would enjoy good laughs and keep busy organizing support for early approval. Behind the scenes with the media, and through Log Cabin, I apprised Republicans, especially Gingrich's people, of FDA's planned delays. It was essential to secure Republican support should intervention be necessary. We all worked to forestall any open support for FDA and TAG from the Democrats. The pragmatic Clinton White House never embraced FDA foot dragging, and Bill Clinton was eager to curry favor with gay voters for his 1996 re-election bid. Besides the President, the other key Democrat was Ted Kennedy. We made sure that Ted understood where gay voters and contributors stood on expeditious approval of the cocktails.

Moreover, while our de facto allies in the pharmaceutical industry rarely criticized FDA openly, nothing prevented their lobbyists from doing so. The pharmas could afford to put the best connected lobbyists to work trolling the Washington swamp. My allies and I were happy to provide them with ammunition. The lobbyists, through private channels, conveyed to politicians of all stripes the complaints of suffering patients, their client's unhappiness with FDA's endemic delays, and the benefits to the public of increased regulatory speed. It all fit into the pharmas strategy for passing an FDA reform bill with the limited, self-interested changes they sought.

The Republicans' control of Congress made them the pivotal political players. Among them were a cadre of outspoken opponents of excessive regulation led by Newt Gingrich. He had long been FDA's most aggressive critic in Washington. Gingrich was particularly valuable because FDA held no leverage over him, and as Speaker of the House he was *de facto* leader of the GOP. Liberal politicians and media had accused Newt of seeking to "gut FDA" and warned that his reforms would launch an outbreak of new thalidomides. Newt, I suspect, wore their slurs as a badge of honor. We were also fortunate in that Newt, ever the realist, rejected homophobia and favored fair treatment for gays. If Time Man of the Year Dr. David Ho was the most acclaimed hero of 1996, Newt Gingrich was the least recognized hero. Perhaps he himself did not realize his impact on speeding the approval of the AIDS drug cocktails.

Speaker Gingrich

At the time, I was still a member of the Advisory Board of Newt's Progress and Freedom Foundation which was focused on FDA reform. By my years of working with Republicans, my newspaper op eds, and leading roles in community protests and meetings calling for faster drug approval, I became too sharp a thorn in the FDA's side for them to ignore. As much as TAG wanted to disregard me and dismiss all Log Cabin Republicans, TAG's mentors in FDA knew this was a luxury they could ill afford. Thus, in the late 1994 and 1995 timeframe I was able to set up meetings with FDA brass, if not Kessler himself, where I made it abundantly clear that Gingrich, Hatch, and other Republicans would not just look the other way if FDA delayed the protease based cocktails.

Writing as Log Cabin AIDS Advisor in an August 28, 1995 letter to Speaker Gingrich, with Kessler and other FDA officials copied, I laid out the case against Kessler's and FDA retaliation and favoritism dealing with the gay-HIV communities, and exposed their recruitment of community allies to shill for their plans to replace accelerated approval with LSTs:

Under your leadership, House committees are for the first time investigating FDA retaliation. Retaliation and favoritism are keys to David Kessler's power and, after drug delay, they are FDA's most common and dangerous abuses. . .. If I attempted to recount all specific instances of FDA retaliation and selective enforcement a letter might grow into a book. Let me limit myself to: (1) discussion of how FDA uses retaliation and favoritism in the AIDS community to enlist and recruit lobbying on its own behalf, (2) an instance of FDA's colluding with its AIDS activist allies to delay approval of AIDS drugs, and (3) a specific retaliation/collusion that has delayed for several months the new breakthrough AIDS drug Saquinivir.

Through favoritism, Kessler turns tax exempt ˙ AIDS organizations into de facto lobbies for FDA. Led by the Treatment Action Group (TAG), these groups use their tax-exempt "nonpartisan" status to pursue activities on behalf of FDA and liberal Democrats. Preeminent among their activities are targeting Republicans (particularly gay Republicans whom, it appears, they would like to eradicate,) and opposing Republican FDA reform proposals. TAG supports FDA delays of full approval for AIDS drugs and lobbies Congress against FDA reform efforts. In late 1992 and 1993 TAG lobbied President Clinton to retain David Kessler, The Great Delayer, including a letter writing campaign. Kessler rewards TAG by making it clear to the drug companies that they treat TAG as their sanctioned representative for the entire AIDS community. Thus, drug companies have come to fear TAG almost as they fear FDA itself.

In June 1994, TAG and FDA held a closed summit meeting in violation of government regulations. Their agenda: to end accelerated approval for AIDS drugs and introduce instead a lengthy program of large scale trials to exhaustively test efficacy before approval of any new AIDS drugs. In July 1995 activists critical of TAG and FDA learned that they had scheduled another closed meeting. Since meetings with the public must be open, the non-TAG activists, including myself, asked to sit in. Kessler not only refused to let us in, he refused to meet with us separately.

Comment: The Gingrich letter then detailed FDA delays in approving the first protease inhibitor, Saquinivir which Log Cabin Republicans had petitioned them to approve earlier. FDA denied delaying the drug, they simply said they needed additional phase II data, an argument we debunked in the letter. FDA was playing their old game implying they needed safety data while ever more efficacy data was their true goal. Saquinivir was notably safe for an AIDS drug. Its efficacy had been decisively proven, though not the exact degree or the optimal dosages. The issue was again turf. FDA was asserting control over the drug approval process by refusing to give the Roche drug the market advantage of earlier approval than its competitors. In short, FDA was regulating the commercial drug market in stealth, something Congress never authorized. The letter concludes: *Saquinivir has minimal toxicity, so safety is not an issue; moreover, its efficacy was established by a large well-controlled phase II clinical trial. A safe, effective breakthrough AIDS drug should be eligible for accelerated approval on the basis of data from a single phase II clinical trial. TAG was happy to provide "community support" for Kessler's delaying tactics by demanding additional data from a phase III trial. The FDA delay of Saquinivir is a clear instance of FDA and TAG working together to thwart the will of a large majority of AIDS patients and their doctors.*

Not wanting to assume too much, I asked Rich Tafel to apprise Gingrich's chief of staff of the FDA's disastrous plan to delay approval of the AIDS drug cocktails. Assurance came that Log Cabin's warnings to FDA would not be idle threats, the Speaker would indeed act if FDA delayed the protease based cocktails—in fact ours was a cause he would gladly embrace. The re-assurance from Tafel enabled me to inform FDA, media, and the community of the Republican determination to scrutinize any FDA delays in approving the protease inhibitors.

FDA's Carl Peck had once told Barry Freehill and myself that he "had dangled before Dingle" (the redoubtable John Dingle, Chair of the House Energy and Commerce Committee) and it was an experience he never wanted to repeat. However, distasteful dangling before Dingle might be, David Kessler knew that kneeling before Newt would be worse. Over the course of that fall I reminded Kessler in various ways that should FDA try to implement the LSTs, the ominous figure of Newt Gingrich would loom large in his future.

Since I had already attacked Kessler's delays and his LST proposals in no uncertain terms in the *Wall Street Journal* and the *LA Times* as well as the San Francisco papers and the gay press, he knew I would say and they would print much worse if FDA blocked the drugs. Across the summer he had begun to realize that many more would join Delaney and me in a rising chorus of severe censure that might soon include Gingrich and other Congressional FDA critics. More than the agency itself, with its crews of intellectually comatose lifers, Kessler was sensitive to public criticism. He well understood that it could spark not just criticism from Congress but actual cuts in his agency's budget. It could even mean dreaded RIFs—reductions in forces—lifers could lose their secretaries and assistants! They might even be reduced to emptying their own waste baskets.

High among Kessler's ambitions was a new campus for FDA to rival that of other agencies, particularly CDC's beautiful new Atlanta campus. For years the agency had been stuck in an aging, almost ramshackle World War II vintage high rise in Rockville Maryland known without affection as Parklawn, and more ominously to the regulated as The Castle. Urged on by myself and activist allies, interests critical of FDA began to complain on Capitol Hill about the cost and waste of a new FDA facility. This doubtless reached the ears of Kessler as well as the lifers ensconced in The Castle, or shall I say imprisoned since the lifers now faced the prospect of never leaving it?

The FDA reform movement and bills in Congress were of great concern to FDA hard-liners and lifers. When Rep. Tom Campbell had launched his FDA reform bill in 1991, a wide majority of House Republicans became co-sponsors. Since becoming Speaker, Newt Gingrich had promulgated what they saw as a radical agenda that included ominous privatization proposals. Moreover, Senator Nancy Kassebaum's FDA reform bill would soon be introduced. It was softer than Gingrich liked, but far tougher than FDA wanted. FDA and its patient shills insisted the agency was just fine exactly the way it was. Indeed, in respect to oversight on manufacturing standards, devices, and supplements, they all sought a stronger, more intrusive FDA. Some advocates longed for the day when FDA could regulate the price of newly introduced drugs. As distasteful as whirlwind approvals for new AIDS drugs were, the politically savvy Kessler understood, even if TAG and the lifers did not, that as FDA entered the 1996 negotiations over the Kassebaum bill the last thing the agency wanted was an avalanche of bad publicity, including noisy street demonstrations from AIDS activists accusing FDA of killing patients by denying access to life-saving AIDS drugs.

It might be sentimental to say that David Kessler wanted to do the right thing; nonetheless, he clearly wanted to do the smart thing. Kessler was extremely ambitious, but, unlike the FDA lifers and their TAG sympathizers, he did not appear to be a hardened ideologue. Clearly, he was smarter and more flexible than most of them. By September 1995 it was becoming apparent that the FDA-TAG large simple trials plan he had laid out in the March *Scientific American* article was looking neither prudent nor intelligent. Researchers from David Ho and Tom Merigan down were openly rejecting it. Hope that the new drugs could save surviving AIDS patients and turn the epidemic around was surging though the community. Perhaps most threatening of all, a solid consensus for FDA reform was developing in Congress. David Kessler must have realized, even if his team at FDA were still foot dragging, that the risks to the agency of delaying the new protease cocktails far outweighed the risks of approving them early. This is all hindsight. At the time Delaney, myself, and our allies feared that FDA would delay approval. We were convinced we had to pull out all the stops to prevent that from happening.

To us the basic situation seemed simple. If you are in a war for survival and someone discovers a new weapon that may work, you use it. You don't wait for time consuming trials to verify that the odds it will work are exactly 99.44% pure. More exhaustive testing to learn more about how the drugs work might make sense for an expensive new biologic for alopecia totalis, but not for an AIDS drug in 1995. In an epidemic with people dying by the tens of thousands you can't waste time pedantically pursuing science for science's sake.

The issue of racial discrimination with the proposed TAG-FDA trials was seldom discussed, yet deeply troubling to those of us who bothered to think about its human consequences. The Republicans were not yet ready to court African Americans let alone gays, but the Democrats knew that lack of African-American access to life saving AIDS drugs could spell political trouble. There was little doubt TAG and their friends would be admitted into the trials; they had always got themselves into the other trials. But most African American patients would either be unaware of the trials or lack the know how to get in. I had met African American AIDS patients in Oakland; they were every bit as scared as the white boys at the other end of the Bay Bridge, but far more lost and alone. Their situation was truly heart rending. Just as previous AIDS trials had reached far too few African Americans, TAG's LSTs would be no different, and many of those who got in would get only the old nukes that we knew were highly toxic and barely worked!

Being *de facto* discriminatory, the TAG-FDA plan was, unethical. Not only would blacks be disproportionately excluded *de facto*, whites outside the main centers, especially in rural areas, would not know how to access the trials. Hispanics and native Americans would be trapped in the same sinking boat. Worst of all, the number of patients who needed the drugs to survive was not in the thousands that might be in the trials, but into the hundreds of thousands. In view of all these dire considerations, for TAG-FDA to push the LSTs seemed an act of monumental hubris. Yet in the fall of 1995 TAG showed no signs of relenting.

The strife between TAG-FDA and the home grown patient advocates came to a head in August 1995. Kessler, bowing to an outraged HIV-AIDS community's demands for input on pending new drug applications for the first protease inhibitors, Saquinavir and Norvir, announced he would schedule an open meeting to discuss strategy for the protease cocktails. The move took nearly everyone by surprise. It was less of a surprise for Delaney and myself because we understood that Kessler was a political animal who could read the hand writing on the wall once his face had been shoved into it, which was exactly what we were bent on doing.

By early September we had secured statements repudiating the LSTs and calling for accelerated approval from major treatment groups including the San Francisco Community Consortium, ACT UP Golden

Gate, Mobilization against AIDS, the National Association of People with AIDS, and even the New York ACT UP Treatment and Data Committee. Leading AIDS doctors across the country openly declared their opposition to the LSTs including Donald Abrams, David Ho, Marcus Conant, Joseph Sonnabend, Mark Feinberg, John Mellors, Stephen Follansbee, Mike Saag, Tom Merigan, Paul Volberding and many others. One distinguished researcher flatly stated that the trials were a dinosaur that could not tell us anything useful. All this criticism doubtless reached the FDA Antivirals Advisory Committee members whose job was to evaluate evidence on the safety and efficacy of new antivirals and make recommendations to guide FDA's approval decisions.

Kessler's unprecedented meeting was scheduled for September 12-13 in a Silver Spring Maryland Hotel. Anyone who signed up could come and speak. Come they did, patients from across the country flew in on their own dime, for some of them almost their last dime. It seemed a stroke of genius on Kessler's part, except in this case genius was thrust upon him by events and determined activists. The meeting would show the FDA antivirals committee members, TAG, the media, and the world where the AIDS community actually stood. It would expose FDA officials to the real community of desperate, suffering patients beyond the Potemkin village scenes staged for them by TAG. Exposure could pressure hardliners in FDA to bow to medical and political realities.

The Silver Spring meeting itself was the most crucial and fascinating, and the most productive, of all the activist meetings with FDA in the 90's. It was held in a fairly large conference-auditorium. Scores of industry people, financial analysts, and media watched and took notes from the back rows. Patients crowded in to express publicly their desperate need for new treatments. The heads and the treatment experts of major AIDS organizations came to voice the concerns of communities they served. All the key activist players, Delaney and his people, all the TAG people, Jules, Ron Baker, myself and many others spoke. I spoke on behalf of Log Cabin Republicans to publicly warn Kessler that any delays of the cocktails would face the scrutiny of Congressional critics led by Speaker Gingrich. As I left the microphone, I glimpsed grimaces of disapproval and dismay cross the faces of the FDA officials on the stage.

There were researchers speaking of course, including David Ho who advanced his view that viral load is not a surrogate marker of HIV disease but a direct measure of the disease itself. That was something Delaney, Barry, Jules, Baker, and I saw as an absolute no brainer, but to TAG and FDA hardliners it seemed a mystery on a par with the Mayan calendar. It was key to the entire debate over expedited approval for the protease cocktails. If Ho was correct, when a drug reduced viral load to undetectable we had proof positive that it would be highly effective in reducing symptoms and extending life.

Two crucial points soon became apparent to FDA hard-liners, the media, and everyone else present: their TAG allies were far outnumbered by activists who wanted the new drugs yesterday, and TAG's ideological stridency was no match for the authentic passion of real patients struggling to stay alive. Beginning with the Silver Spring meeting, over the course of the fall, Kessler maneuvered to distract from the untenable position he had taken in his March *Scientific American* article. In the process, he was distancing himself from TAG, moving toward Dr. Ho, Delaney, myself, and the great majority of AIDS patients.

Delaney and I, along with our many allies, left the meeting feeling like victors. While we believed we'd won, we did not know how complete our victory was until FDA approved Roche's Saquinavir with unprecedented speed at the antivirals committee meeting in December, and soon followed with Abbott's Norvir and Merck's Crixivan in March 1996. As mentioned, FDA told Merck to be ready for approval in three years. FDA's forced change of plans took the company by surprise. It needed to ramp up factories at breakneck speed, set up a special distribution system through an outside company, Stadtlanders Pharmacy, to get the drugs to patients on time. The three protease drugs worked in cocktails with other already approved drugs like 3TC, the old nukes, soon to be approved Viramune, and a powerful new drug, Sustiva. The cocktails, which varied like cancer drug cocktails, proved far more effective, longer lasting, and usually less toxic, than any monotherapy. A new day had dawned for one million HIV infected Americans.

Indeed, at the March 1996 meeting Commissioner David Kessler privately thanked Jules Levin and myself for our roles in pressuring the

FDA to get the drugs out immediately. This was gracious on Kessler's part. I believe that Kessler made an initial mistake out of loyalty to the agency, or maybe just going native with the culture of FDA. At least he was honest enough to acknowledge his mistake. Nonetheless, neither the FDA nor Congress, nor the Administration ever acknowledged any debt to the AIDS activists for saving the nation from approval delays that would have cost tens of thousands of lives, severely damaged FDA's reputation, and brought harsh censure and demands for far-reaching reforms.

Early approval of the cocktails prevented a monumental healthcare disaster and regulatory scandal. Because the near disaster has yet to be acknowledged, there have been no thorough scholarly studies of events and decisions inside either the FDA, the researcher profession, or the drugs' corporate sponsors. Such studies might give us valuable information on how things actually work within the FDA bureaucracy, as well as how they deal with the companies and patient activists. Indeed, they could point out needed reforms.

Moreover, they could yield important insights into a crucial period in the history of HIV, the LGBT community, and our nation itself. Unfortunately, all we have is activist and press accounts from the time gathering dust in libraries and closets like mine. With each passing year records are destroyed, events fade, and key players pass from the scene their memories lost forever, and lost with them our chance to learn what we must do to avoid repeating mistakes that led us toward the brink of a horrific and entirely avoidable disaster.

The most decisive factor in the drama of FDA's turnaround was the courageous patients who refused to take early death for a fate. The patients inspired the activists, researchers, and doctors to act, and their passion for life sustained our resolution. They were the fire in our bellies and our guiding lights. Never before had a large group of patients revolted against the regulatory and research establishments to demand faster and better results—to demand a chance to live! And it has never happened since.

These patients outrage against their fated premature deaths and pent up anger over their years of oppression as gay people gave them passion, courage, and resourcefulness. Without their passion driven urgency, the research that led to the protease drugs would never have moved as fast as it did. Without their passion, FDA culture, not tailored for life threatening illnesses, let alone for a deadly epidemic, might have delayed the cocktails by three years while far more additional Americans would have died of AIDS than were killed in the entire Vietnam war. The human and fiscal cost of the epidemic would have exploded, and the suffering would have been worse by being wholly avoidable. Resulting delays in implementing treatments in Africa and across the world, would have caused the preventable loss of millions of lives. Indeed, the AIDS patients and their activists helped save the lives of millions by saving FDA from itself.

Ours society remains loath to recognize the heroism of LGBT people asserting their rights and dignity as human beings. Bigots insist that would be tantamount to sanctioning and even promoting homosexuality. We all live under the curse of that wicked Old Testament text, Leviticus 20:13. LGBT people fail to recognize their heroism because it is difficult for them to face how badly they have been hurt, how unjustly treated. It's like struggling to recall childhood abuse that the victims repress deeply. Far easier for the victims to believe that somehow they deserved the abuse and accept guilt for their cruel fate. Guilt requires less effort than anger, though it can do more damage. As Harvey Milk lamented, it's much easier to live in closeted shame than to step forth and fight for justice.

There is no museum commemorating LGBT Americans on the Washington Mall, no politician dares suggest such a thing. Yet there are many great LGBT Americans whose contributions deserve memorial and celebration. We are best known in letters and arts, which define the very spirit and character of a nation. We have given America a disproportionate number of her greatest writers, composers and artists. These include writers Walt Whitman, Herman Melville, Ralph Waldo Emerson, Henry James, Hart Crane, Gertrude Stein, James Baldwin, Tennessee Williams, composers Aaron Copland, Leonard Bernstein, Samuel Barber, Billy Strayhorn, painters John Singer Sargent, Georgia O'Keefe, Thomas Eakins, Andy Warhol, Keith Haring, and many others. Indeed, LGBT people shine in all areas of human endeavor, including civil rights with

Barbara Gittings, Frank Kameny, Bayard Rustin, Barbara Jordan, Jim Foster, Harvey Milk, and the many uncelebrated AIDS activists.

Along with everyone else, we have sacrificed lives in all America's wars, built its railroads and skyscrapers, and maintained its professions. As a group we have contributed as much and sacrificed more for America than other groups our size. Silence, the head bowed to injustice in secret shame, is our greatest sacrifice. Our contributions are made in spite of denial of equal rights and fair recognition, in spite of demeaning abuse, and the quiet marginalization that continues apace to this day.

Like Dave Olson, Jim Foster, Steve Wright, Jesse Dobson, Duane Dugger, and so many other unsung heroes, the patients who came to Silver Springs acted on the hope of saving others from the disease that would soon snuff out their lives. Their courage made a decisive difference in the lives of countless future HIV patients, and a huge unacknowledged difference to our nation. That heroism remains unsung because they were routinely devalued for being gay and still are so devalued, as are all LGBT people everywhere.

Martin Delaney, however, did receive limited recognition. TAG did as well, in TAG's case it was, in my opinion, misguided and undeserved. Their recognition was a case of the liberal straight establishment again presuming to decide which plantation gays would be anointed as leaders, and of course they chose those they felt most comfortable with, the ones who were unfailing in their allegiance to the liberal agenda and unquestioning in their fealty to a protectionist FDA.

Delaney wasn't in it entirely for himself, but he longed to be recognized as the national leader of treatment activism. His desire for recognition was not a bad thing, gays desperately needed and still need recognized heroes and leaders. But Delaney made compromises on underground drugs and with FDA and TAG that left him a more flawed hero than he might otherwise have been. From my conversations with him, I know that he grasped intellectually the need for incentives for drug research and that an absolutely crucial incentive was to reduce regulatory delays. However, like many gay people, his loyalty to the Democratic party and its priorities was a given, and in the end a hindrance to his flexibility, and integrity.

Delaney understood that FDA was wasteful, and put expanding its bureaucratic turf above patients' interests and even their lives. But he did not believe FDA's defects could be remedied. My libertarian allies and I rejected the liberal's tacit assumption of the God given authority of FDA's regulatory hierarchy. We were willing to work with Republicans to save people with AIDS, even though we harbored scant hopes of being rewarded and knew we would face harassment, abuse, and be ostracized.

Unwilling to challenge FDA, Delaney jumped into the underground which gave him momentary fame and some coveted adulation at the cost permanent tarnish. But in the most important decision of his activist career he extended an olive branch to his chief activist adversaries, Barry Freehill and myself, and broke with the FDA and TAG to save untold lives. Delaney was a political animal, but not every political animal risks doing what is right to save others. In truth, all too few undertake that risk. Martin Delaney deserves to be remembered for doing the right thing when it mattered most. He was a bona fide anti-hero, but was he a hero still? Well, many straights regarded as heroes have been more tarnished and done far less. I won't cite names, but some of them are known everywhere.

TAG and the gay leftists wanted to consign me along with all the Log Cabin Republicans, to the outer darkness where they felt gay Republicans belong. We decamped the plantation, that made us non-persons deserving zero recognition for our roles in speeding access to the cocktails. Since FDA remained a vital liberal icon, the gay community's long and fateful battle with a hidebound FDA would not be acknowledged for what it was, a despised minority's valiant struggle for dignity and survival against bureaucratic arrogance, inflexibility, and bias.

PART IV: Outcomes

Chapter 1
1996 Persons of the Year

The pivotal role of scientific research in defeating HIV is evident in the long, contentious dispute between Robert Gallo and Luc Montagnier over who first discovered the retrovirus that causes AIDS. The stakes for reputations and revenues from licensing fees were huge. Beginning in 1983 and not resolved until 1987, the wrangle was complex, arcane, and ugly. The compromise resolution credited Montaigne with first isolating the virus and Gallo with proving it to be the cause of AIDS. Another eight years passed before researchers, building on these discoveries, developed the drugs that made HIV disease a manageable condition. The first of the new protease drugs were from three different companies and their development involved executives along with scores of doctors and researchers. Complexities notwithstanding, with these drugs humanity won a monumental victory over a terrible adversary. Victories deserve celebration, and celebrations demand heroes. So what hero would lead the AIDS victory parade?

People always love heroes and sometimes actually need them. A true hero takes a risk when others hold back in sloth, fear, or caution. He gathers unto himself the collective power of his following. The hero must have insight, resourcefulness, courage, and the will and ability to lead. Charisma helps but does not guarantee success. He must lead the troupes into the fray, grasp the great idea others miss, break a path through a wilderness where his fellows are stumped or lost. She carries the banners of truth into the unknown, and crosses stormy waters risking defeat and destruction. Envision Florence Nightingale dodging bullets on a battlefield, Galileo facing the inquisition, Lincoln signing the Emancipation Proclamation, Washington crossing the Delaware (on the next page),

or dying AIDS patients demonstrating against FDA. Heroes symbolize
their group's energy, initiative, and achievement, as Jung would say the
hero becomes a mana-personality who gathers and evinces the mighty
energy of an archetype holding sway over the people.

But often, especially in modern science and technology, the one
we identify as the hero is just the most articulate, prominent, or boldest
member of a group or team spearheading a major achievement, a victory
for the public, or for all mankind. Dr. David Ho became the most visible
member of a group of medical researchers who by 1996 had developed
drugs to defeat, or at least neutralize, a great enemy of mankind, the human
immuno-deficiency retrovirus or HIV. Others were envious of the
recognition he got, felt their discoveries were as or more crucial, but they
did not step forward to lead in efforts to overcome the obstacles to getting
the benefits of their work to the patients. They played safe, not wanting to
offend FDA or NIH. David Ho led morally, as well as scientifically, by
challenging obstructive bureaucratic thinking and so was justly anointed
hero of the war against AIDS.

Thus, *Time* named David Ho 1996 Man of the Year for being the
stand out leader among the scientists and researchers pioneering the
treatments that made HIV disease manageable. Media accounts glazed
over the momentous debate around Dr. Ho's compelling scientific
argument that made a reluctant FDA approve the cocktails in record time.
The FDA dismissed HIV viral load as an unproven disease marker, and
demanded large simple trials to document symptom reduction and

longevity increase to prove the marker a reliable measure of the disease. Dr. Ho, unlike the others, stepped forward to challenge FDA by asserting that HIV viral load was not a surrogate marker, but rather a direct measure of the disease itself.

His public challenge of FDA's position on viral load, which reflected his laboratory work on viral kinetics, made David Ho heroic. He repeated the challenge in conversations with activists, media, and other researchers. At the September 1995 public meeting to discuss early approval of the protease based cocktails, Ho again challenged FDA's position on markers. Ho was a gambler. To win gamblers must assess the odds and then take a risk, but risk taking requires the courage to face the danger of losing. Risk taking is a defining feature of heroism. Like all bureaucracies, FDA is risk averse. Courage is never a virtue characteristic of bureaucrats, nor is it at all conducive to work in a bureaucracy. Caution, not courage, is their watchword; caution is infectious, and it can paralyze. Researchers working in the shadow of FDA often are cautious to the point of cowardice. Ho showed courage rare for a drug researcher in challenging the powerful regulatory agency on the science and by backing its critics among the patient community activists. Others were not as ready to risk their careers to save the patients. David Ho deserved his honor in a moral sense that has not generally been recognized.

A full, accurate, truthful assessment of the FDA attempts to delay accelerated approval for the antiretroviral cocktails would challenge the myth that the agency is a benign protector of public health. It would show on one hand that the political resistance to the patients fighting FDA delays came from Congressional consumer protectors allied with FDA. On the other hand, the patients' political support came from libertarians seeking regulatory reform and accountability, chief among them the man big government lovers all loved to hate, Speaker Newt Gingrich. It would celebrate the courage of David Ho and many other researchers and clinicians in putting patient's lives above their own professional relations with regulators. But these are not angles the establishment wanted to stress. So the facts and valuable lessons of history have been casualties.

FDA delays on approval of drugs for deadly diseases has long been and continues to be a stock criticism of the agency. Elon Musk nailed the underlying problem with all regulators which is nowhere more evident than with FDA:

> *There is a fundamental problem with regulators. If a regulator agrees to change a rule and something bad happens, they can easily lose their career. Whereas if they change a rule and something good happens, they don't even get a reward. So, it's very asymmetric. It's then easy to understand why regulators resist changing the rules. It's because there's a big punishment on one side and no reward on the other.* 22

In short, bureaucracy makes regulation the enemy of innovation. The lesson here is: "First do no harm" must apply as much to harmful caution and precision for precision's sake as to ill-considered creativity." The Hippocratic oath is Janus faced. But our bureaucracies see only the face looking backwards.

It would have been of little consequence for FDA, or to public health, if the agency had hurriedly approved more lackluster AIDS drugs. All the drugs worked poorly and tens of thousands of the patients were at death's door. They wanted a chance to try any drug that might save them or just give them a little more time. But the FDA wanted to take a stand for its regulatory turf, procedures, and authority. Valuing bureaucratic power above doomed patients' need for extra time and their freedom to choose, it was unwilling to grant them the dignity of dying in battle. Thanks to heroic researchers like David Ho, backed by intrepid patient activists and the favorable political forces of the time freedom won, but freedom's victory is never assured.

Chapter 2
Congress Passes an
FDA Reform Bill, Finally

Background political events powerfully influenced the dramatic 1994-1995 struggle to approve expeditiously the AIDS drug cocktails. The movement to reform FDA, pushed by Speaker Gingrich and others including democrats, was gaining strength in Congress and support within the Clinton Administration. These developments made accelerated approval of the protease cocktails the only rational option for FDA, as David Kessler must have realized at some point. During 1995-96, I was involved in formulating Senator Nancy Kassebaum's FDA reform bill and advocating for its passage. One of my objectives was to collect chits toward insuring that any FDA reform bill would protect accelerated approval for AIDS drugs. I laid out my support of the Kassebaum bill in an opinion piece in the Feb 8, 1996 *Wall Street Journal*:

> *At long last, Congress may bow to public pressure and bring at least a measure of accountability to perhaps the most unaccountable of federal regulatory agencies, the Food and Drug Administration. Congress last revamped the FDA in 1962 when, panicked by the thalidomide disaster, it gave the agency a blank check. Throughout the next three decades, the FDA inflated its powers until regulatory gridlock became a worse menace to public health than thalidomide ever was. . . While Senator Kassebaum's reforms employ cautious means, the radical goal of making FDA accountable would modernize the agency that has stood defiantly against the wishes and best interests of the general public for too long. . . The bottom line: Scientific and technical advance makes the drug development process safer and less in need of regulation.*

The FDA ignores these advances in safety. Instead it imposes an escalating burden to reduce drug risk to an absolute minimum, damn the cost. How does it get away with selling the public its wasteful regulatory Rolls Royce? The answer is simple—FDA imposed costs are hidden. Just as companies must prove their new products safe and effective, the FDA should have to prove that its procedures expedite medical innovation and are cost effective.

The heart of Mrs. Kassebaum's bill is the patient's right to better treatments. She feels the anguish of desperately ill patients denied experimental therapies by the FDA. Her bill will allow earlier access to medicines and hasten approval of drugs and devices for life threatening diseases.

Comment: Most likely at the behest of their mentors in FDA, TAG, under the misnomer "The Patient Coalition," formed a new group dedicated to defending FDA's powers. Perhaps intimidated by the Patient Coalition, the other major AIDS groups sat on the sidelines. It is shocking in retrospect that neither TAG nor the FDA hard-liners appeared to have learned anything from their recent near catastrophe in attempting to delay for three or more years the protease based cocktails. Of course, when no one calls them to task for their mistakes, most people's errors teach them nothing, and the public learns nothing. History's mistakes are thereby set up to repeat themselves.

The FDA is not subject to independent oversight. In the absence of such oversight Commissioner David Kessler's FDA can be as politically motivated and as arbitrary as the FBI under J. Edgar Hoover. AIDS drugs, like the new protease inhibitors, are moving fast because AIDS activists have political clout; but treatments for diseases where activism is rare face arbitrary delays and obstructions. . .. High safety standards are maintained under Sen. Kassebaum's bill. However, the standard of effectiveness, that sacred cow of consumer protectors, is clarified and updated.

Comment: TAG and FDA again claimed they wanted to know more about "how the drugs worked" before approval. Delays in life saving medicines for the purpose of satisfying intellectual curiosity were one of the chief obstacles the Kassebaum bill was designed to remove.

No longer will the FDA be allowed to delay new drugs while it tests their effectiveness relative to drugs already on the market...

When George Bush lost to Clinton, FDA immediately aborted reforms started by the Bush Administration. The FDA cannot be trusted to reform itself, Sen. Kassebaum has wisely concluded.

My support of the Kassebaum bill in the *Wall Street Journal* put me temporarily at odds with the Progress and Freedom Foundation which, wanted to go further. I thought their plan was better, but was willing to take half a loaf rather than risk getting nothing after such a long struggle. As it turned out, we did not even get half a loaf that year. A Republican staffer offered me an explanation. Both parties, he confided, wanted to retain an incentive for the pharmaceutical industry to fill their campaign coffers during the 1996 election year. At least the two parties were cooperating!

A reform bill similar to Kassebaum's finally passed in 1997 after she had left the Senate. Ever beholden to their FDA allies, TAG's Patient Coalition fought tooth and nail to stop that bill, and Delaney, along with the main AIDS groups, sat on the sidelines. Kennedy's staffers complained to me that TAG had become a big nuisance demanding repeated meetings just to restate FDA's boilerplate arguments. The bill was a done deal once Kennedy signed on, much to the rue of TAG and, one assumes, FDA itself. Bitter enders ever, TAG took the unprecedented step of condemning Ted Kennedy in a final statement that lavishly praised Jack Reid (D-R.I..), the major Senate hold out against FDA reform.

The only AIDS treatment activist invited to attend the bill's signing in the White House was yours truly. There were two main reasons for this: Republicans, especially Senator Hatch, requested that I be invited; FDA's ever loyal Manhattan minions, fought passage of the bill, while other activists, not wanting to take on FDA, declined to support it. My seat was immediately behind Senators Hatch and Kennedy. Kennedy had come to recognize that the bill was an important step forward for many patient groups. By 1997 the AIDS activists battle with FDA had been won, with the important exception of FDA's continuing delays of HIV rapid testing. Since then, the agency has met reasonable requests to expedite drugs in the area of HIV. Would that cancer and other patient groups could say the same!

However, some of the FDA reforms that AIDS activists sought have yet to be fully implemented. One major reform waited until May 30 2018 when President Trump signed the "right to try bill" streamlining procedures for terminally ill patients seeking to try experimental treatments. In the November 17, 2017 *Washington Blade* I wrote one of the few op eds in support to this bill which yet once more was bitterly opposed by TAG and FDA:

> *The dilemma of Americans denied access to investigational drugs is not peculiar to AIDS patients of a bygone era. Today's patients with terminal cancer and rare diseases too often find they must leave America to try the newest treatments, if they can afford to leave. Even the prominent and highly educated are driven to try ineffective or dangerous remedies, as was the revered Coretta Scott King before her 2006 death in Mexico. America needs to make the right to try investigational drugs a civil right for all dying patients. Indeed, the right to try is part and parcel of the right to life.*

Trump's bill signing culminated a movement that began with frustrated AIDS patients and advocates demonstrating and enduring beatings from the police in the plaza before the Federal Building in San Francisco. No AIDS activists were invited to Mr. Trump's signing nor was the gay community recognized in any way for its sacrifices on behalf of the cause his bill furthered. Republican sins of omission again? Or maybe I should just say, thank you Vice President Mike Pence!

Chapter 3
New Era, Different Challenges
(1999: 16,762 AIDS deaths)

The approval of the three protease drugs ushered in a new era in HIV-AIDS and for the LGBT community. With HIV no longer a death sentence, patients' lives could become almost normal again. The "Lazarus effect," sudden recovery from a near death state to normal health, was sweeping the HIV community. Patients could return to their jobs and careers, resume home life with their families, and start planning for the future---with one important caveat: they must have uninterrupted access to proper medication and care.

For the activists that caveat held a whole new set of challenges. The focus of their energies shifted from FDA, NIAID, and NIH and drug company trials and researchers, to providing access to testing, treatment, and care. It was a formidable task that required many activists, including myself, to reinvent our roles. The new drugs were not a cure, patients had to be engaged and retained in care so that their viral loads could be regularly monitored to insure that their cocktails were working for them. Moreover, HIV had impaired their health, and the disease, along with toxic drugs to manage it, continued to damage them. Hence, they had more illnesses than HIV negatives whose ages and backgrounds were otherwise similar. The HIV positives remained alive but became increasingly vulnerable as they grew older.

Several hundred thousand positives would need to be maintained on the cocktails and retained in care. The vast expansion of treatment and care had to be paid for, professionals needed to be trained, and new facilities established. Medicaid, Medicare, and private insurance would take care of the patients they covered. However, many HIV patients were either not covered, or incompletely covered. The Ryan White Care Act, established by Senators Hatch and Kennedy in 1991, had been set up to fill in this gap. RWCA would need massive expansion of its programs and funding, particularly ADAP or the AIDS Drug Assistance Program. ADAP is a joint federal-state safety net established for those who lack other access to the drugs. ADAP is vital, because it allows patients to remain working who otherwise would need to spend down their resources and quit their jobs to qualify for free care under Medicaid. This feature of ADAP appealed especially to Republicans.

Enter Bill Arnold and Dorothy Keville to establish the ADAP Working Group, a joint community-industry effort to insure that the Federal and State governments funded the costly medications. Under their leadership ADAP soon fulfilled a critical role in the domestic epidemic. Indeed, ADAP became a precedent and paradigm for the PEPFAR and Global Fund programs initiated by President Bush in 2002-2003. ADAP was a small program in 1995. The approval of the HIV cocktails meant that its funding must be expanded by multiples which would require appropriation increases from a Congress and a President struggling to curb deficits. Each year during the late 90s, and several years beyond, ADAP needed major increases. It was the task of LCR, and myself as their AIDS Advisor, to insure that the Republicans who controlled Congress understood the urgent need and put their shoulders to the wheel.

AIDS from its inception has been a "political" disease because of the stigma attached to its most numerous victims, gays and injection drug users. The HIV and LGBT communities have long been merged at the hip with leftist politics. This liability fraught alliance is again problematic in the new political conditions brought by Donald Trump and the rise of Sharia Islam. The political path to ending HIV in America, as well as to improving healthcare has required and will continue to require working with both parties and all stakeholders. There is no better illustration of this than with ADAP.

In the early years of very rapid ADAP budget increases, the Republican Chairs of Appropriation in the Senate and House, Senator Mark Hatfield and then Arlen Specter, and Rep. John Porter in the House understood the overall needs. So did Nancy Pelosi who did much of the heavy lifting with the Democrats. The ADAP Working Group and Log Cabin Republicans helped explain the value of the program to the committee members. Since the Republicans were in charge of Congress, they had to take the lead. The Clinton White House saw this as an area they'd happily cede to Congress. Partisan rancor was less then compared to today; although dissension over drug pricing between the community groups and with the pharmaceutical companies often flared up.

For many years the ADAP Working Group's efforts persuaded conservative Congresses to repeatedly increase funding for what was viewed as a liberal "entitlement." Arnold and Keville, like Rich Tafel, understood that leftists demonizing conservatives would mean fewer patients getting the drugs they needed to stay alive. So they, lifelong Democrats both, neither demonized conservatives nor canonized progressives. They kept the focus on the needs of the patients and the value of the treatment for both the patients and long term public healthcare costs. Their work is a veritable case study in effective advocacy.

Astute, community leadership, like theirs', will be needed to steer the ship of AIDS treatment and care through the challenges we face under Donald Trump and his successors. The HIV advocacy groups would do well to remember that, had the community relied exclusively on partisan leftists, the FDA might have taken additional years to approve the drug cocktails, ADAP funding might have been perennially short, and rapid HIV testing would have waited many more years in a regulatory deep freeze (see Appendix I). Indeed, it took a Republican in the White House to initiate and implement PEPFAR and the Global Fund for AIDS and Malaria.

There were regional conflicts pitting the South, where the epidemic was spreading rapidly, against New York and California which had older more stable epidemics. Funding flow did not always keep up with changes which generated dissatisfaction and conflict. Because the advocates were accustomed from an earlier period to dealing with a high level of conflict, confrontation had become habitual. Nonetheless, the conflicts didn't reach previous levels, mostly because there never was as much at stake: with the new drugs protecting them, people were less tense. Fighting to improve your life is never as dramatic or desperate as fighting to save your life.

A major issue became HIV denialism, a pernicious theory advanced by an opportunistic UC Berkeley professor, Peter Duesberg. Distrust of the drug companies, stirred by activist demagoguery as well as the companies own greed and moral insensitivity, fed tragically misguided support for Duesberg. AIDS is caused, he maintained, by a complex of factors including consumption of recreational drugs, the toxic antivirals used for treatment, dangerous sex practices of homosexuals, and poor nutrition. HIV was dismissed as a mere passenger virus. Reputable treatment activists joined with distinguished AIDS clinicians and researchers to oppose this dangerous scientific heresy. Here Martin Delaney at last got a chance to lead a united HIV treatment activist community.

Studies estimated that adaptation of the Duesbergian heresy by Thabo Mbeki, President of South Africa, resulted in delays in introduction of ARV therapy that were responsible for 330,000 excess AIDS deaths and enormous numbers of preventable infections.[23] Just as FDA has never been held to account for delaying either rapid testing or DDI, DDC, and D4T used in combination therapy, or trying to delay the antiretroviral cocktails, efforts to hold Duesberg accountable failed. Letters of complaint to the University of California at Berkley years later in 2010 prompted an inquiry which ruled that Duesberg's theories were protected by the principle of academic freedom. He remains today an Emeritus Professor in good standing with that august institution.[24] For this travesty we must in part blame stigma and the associated systematic devaluation of LGBT people. Had Duesberg denied the holocaust or postulated inferior mental abilities among women or Africans, would the University of California have dared to rule his deleterious notions protected by academic freedom?

The Duesberg case raises serious questions about the morality of delaying, restricting or impeding access to life saving therapies. The obstacles to discovering effective treatments are many: incompetent research, misleading research, prohibitions on types of research, lack of financial resources or incentives for research and development, ideological biases, regulatory rigidity, corporate avarice, and researcher rivalry and envy. Once treatments are developed, many patients may encounter a societal failure to provide adequate healthcare access. Some instances are due to human stupidity or ideological rigidity; these are unacceptable but not quite criminal. However, culprits like Duesberg who impede access by promoting falsehood for personal gain, fame, or power, cross into the realm of moral turpitude. Evil and criminal are not words too strong for such perpetrators of deadly delays.

The indisputable fact of the efficacy of HIV cocktails for millions of patients across the globe refuted Duesbergism, although never to his satisfaction apparently. The story of how these drugs continued to turn back the worldwide HIV epidemic is one for another work with a different set of characters and author. While we wait for a vaccine and a cure, countless HIV patients are able to live normal lives with the help of the anti-HIV cocktails which have proved to be one of the great triumphs of medical science in our era.

****

So what happened after 1996 to the main players and institutions in our story? Barry Freehill returned to his profession as a chemical engineer, he still lives in his Castro District home near Davies Hospital. Other San Francisco activist survivors also resumed their lives in a society that quickly forgot their suffering, sacrifices, and achievements. Martin Delaney led Project Inform almost until his death in 2009, the treatment advice they gave was generally well founded and needed.

The Treatment Activist Group, and its members, continued to secure favorable publicity and receive generous grants: $500,000 from the MacArthur Foundation and $4,700,000 from the Bill and Melinda Gates Foundation went to Mark Herrington alone. Edward Wyatt, who wrote the TAG inspired *Barron's* article that could have stopped AIDS research dead in its tracks had other AIDS activists failed to oppose it, is now Senior Communications Officer for the same Gates Foundation.*25*

FDA, supported by their trusty sidekicks in TAG, has vigorously resisted all efforts at fundamental reforms including the 2018 "right to try" act. David Kessler, however, left the FDA a somewhat more relevant protector of public health and went on to head the Yale Medical School. The agency continues to impede medical progress in many areas as its bureaucracy struggles for relevance in the face of bewildering advances in medical science and technology. Its motto remains, 'Never Forget Thalidomide!'

The HIV drug companies continue to make splendiferous profits, from which they frequently gave alms to activists, most generously to FDA approved activists while passing over those who sacrifice to get their drugs approved by FDA.

Following Dave Olson's wishes and what became part of my identity, I remained an AIDS activist. Under Bush 43, I served on the Presidential Advisory Council on HIV-AIDS, PACHA where I pushed for rapid testing and the development of PEPFAR. In 2001, I became a political consultant to the AIDS Healthcare Foundation and remained so for fifteen years. During that time AHF grew into a billion-dollar giant, the world's largest AIDS treatment provider and the largest non-profit based in the LGBT community. In 2016 differences over AHF's using 340B drug discount program funds for political purposes unrelated to AIDS ended our relationship. I returned to Shakespeare, Jung, and my youthful ruminations on God and time to write a philosophical treatise, *Shakespeare and Jung—The God in Time* along with a volume of criticism, *Shakespeare's Identities*. Not wanting to go to my grave leaving untold the story of AIDS activists, many of them beloved friends, saving FDA from an unprecedented disaster entirely of its own making, I penned the current account. As of this date, I am busy working on two additional books. The friends I've lost to AIDS and other killers remain alive in my memories.

Conclusion
What Can We Learn?

"I learned to scent out what was able to lead to fundamentals
and to turn aside from everything else, from the multitude of things
that clutter up the mind."

Albert Einstein

If we ask "what did we learn?" the answer is too short to fill a chapter—two words will suffice, *almost nothing*. More productive is this question: what can the AIDS epidemic teach us about bureaucracy, regulation, freedom, and activism in a true existential crisis? Let me begin by citing from my June 4 1995 opinion piece in the *Los Angeles Times* titled "FDA's Caution is Killing People." The timing of the piece was crucial because it fell midway between Kessler's March 1995 *Scientific American* attempt to resurrect the old FDA over the dead bodies of tens of thousands of AIDS patients and the September 1995 convocation after which, Kessler, measuring the opposition, decided a white flag was FDA's and his own best survival weapon. I quote it because it sums up the issues at the time and explores the history and philosophic roots of what many AIDS and cancer activists came to believe was wrong with FDA's bureaucratic hyper caution and regulatory feather bedding.

> *During the 1950s, drug approval was a relatively quick and simple process. Then came thalidomide. European regulators had approved this tranquilizer without realizing that it could affect a fetus, and several hundred birth defects resulted worldwide. Capitalizing on the tragedy, liberals in the Congress expanded the Food and Drug Administration's powers and altered its priorities. . ... After 1962 a highly bureaucratized system of drug approval emerged. With each passing year, that system grew more dilatory, more unbalanced, and costlier to patients. . ..*

FDA's top priority became---and remains---prevention of new Thalidomides. Much of our gross national product is spent on prevention: national defense, policing, flood and fire control, sanitation, auto safety, anti-terrorist measures, and home alarm systems. Our prevention needs are boundless, but resources are limited and must be used wisely. Too much allocated to a minor need will leave major needs neglected. Ideally, the greatest good for the greatest number should determine priorities. Narrow self-interest often prevails. Thus defense contractors build weapons the country doesn't need. And FDA churns out burdensome regulations that delay drug development and approval and actually harm patients while raising drug costs.

To better understand FDA's narrow priority, we need to see it in light of the range of problems that besets regulators. The rarest kind of problems are the thalidomides, drugs approved before their safety hazards are known. Even with the pre-1962 FDA, this kind of problem was never a threat comparable to hospital infections, medical errors, or even food poisoning. But since Congress stood ready to blame FDA for mistaken approvals, but not other mistakes, the agency made preventing new thalidomides its priority. Through scare tactics and deception FDA sold the public on this priority. Rational priorities would seek a balance that minimizes deaths caused by both mistaken approvals and delays. Rationality and balance are hard. Delay is easy and deals made in hell are tempting.

A recent FDA delay resulted in 3500 deaths—those kidney cancer patients who by FDA's own figures would have been saved if Interleukin 2 had been approved as quickly here as it was in Europe. These kidney cancer deaths far exceed the number of babies deformed by thalidomide. . .. Congress has tolerated FDA delay because its dangers are difficult to prove. Individual patients usually do not know about the unapproved drug or device that could save their lives. Patients who suffer the most terrible loss from FDA delays cannot protest from their graves. Fearing retaliation, drug companies avoid blaming FDA for the delays and shoulder FDA's blame themselves.

Few people grasp the complexities of drug development. Few politicians bother to evaluate carefully either FDA's priorities or the human cost of regulatory delays. Consequently, we've lacked effective Congressional oversight. Without oversight rational policy perishes, and deceit flourishes.

Enter David A. Kessler, FDA's answer to J. Edgar Hoover. Kessler's FDA boldly sets its own priorities. It pursues favoritism, retaliation, and selective enforcement without conscience. It has made drug efficacy testing a worse bargain than the Pentagon's $600.00 toilet seats.

Harsh on Kessler, but my objective was to force him to face the concerns of real AIDS patients, and stop hiding behind FDA's shills. Parts of the op ed's message may have gotten through to him during that summer of mounting pressure as it must have become increasingly evident that the safest course for the agency was to abandon TAG and their shared ideology, and instead confront the political, medical, and existential realities of approval delay. The fate of tens of thousands of AIDS patients hung in the balance, but that surely took a back seat to the fate of the agency itself. FDA was, after all, a bureaucracy, and bureaucracies ever put their own interests above broader societal and human concerns. The endemic immorality of bureaucratic over-reach may be the greatest problem facing our vast and growing urbanized human population in the twenty first century. No nation is free from it, it varies only in degree and cultural coloration.

FDA's failed early 1995 attempt to delay AIDS drugs and the subsequent 2003 defeat of their efforts to delay HIV rapid testing are pivotal lessons about regulation that are far more instructive than the thalidomide delay that saved a few American children from birth deformities. However, the FDA and its political, business, and media allies continue to beat their drums on thalidomide while mum's the word about FDA attempts to delay the AIDS drug cocktails or its actual delays in approving HIV rapid testing (Appendix I), or delays in approving drugs for cancers and other fatal conditions, not to mention delays in approving innovative devices and non-drug therapies or FDA's recent, disastrous delays in implementing Covid 19 testing. After all, we wouldn't want to embarrass the agency with the truth, would we? Certainly not if we plan to be doing business with them. The truth might vindicate some libertarian and Republican critics, and we would never want to do that!

As a consequence of the liberals "gentlemen's agreement" to protect FDA, a near catastrophe of shocking proportions was quietly covered up, and a dangerously imbalanced perception of the risks and benefits of the FDA's feather bedded drug approval procedures has been perpetuated into the 21st century. There are more shades of cover up than there are shades of grey, but all of them are in a gray area morally if not legally. This one was very dark grey. At the time no one bothered to expose FDA, we were all too relieved to have viable treatments for HIV disease at long last. It was the most common type of cover up, where people do not bother to get out the truth because they don't care what happens once they've gotten what they want. These may be the most dangerous cover ups because they are rarely exposed, so their lessons go unlearned and we are set up to repeat even the worst mistakes of the past.

Readers may be asking why I so belabor my point that FDA's attempt to delay the AIDS cocktails could have cost tens of thousands of lives. Here's why: it is the most crucial lesson from the agency's history of drug regulation. Yet few know about it, even though it is vastly more consequential and instructive than thalidomide. Above all, it offers the single most important warning/lesson from the histories of the AIDS epidemic and of FDA drug approval.

To avoid recurrence, this near disaster must be recognized and understood. History does repeat itself with variations. FDA, however, has done its best to pull the wool of collective amnesia over the eyes of the public and Congress. So, while mums the word on FDA's ignominious attempts to delay AIDS drugs, we still hear time and again their "broken record" refrain about the "heroic" delay of thalidomide.

In 2010 Dr. Francis Oldham Kelsey, who is credited with preventing a worse thalidomide disaster by delaying approval of that drug, was awarded the first Francis Oldham Kelsey Award for Excellence and Courage in Protecting Public Health, and earlier in 2000 she was inducted into the National Women's Hall of Fame. The FDA has never publicly acknowledged, let alone thanked, the gay activists and their doctors for saving the agency from a disaster far worse than the hasty FDA approval of thalidomide might have been. AIDS activists have never received official recognition of their crucial role in expediting FDA approval of the cocktails. As long as the facts of that decisive year 1995 are ignored, obscured, and denied, its lessons will not be learned. High on the list of those unlearned lessons will be: 1) the dangers posed by regulators who hold others accountable but are never themselves held accountable; 2) the cost and the shame of America's continuing and pervasive reflex devaluation and marginalization of LGBT people.

President Trump has stated his admirable goal of further streamlining the FDA and other regulatory bodies in order to speed research, development, and approval of new medications, vaccines and diagnostics. In his speech to Congress of February 28, 2017 he said: *"Our slow and burdensome approval process at the Food and Drug Administration keeps too many advances . . . from reaching those in need. If we slash the restraints, not just at the FDA but across our Government, then we will be blessed with far more miracles."* To accelerate access to new drugs, biologics, devices, diagnostic tests, and other treatments for killer diseases, the President and his successors must be prepared to take on a recalcitrant FDA to make it accountable the same way AIDS activists did in the years leading up to 1996, and the same way President Bush did for HIV rapid testing in 2003. The recent FDA delays in the Covid 19 diagnostic test indicate much work remains to be done.

As a surviving leader of activism during the AIDS epidemic and gadfly against the costly fiascos FDA has covered up, let me suggest one key activist strategy for those in similar future circumstances where tens or hundreds of thousands of lives depend on rapid development and approval of new treatments: **Go to the President, ask him to declare a national health emergency and issue an executive order limiting FDA efficacy testing for approval of new treatments, diagnostics and vaccines for the problem to basic evidence of efficacy. In 2003 George W. Bush overrode FDA objections to make HIV rapid testing available. Future Presidents should do likewise when faced with deadly epidemics. The current Covid 19 epidemic will likely prove to be an instance where this approach is/was needed.** It could forestall much waste, folly, suffering, and death.

AIDS patients can now live long enough to succumb to diseases of aging like Alzheimer's and cancer. Unfortunately for everyone, the drugs we have for Alzheimer's and many advanced cancers are, like the early AIDS drugs, woefully inadequate. Moreover, development of and access to better treatments is crucial to the quality of life of all older Americans as well as to the solvency of Medicare and Medicaid. If President Trump and his successors are serious about speeding treatments and a cure for Alzheimer's, and about preventing and curing more cancers, they must heed what AIDS activists discovered: **the most potent incentive for rapid drug development is cutting regulatory delays and the burden of regulatory costs on drug research and development. But the greatest lesson is a moral lesson: safeguarding the lives, health, and freedom to choose for patients must take priority over rigid adherence to bureaucratic procedures. Jesus said, "The Sabbath was made for man, not man for the Sabbath," (Mark 2:27). Likewise, under our Constitution the government and its agencies are established to serve the citizens, not the other way around.**

Under the constitution federal bureaucracies have no power except what Congress and the President grant them. Yet in our era federal bureaucracies have grown massive, powerful, enormously complex, and increasingly unaccountable. Their size and complexity enables them to arrogate power to themselves, and it makes effective outside oversight increasingly difficult, and rare. President Eisenhower warned against the perils of the military-industrial complex, but that is only one of several powerful complexes prone to dangerous abuses. Less understood is the formidable and potentially dangerous complex centered on the healthcare industry and its regulators. Without vigilant oversight and accountability, our feather bedding healthcare-regulation complex threatens to bankrupt the country with cost overruns while delivering inadequate care to our citizens.

President Trump and his successors need to protect and expand the freedom of all citizens to access care. Equally important, they need to foster a national conversation about improving incentives for developing better medical treatments and care. To this end we must change the priority of the regulatory process from prevention of thalidomides to speeding development of better, less costly treatments and actual cures for all diseases. We must frankly acknowledge that excess caution and regulatory feather bedding at the FDA and other healthcare regulators often impede innovation. For FDA an essential first step in this direction would be honest and open recognition by the nation itself of what actually happened in 1995. That must include exposing why the FDA attempted to delay lifesaving AIDS drugs for additional years, what that delay would have cost, and how it was avoided. This is something every healthcare policy maker, indeed every educated American should know.

There is another important lesson specifically for the LGBT community and all marginalized minorities. When AIDS threatened our survival, we found ourselves powerless at the mercy of unelected, unaccountable bureaucrats in a federal agency whose practices would have given Franz Kafka vertigo. If AIDS had instead posed an existential threat to a potent, politically organized minority would they have had to mount street demonstrations and kowtow to politicians to get FDA to approve expeditiously the drugs their people needed to stay alive? **Bottom line: survival in a bureaucratic mass society requires political skill and clout.**

****

How much difference did AIDS activism really make? How much is reality and how much is hope or hype? A key to the impact of AIDS activism lies in the ways it energized momentous trends that still have a long way to go. These trends may not change human nature itself, but they can change the ways we understand, view, and express human nature.

Civilization is the domestication of humanity. Animals we domesticate can revert to the wild, even as civilized countries, like Hitler's Germany, Stalin's Russia, Mao's China, and Pol Pot's Cambodia can temporarily throw off the trappings of civilization to revert to savagery. But once civilization makes a significant advance, the steps backward tend to be temporary, although in the long view of history temporary may encompass entire lifetimes.

Over the millennia humanity has devised, morals, ethics, and religions to more or less civilize our populations. However, these must be sustained by institutional bureaucracies. We have yet to learn how to insure that bureaucracies themselves submit to the values and ethos of civilization. They habitually place their organizational interests above the rights and freedoms of society and its citizens, rights and freedoms they were established to protect and serve. Lacking accountability, they allow their officials to equate their own selfish concerns with the welfare of the institutions themselves. Thereby, is tyranny born, bred, and rationalized. FDA's delaying innovation is but one example among far too many.

Our era provides manifold examples of bureaucratic abuse: the Soviet, Nazi, and Maoist experiments, the Catholic Church's infinite regress of cover ups for pedophilia; Islam's failure to adapt Sharia to basic human rights and curb Jihadist extremism; Colleges and Universities that offer indoctrination instead of education and burden students with heavy debt preparing for jobs that may not exist; corporations that pollute society through sale of useless, destructive products; featherbedding professions that make essential services unaffordable; Orwellian government agencies and tech moguls manipulating information in order to control what we think, feel, and believe; the military-intelligence complexes pursuing insane wars; and those who deny the perils of environmental degradation to protect their economic advantages. These abuses compromise or abrogate something essential to realizing our full humanity—our freedom.

Occasionally, too seldom of course, some brave souls take a stand for freedom against institutional dysfunction. Harvey Milk showed the LGBT community, and me, that we must stand up to bullying. The AIDS activists followed suit, and they inspired other LGBT people to stand up for their rights, dignity, and essential freedom as individual human beings. In the wake of the inspired examples set by AIDS activism we experienced startling advances in LGBT freedoms and rights, like serving in the military, adoption, and marrying whom we love. Millions of our people moved out of the shadows into the daylight of life in Western societies.

Indeed, the gay civil rights movement of the last two decades was nourished from the corpses of patients who died fighting AIDS and the sacrifices of those who battled any way they could against an inflexible FDA. AIDS activists taught patients in all disease areas to aggressively take charge of their health. They taught the mainstream of American society that LGBT individuals deserve respect, like us or not, and we are entitled to the same freedoms as others, like it or not. But these are lessons America is still learning.

Today we suffer collective amnesia about the struggles of that period. We need to learn from and honor those who sacrificed for something bigger than themselves, and bigger than they understood. Too many LGBTs lack pride in themselves and in our community. LGBT youth in America is bedeviled by stigma, identity crisis, and widespread bullying, both subtle and overt, as evidenced by suicide rates shockingly higher than that of their heterosexual age peers. Civil rights protections readily extended to other minorities are still resisted, resented, and partial for LGBTs. Acceptance of Sharia proponents by the Democratic party calls into question the liberal LGBTs mono-strategy of reliance on one party. Yet the prominence of that smiling purveyor of stigma, Vice President Pence, douses hope for an effective Republican alternative anytime soon. The challenges for LGBTs are still urgent for all but the most privileged among us. As a movement we are in no position to lose our sense of urgency.

PART V: Loose Ends

The following appendixes explore four weighty issues: 1. FDA's delay of HIV rapid testing; 2. drug pricing; 3. the political dilemmas LGBTs pose and face; 4. Vice President Pence's promotion of stigma for political gain. These materials did not fit easily into the narrative, but are critical to understanding the dynamics of the epidemic.

APPENDIX I
A Counter to FDA's Thalidomide Mythos:
FDA Delays of HIV Rapid Testing Cost Lives

It is not hard to find other definitive examples to counter FDA's thalidomide rational for feather bedding regulations that delay approvals of new drugs and medical technologies. The challenge is to look in the right places. FDA rimes with delay, and the agency does not limit its deadly delays to biotech and pharmaceuticals. It also delays devices, laser and light treatments, and new diagnostic tests; sometimes without valid safety considerations, but nonetheless with lethal consequences to those who need the technologies. To better understand the threat that FDA's excess regulation posed by delaying the drug cocktails, it is helpful to jump ahead several years to a dramatic and well understood instance where FDA delay clearly cost many lives and resulted in thousands of avoidable HIV infections. At issue was the agency's determined efforts to delay implementation of HIV rapid testing.

Before you treat you must test to find those in need of treatment. HIV rapid testing had been developed well before it was finally approved for widespread use in the US in 2003. When President Bush entered the White House in 2001 HIV rapid testing was stalled in the FDA by the hyper-bureaucratic Clinical Laboratory Improvement Amendments (CLIA). These featherbedding regulations codified the special interests of the laboratorian profession by protecting and expanding their jobs. Too little attention was paid to the costs or need for CLIA's superfluous procedures. Regulation for regulation's sake can be worse than no regulation: CLIA too often provides the proof.

For years the entire spectrum of AIDS community groups across the country had called for FDA removal of the outdated and useless CLIA impediments to rapid HIV testing. NASTAD, the National Association of State and Territorial AIDS Directors, strongly pushed for reform. The demand for reform was as spirited in liberal of the big states, like New York and California, as in Tom Coburn's Oklahoma or Kansas. Even the diehard New Yorker consumer protectors who had demanded FDA delay the protease cocktails to test their precise degrees of efficacy opposed FDA's foot dragging on HIV rapid testing.

President Bill Clinton could have removed the block. And he might have done so had the community been willing to pressure him. Clinton was a political animal who responded to political pressures, positive as well as negative. In a democracy it is the responsibility of stakeholders to build support for the changes they need, and not to rely on paternalistic political bosses to hand them change gift-wrapped on a silver platter. Clinton was not a bad AIDS President, although he later acknowledged, correctly, he could and should have done much more. He would have done his job better had the community been willing to do its job of pressuring him on testing, not to mention speeding AIDS drug approval. Because support for gay and HIV rights was recent and hard won, and still under attack by bigots and some Republicans, many in the community were afraid to put effective pressure on the Democrats even to save lives. Feeling no real pressure to take on the clinical laboratorians, the FDA, and their consumer protector shills in Congress, Clinton left the job undone.

George W. Bush's election became a game changer. Now we had a President the community did not mind pressuring. Even better, Bush was a President we did not need to pressure once he understood the stakes. An array of major AIDS groups including, NASTAD, AIDS Action, AIDS Healthcare Foundation, Project Inform, Florida AIDS Action, Log Cabin Education Fund, SF AIDS Foundation, and many smaller groups saw an opportunity to change CLIA-FDA's obstructive testing regulations. Indeed, AIDS offered many opportunities for George W. Bush, and he rose to the challenge to became our most effective AIDS President so far. For the first time Bush chose an openly gay man, Scott Everatz to head ONAP, the Office of National AIDS Policy. He also appointed several openly gay activists, including myself, to the Presidential Advisory Council on HIV-AIDS or PACHA. Most important, he put a power player, former Congressman and future Senator Tom Coburn, in charge of PACHA.

There was, however, strong opposition, within what today might be called the deep state bureaucracy, against suspending CLIA regulations because it would involve a minor, although unprecedented, truncation of FDA's regulatory turf. These complex and cumbersome regulations required laboratory verification of all HIV test results, the subject had to be tracked down when results were verified up to two weeks later. Once contacted, she or he would need to meet with a specially trained councilor to receive the results. The justification for these complex procedures was hopelessly anachronistic. When an AIDS diagnosis was a death sentence before the cocktails, there was a danger that patients, if not properly counseled, might do something rash upon learning their diagnosis. Suicide was feared, and in a few instances patients attacked the spouse or person whom they suspected had infected them. However, it was 2002 and AIDS had been a manageable disease since 1996.

Rapid testing gave the patients their test results within minutes. It eliminated the problem of locating them and the unwieldy procedures for informing them. Upon being told they tested positive in a rapid test, they were given a second confirmatory test, necessary because the rapid tests were highly accurate but not perfect. After confirmation, the process began for transferring the positives into regular care and treatment. With the old, sluggardly CLIA methods, many patients from marginalized groups, such as homeless people, sex workers, addicts, migrants, and non-English speakers, simply slipped through the cracks, never learning their HIV status, never getting treatment, and continuing to infect others.

Rapid testing made it easier and less expensive to test larger numbers of patients per year. Once it was enacted, some organizations, like AIDS Healthcare Foundation (AHF), established fleets of testing vans to make testing convenient in areas of high HIV infection, and in problematic neighborhoods. They would also set up on the streets or in the parking lots of popular bars at night. Tens of thousands of new cases were found by rapid testing, cases that would otherwise have festered until they wound up in an emergency room with a destructive opportunistic illness.

A crucial reason to get every HIV positive person tested is essentially psychological. Once patients know they are positive, they tend to change their behavior. Most people, even the dysfunctional, do not want to transmit a potentially fatal disease to others. The statistics from the 2016 CDC surveillance report demonstrate the importance of testing every HIV positive person and getting them into treatment. (X) Consider:

- The 15% of HIV infected who did not know their status accounted for 38% of new cases
- 23% who knew their status but not in care, 43% of new cases
- 11% in care but not virally suppressed, 19% of new cases
- 51% virally suppressed accounted for 0 new cases

The last statistic is key: it means that if every HIV positive person were in treatment and virally suppressed, there would be no new cases of HIV! The dreaded disease would begin to disappear. Researchers have proven that non detectable equals non transmissible. While it is not yet possible to rid the body of HIV, in most patients we can reduce the virus's numbers to non-detectable, that is non-infective, levels. To a significant degree because of increased rapid testing, new cases of HIV in the US, according to CDC figures, fell 9% from 2010 to 2016.

Even with a receptive President, a politically astute, highly motivated PACHA Chair in Tom Coburn, the unified support of the entire HIV patient activist community, not to mention that of the scientific and medical establishments and the healthcare industry, implementing rapid testing over the figurative dead body of FDA was no cake walk. The clinical laboratorians had their lucrative featherbedding at stake, and FDA, a true bureaucracy, was loathe to part with a single centimeter of its regulatory turf. To our dismay, we found that officials in the White House and HHS were reluctant to take on FDA. Fortunately, the issue pitted CDC against FDA. CDC clearly recognized the value of rapid testing for reducing new infections. Although reluctant to challenge FDA directly, CDC was happy to see the activists do it, and so they gave us critical information in service of the cause. Dr. Bernard Branson proved especially valuable in that regard.

As Log Cabin AIDS Advisor, I led the activists on PACHA with this issue; our push for rapid testing began when Tom Coburn became Chairman in 2002. Partly because Coburn elevated the Council, PACHA members were able to set up high level meetings with Secretary of HHS Tommy Thompson and Domestic Policy Advisor Claude Allen.

Thompson and Allen were instrumental in persuading President Bush to overrule the FDA and implement widespread rapid testing. Crucial to this and many other AIDS successes under Bush was Dr. Joseph O'Neil who became National AIDS Policy Advisor in 2002. O'Neil brought to the position deep knowledge and wide experience of the disease and AIDS policy issues. He established an excellent rapport with President Bush which led to a Presidential prioritization of AIDS that benefited testing policies, the Ryan White program, and proved instrumental for the creation of US international AIDS efforts with PEPFAR and the Global Fund for HIV-AIDS and malaria. Joe O'Neil knew what needed to be done, and how to get it done quickly.

At the time I was a consultant for the AIDS Healthcare Foundation, an energetic proponent of rapid testing and of PEPFAR. NASTAD, under the leadership of Julie Scofield and Dr. Mark Loveless, had made approval of rapid testing their goal for the year. Laura Hanen led their effort in the field and Karl Milhoun, the Kansas State AIDS Director, was key. Gene Coppello of Florida AIDS Action along with other local groups across the country pushed hard for approval. We all worked with Dr. O'Neil to achieve major advances in testing which we had long supported, but did not expect to achieve so rapidly.

One event in this story stands out above all others as the iconic image of how and why things worked out as they did. In late 2003 President Bush invited about 60 key people working on rapid testing to the White House to announce his plan to waive the CLIA obstacles to rapid testing. Nearly everyone rose to give him a standing ovation. The sole exceptions were Acting FDA Commissioner Lester Crawford and his two associates who sat staring at their shoes. If only I'd had a cell phone camera with me to record that emblematic sight!

Bush's action was unprecedented. The President as chief executive has the constitutional power to overrule FDA on discretionary matters and to waive obstructive rules, but no one before Bush 43 had done it. In retrospect, one cannot help but speculate that if Presidents Bush 41 and Clinton had declared the AIDS epidemic a national emergency and relaxed FDA standards for AIDS drug approval. Doing so would not have required Congressional approval since judgements upon the degree of efficacy were up to the executive branch. Although safety testing would have remained in place, an executive order could have required that all AIDS drugs approved for safety must be given accelerated approval for marketing once we had basic evidence for some degree of efficacy in some patients—No more delays for lengthy testing to determine the exact degree and parameters of efficacy, or for FDA to flex its muscle over drug marketing, no more hapless patients resorting in desperation to unsafe and useless underground drugs!

FDA will of course deny that they delayed rapid testing implementation, though every activist who worked the issue knew otherwise. (FDA has never admitted to unjustifiably delaying anything!) They insisted that their reservations on rapid testing were prudent and reasonable, just as they habitually intimate that their delays for efficacy testing are really about drug safety. However, this time the community activists' argument that the CLIA testing regulations were outdated and obstructive was solidly, if tacitly, backed by the prevention experts at CDC. Along with state AIDS directors and the major AIDS groups, CDC had started to call for accelerated development of and access to the invaluable detection system early in the second Clinton Administration.

The technology had functioned without significant problems for some time in Europe, as reported in one of the few articles available on this subject:

> Rapid HIV testing is well established in Europe. Since 2000, a rapid HIV test called MiraTest has been available over the counter at pharmacies in the Netherlands, Greece, and Hong Kong, and for €19.50 can be ordered online at Dutch Web sites for delivery by mail though, again, it is not authorized for distribution here. (See Anne Paxton, "Rapid HIV test whips up waiver debate," Cap Today, Feb., 2003) **26**

The article cites, though it does not fully credit, the key role of the AIDS activists in implementing rapid testing in the US. From the same article:

> AIDS patient advocates have added their voices to those of other waiver proponents. Last year, nearly 100 U.S. AIDS organizations issued a call for broad-based rapid-HIV testing.

"Limiting who can administer the tests and where they can be administered perpetuates this epidemic by disallowing testing at community outreach sites," noted Florida AIDS Action.

The group's Executive Director, Gene Copello, Ph.D., remonstrated, "We are trying to win a war and we've been shown this wonderful new tool, and now we're being told we may not be able to use it in the most effective manner possible."

The article stresses the obstacles the old CLIA system presented for follow up and transference into care.

According to the CDC, in the last few years 9,600 HIV-positive people did not return to the publicly funded site where they were tested to find out their results. . .. Dr. Branson predicts that a rapid HIV test will slash these numbers. In a study at Johns Hopkins Medical Institutions' emergency room, when a specimen was sent to the laboratory, the turnaround time averaged 180 minutes. Sixty percent of the patients left before receiving their test results. [Today the turnaround time is less than 15 minutes. --JD]

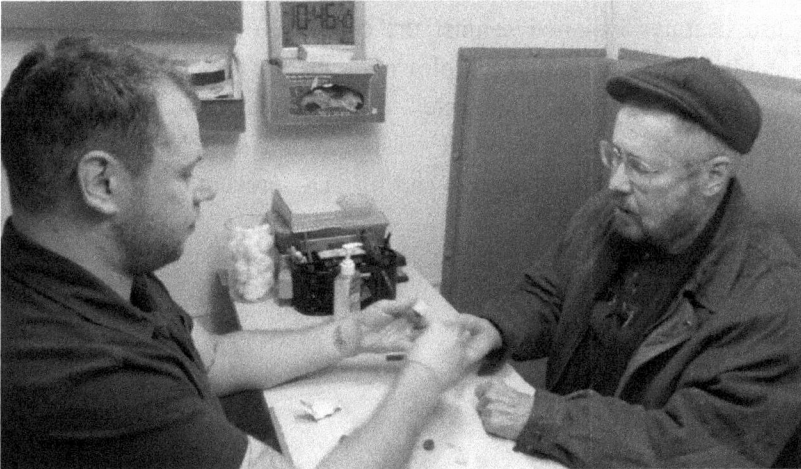

**(The author getting a rapid HIV test
in a Las Vegas AHF testing van, 2015)**

As I recollect, among those who played the most consequential roles were, first Tom Coburn who worked directly with the White House and Dr. Joe O'Neill the President's AIDS Advisor; but also Julie Scofield, Mark Loveless, and Laura Hanen of NASTAD, Gene Copello, Coburn's staffer Roland Foster, Marsha Martin of AIDS Action, and Brent Minor, Anita Smith, Abner Mason, Jackie Clements, Reverend Sanders, of PACHA, along with Karl Milhoun, the Kansas AIDS Director, and Michael Weinstein President of AHF. My main role was to bring together this extremely talented and committed but diverse group of activists who in some cases were less than eager to work with each other.

Problems in implementing rapid testing, which tests worked best, diverse state rules, how to set it up, etc. remained. Altogether, FDA caused delays of up to two years. The number of lives lost through delayed detection are difficult to calculate, as are the new infections that might have been prevented by earlier development and accelerated implementation of the technology. However, it seems certain that FDA's delay of rapid testing cost far more new HIV infections than their much vaunted caution on thalidomide saved from birth defects. When we compare the two cases, the importance of calculating tradeoffs in delays in approving medical innovations becomes evident. The delay of rapid testing was particularly inexcusable because the risks were miniscule relative to the vital benefits. We had the chance of a couple of suicides and spouse beatings weighed against the certainty of saving thousands of people from advancing into full blown AIDS, and tens of thousands from being infected by the undetected cases. Today millions of people worldwide have received rapid HIV testing. It is a linchpin of the PEPFAR and Global Fund HIV programs and of CDC prevention efforts here in America.

APPENDIX II
Larry Kramer's Cyclopean Distraction: Corporate Greed

Screenwriter, novelist, and true founder of the AIDS Coalition to Unleash Power (ACT UP) Larry Kramer wrote "1112 and Counting" in the March 1982 *New York Native*, becoming thereby the Paul Revere of the AIDS activist revolution. The first step toward solving a public problem is focusing attention on it, and Larry Kramer had an undeniable talent for that. The next step is recognizing it officially. Here President Reagan failed lamentably, but his Surgeon General C. Everett Koop finally stepped into the breach and found a surprising ally from the world that gave Reagan his start—screen legend Elizabeth Taylor.

While Koop and Taylor made AIDS activism respectable, it was the mercurial Larry Kramer, the pied piper of ACT UP, who selected the topics for its most obstreperous messages, for better or for worse. Kramer was on the mark about the slowness and lack of urgency among government agencies and officials. He was Mr. Urgency, and urgency was needed in many areas. Although he was perpetually energized about the interminable disputes over drug pricing, drug cost--as distinct from insurance coverage—is not often a problem for individual AIDS patients. However, pricing became a distraction from much more urgent problems, such as minority access to care and FDA caused delays in development and approval of new medicines.

Soon after AZT was priced at the then unheard of cost of $30,000/year, a group of Kramer inspired New York ACT UP zealots led by the intrepid Peter Staley scaled the walls of the North Carolina headquarters of AZT's maker, Burroughs-Wellcome, to protest the drug's outrageous price. AZT was a re-formulation for AIDS of an old drug developed by NIH for cancer. The government paid the bulk of its development costs. So the price seemed unconscionable not only to the activists but to the media, the politicians, and the general public. Indeed, the price was unconscionable in view of the drug's low research and development costs, its marginal efficacy coupled with high toxicity, and in exploiting the desperate need to get out something, anything, to curb the AIDS virus.

The New York ACT UP actions forced Burroughs-Wellcome to release AZT at the lower but still exorbitant list price of $10,000/ year in March 1987. Twenty-five years later in 2012 an important new HIV drug, Stribild, was released at $28,500. In 2012 dollars the $10,000 price of AZT would be $21,577. Here's the rub: few patients paid the high list price for AZT and even fewer paid it for Stribild. More important, Stribild is, unlike AZT, highly effective with minimal toxic side effects; in short, its clinical value is far greater. Still, Stribild's price indicates that the decades of drug pricing activism Kramer initiated had only modest success in restraining the list prices of new AIDS drugs. Notwithstanding, much of the energy and *animus* of AIDS activism has focused on pricing. Decrying drug pricing became and remained the movement's equivalent to waving the blood shirt. The major positive effect of pricing activism was not in restraining drug list prices, but in something more important: motivating government and the drug industry to set up programs that insure drug access to those who lack it.

There have been egregious abuses, like AZT's initial price, which periodically ignite calls for price controls that always lead nowhere. Out of apparent inability to restrain overweening greed, some companies regularly make pricing and PR blunders that bring down the wrath of patient communities and media on their heads. An early example was the pricing of Astra's CMV retinitis drug Foscarnet at $21,000/year in 1991. Astra was so recalcitrant about negotiation that activists felt compelled to take extreme actions. Tim Kingston in the Feb 13, 1992 *SF Bay Times* reported:

> *When it became clear that the lobbying efforts with Astra were ineffectual, ACT UP Boston and TAG decided to play hardball. On January 27 at 7:30AM they struck Astra's corporate*

headquarters. Eight activists chained themselves under four rental trucks that blockaded Astra's offices . . . 12 activists were arrested under full glare of CBS evening news. . .. What particularly enrages activists says Peter Staley of TAG is that, "This is a drug that got expedited review process by the FDA because of ongoing pressure from activists."

Astra, in an act of singular callousness, stubbornly resisted providing their drug to indigent patients through a patient assistance program. Raymond Schmidt of ACT UP Boston noted, "it took a series of protests including vigils outside the home of Astra's CEO to get the program in place."

(Peter Staley being handcuffed at Astra demonstration.)

Astra's was yet another a case of a drug company being its own worst enemy. A more recent and even more extreme instance was the infamous Turing Pharmaceuticals price increase of Daraprim from $13.50/tablet to $759/tablet. These sensational abuses set the media abuzz which incites posturing politicians to demand drug price controls. Predictably, the pharmas mobilize their battalions of lobbyists who so far have always succeeded in blocking systemic reforms. Once the sensation subsides, the companies return to their tried and true strategy of raising prices modestly above the CPI to achieve by stealthy increments a major long run increase. Ambitious activists and politicians get publicity and K Street lobbyists rake in lucrative fees, while the patients gain nothing.

However, there are at last signs of change for the better under President Trump, though DC gridlock threatens to once again stymie reform.

A realistic view on drug pricing requires recognition of three critical factors. First, the more revenue a pharmaceutical company expects to generate, the greater the resources it will put into developing its drug and the greater risk of drug failure it will assume. Drugs that cannot bring in big revenue do not justify risking high development costs; they may never be developed no matter how effective they might prove. Hence, too few drugs for rare diseases are developed because the market is often inadequate to recoup R & D expenses. Second, even developing drugs for diseases with large patient populations, like HIV and some cancers, is costly because the successes must pay for both themselves and the failures, the drugs that don't work and never are approved. The paths of AIDS and cancer drug development are marked by the tombstones of costly failures. Finally, thorough testing and documentation of efficacy under mandatory FDA procedures and strict standards is exceedingly, and often unnecessarily, expensive.

Moreover, pricing activism has its dangers: if the activists message about their will to resist high prices is too intimidating, the corporate bean counters may determine that particular drugs will be too risky and nip promising research in the bud. Some potential AIDS drugs, such as the low toxicity nucleoside analogue AZDU, were never developed because they lacked profit potential. True AZDU was not a very effective drug, but like AZT, ddC, ddI and D4T it might have helped a few people make it to the cocktails because, unlike the other nukes, its toxicity was very low. Drugs that do not work for the majority may work for some, but only if they are developed.

Our bodies are all unique, even where our minds appear to be cloned from our cultural milieus. AZT's effectiveness did not last for most patients, yet it kept some alive for years because the drug's tolerance and efficacy varied greatly among patients. Having more drugs that worked for only a minority or worked poorly for the many, like AZT, ddC, ddI and D4T, would nonetheless have extended, more lives. Any patient who could have lived long enough to take the cocktails might have experienced the Lazarus effect and be alive today. That is why I pushed for approval of ddC, and then for AZDU when no one else did. The experts told me AZDU would help too few to be financially viable. Having lost so many friends, I had an emotional, rather than financial, view of the value of individual lives. Unlike the bean counters, I understood feelingly that dying in early adulthood is a terrible thing.

An absolutely critical factor in drug pricing is usually overlooked: very few patients pay out of pocket for drugs for expensive diseases like AIDS, auto-immune disorders, and cancer. With a patient who cannot spare more than $100/mo. for a drug, it does not matter if the drug is priced at $500 or $5,000, neither is affordable. Most AIDS patients have either private insurance, Medicaid, Medicare, or VA, all of which reimburse for HIV drugs, though sometimes the insurance copays are oppressive. In that case ADAP usually steps in to cover the copays. Patients who cannot get treatment because of drug cost generate very bad press for the drug makers along with political pressure to reduce all drug prices. To prevent AIDS patients from falling into the cracks between government programs, drug companies worked with activists to develop elaborate PAPs or Patient Assistance Programs. The PAPs also provide tax breaks for the companies. They combine smart politics with good PR. As long as the giveaways are significantly smaller than actual sales, they cost the companies little or nothing.

Thanks to activist diligence, led by the ADAP Working Group and NASTAD, ADAP is usually funded to meet the needs, and the program has been stable since 2008. Moreover, the Fair Pricing Coalition or FPC, founded by Martin Delaney, Linda Dee, and Linda Grinberg, has been a conscientious watchdog ready to call out serious offenders. FPC meets with the company sponsor each time a new drug is introduced in order to negotiate a price that will not break the ADAP budget. FPC also monitors price increases. All this does not mean that price increases have been reasonable and justified, but it does mean that they seldom impact individual AIDS patients access to life saving medications.

What is true for an organized patient community like HIV-AIDS is not the case for many other diseases and conditions where patients may have to spend themselves into poverty to qualify for public assistance to get drugs. I developed Crohn's disease, aspergillus, and severe psoriasis in 2009 only to learn that multiple reimbursement options available to AIDS patients are seldom available for others. My yearly drug costs are several times those of a typical HIV patient. For all their drawbacks, other disease groups could use a Larry Kramer and a Peter Staley.

The prophet Jeremiah appears to be Kramer's dominant archetype inspiring his bitter complaints about the speed of medical progress, and angry harangues against the "greed" of his personal Cyclopes, the pharmaceutical industry. All the while, he turned a blind eye to the shocking immorality of FDA's self-serving regulatory delays and to the agency's collusion with an illicit drug underground. Jeremiahs reserve the right to pick their outrages and targeted villains, it appears. Yet Kramer and too many of the ACT UP people who followed him viewed drug pricing strictly, and inappropriately, in moral terms. Too many bought FDA's pretext that costly drug approval delays are a matter of scientific "need" to fully explore every hypothesis however unlikely. In fact, delays mostly result from featherbedding practices prevalent in the agency's bureaucratic culture. Delays pad existing FDA jobs and create new jobs for FDA lifers. FDA, like DOD and other bureaucracies, sells featherbedding under the guise of public safety.

Kramer, oblivious to the characteristic sins of modern bureaucracy, took an almost medieval perspective. High drug prices, like usury, exploit misfortune: because they profit from suffering they are immoral. It is tempting, though perilous, to speculate on the psychological roots of his article of faith, that pharmaceutical profits are morally heinous compared to other forms of profits. One may, however, note that avarice is the kneejerk bugaboo of the left, just as lechery is that of the right.

Kramer's monomaniacal *animus* against drug company profits made no sense to me, or to my early activist colleagues. Even Delaney always took Kramer's ravings with a grain of salt. We knew the drug companies would never be candidates for sainthood, but we all understood that these corporations must be operated as businesses accountable to their investors. Not so Larry Kramer. The first time I met him back in 1989 at a Roche meeting, he told me, "We may be useful to them, but you need to realize that they (the drug companies) are never our friends." What I did realize with more experience was that there was no they in they. The companies and their people are all different, a few deserve a fair degree of trust and admiration, some merit censure and condemnation, and most are somewhere in the gray zone. I also realized that in the AIDS world the least trustworthy players were government bureaucrats and politicians. Republicans would betray us whenever they feared support from anti-gay bigots might be at stake, and Democrats too would betray us at the behest of their own special interests, the preeminent one being FDA itself. Neither party had qualms about making gays and people with AIDS feel dispensable when they were in conflict with other political priorities.

In a speech delivered in absentia to the 2018 US Conference on AIDS Kramer served up his same old menu in spades. Kramer's rhetoric may be demagogic, so be forewarned, but it is typical ACT UP rhetoric on drug pricing and consistent with Kramer's entire incendiary career. He begins and ends with moral outrage worthy of the prophet Jeremiah:

> *The pharmaceutical industry is evil incarnate. Their greed is beyond comprehension. To withhold drugs that can save lives and make them available only to the rich is, as I have said, evil. It is allowing people to die. It is murdering them. That America has allowed such behavior makes a farce of God and Christianity and democracy.*

I site specifically our own experience with Truvada and its distributer Gilead Pharmaceuticals. Gilead did not finance Truvada by itself; it was also financed by the American taxpayer via grants to the NIH, with which Gilead shares the patent. Dr. Fauci is the official NIH mouthpiece that announced to the American People that everyone with HIV should take Truvada. He then provided no help or information on just how we can pay for his recommendation.

At the same time Gilead is fucking us over with Truvada they are doing the same with a number of other AIDS and hepatitis meds they are controlling. They have made many billions of dollars claiming they are saving us. A drug that cost peanuts to manufacture is dumped on each of us for tens of thousands of dollars. They are all too expensive for most patients to afford. How unchristian, how undemocratic, how selfish can you be?

How does Gilead get away with this? We are all helping them to do it. They pour millions of dollars into organizations like this one to keep us quiet. By taking their money they are enslaving us while they continue to rob us blind. Why they are even a sponsor of the new wonderful gay series POSE, using their commercial time to show the world what wonderful things they are doing.

Kramer contends that the drug companies are robbing us blind by charging thousands of dollars for drugs whose manufacturing costs are minimal. Odd isn't it that he does not levy the same charge against Apple, Google, Facebook, Microsoft, or Disney whose gargantuan profits dwarf those of even the drug companies and whose intellectual property based products often cost as comparatively little as drugs to physically manufacture? Or how about his own revenues from writings and films? Does he grasp the concept of intellectual property? Can he not see that the value of drugs is not as manufactured goods, like automobiles and refrigerators, but more like software for the human body? —their worth resides overwhelmingly in intellectual property. The one industry more profitable than pharmaceuticals is high tech, Silicon Valley. Why should developers of intellectual property that alleviates suffering and extends life be denounced as greedy profiteers while developers of other forms of intellectual property are left free to charge all the traffic will bear?

Kramer mirrors the medieval mentality that forbade usury because profiting from another's distress was deemed immoral. His condemnation of greed is highly selective--that is, limited to pharmaceuticals. Let's get some perspective! Most business depends on profiting from meeting distressing needs. Grocery stores and restaurants profit from selling food to ward off hunger. Should Whole Foods and McDonalds be required to give away bread and burgers? After all, people die in a few weeks without food, and starvation is a truly horrible death.

Why single out Gilead, the leading AIDS drug company? Their drugs are expensive but often less so than those for cancer and other killer diseases. Yes, their drugs are too expensive for most patients to afford, that's the reason we have private insurance, Medicaid, Medicare, VA, ADAP, and Gilead's own generous PAPs. Why single out drug companies? Doctors and hospital and clinic staff do not work for free, nor for that matter do the staffs of the ubiquitous non-profit AIDS service organizations. The average 2018 income of an infectious disease doctor in the US was $265,000, whereas the average workers' salary was $47,000. Does Kramer think doctors are morally obligated to work for $47,000 to make healthcare affordable? In our society everything is expensive, housing, medical care, schooling, transportation, entertainment, utilities, food, taxes, not just pharmaceuticals. High drug costs do hurt many people, including people who have my conditions, Crohn's, psoriasis, and aspergillus, but very few of those who cannot access treatment because of high drug prices are HIV patients.

Kramer assumes, quite mistakenly, that the mono-cause of high HIV drug prices is the greed of the drug companies. Drug company research is financed by investors who will withdraw their money if these companies cannot offer returns competitive with those other sectors. Many crucial drugs, such as Gilead's breakthrough cure for hepatitis C or HCV, Harvoni, were originally developed by small biotech companies. Some of these companies never go anywhere, others hit the jackpot and sell out to bigger companies, as in the case of Harvoni's original developer Pharmasset. But venture capitalists fund these companies research because they hope to hit the jackpot—outlaw the jackpots and their risk capital will evaporate.

If Kramer and the street activists succeed in dramatically reducing HIV drug profits, that would help very few individual patients. Instead it would hurt the patients who could be saved by those drugs the companies do not develop because they would not be profitable. Targeting drug company profits can harm future HIV patients without benefiting current patients. But it gets certain activists and their groups media attention, which is indispensable for fund raising from liberal foundations who too often feel noble when funding noisy, useless, and unscrupulous activists. Focusing on drug pricing is legitimate, but not to the point of monomania. It can degenerate to yet another bootless form of virtue signaling.

The need for better drugs in many diseases, including HIV-AIDS, is even more urgent than the need for cheaper drugs. Our costly, troublesome HIV disease management with drugs that have known and unknown toxic side effects is a poor long range solution. To end AIDS, we must ultimately couple an effective vaccine with a cure. To get new vaccines and cures for an array of diseases we need research and development which will not be done under our capitalistic system if we take away the prospect of healthy profits. Socialism is no solution. Pharmaceutical innovation is almost non-existent in socialistic systems. Can anyone name a valuable drug that came out of the old Soviet Union? Larry, Bernie, anyone?

This does not mean activists should capitulate on high drug costs. We need reduction in overall medical costs to expand access to everyone. But our first priority must be unnecessary expenditures, the waste--Such as money spent on conforming to FDA regulations that cannot be justified on a cost-benefit basis. All healthcare expenses, including those of non-profits grown rich on the little known but vast and unaccountable 340B Federal drug program, should be subject to rigorous cost-benefit analysis and oversight to reduce waste. Profits and waste are not limited to private industry. The government agencies all have their own ways of profiteering, as does the non-profit sector that in some capacities serves everyone in society. The profits of the non-profits lie in all the well-paid jobs with desirable perquisites they provide their employees, largely at taxpayer expense.

The non-profits all seek taxpayer dollars to finance more and better paying jobs for themselves. Aren't drug companies doing something similar? What are the differences between a for profit company and a non-profit? A key difference is that the companies rely on investors risking their capital, whereas non-profits, like government bureaucracies, get their capital, directly from taxes or indirectly via tax exemptions. Another crucial difference is that fiscal accountability is more prevalent and effective with private enterprise because private investors are strongly motivated to withdraw their funds when the companies fail to show results. With non-profits, as with government, accountability is the Achilles heel. Taxpayers rarely have an option to stop feeding the bureaucracies gaping maws. The sun rarely sets on government programs and policies that have out-lived their usefulness or were ill-advised from the onset. Like other bureaucracies, non-profits fight for more funding long after their original raison d'etre` is diminished or gone forever.

One solution to the HIV drug access-pricing problem that is rarely discussed but deserves serious consideration is federally guaranteed access to drugs and care for all American HIV patients. Putting all HIV patients in care is after all the only currently available way to stop the spread of this infectious disease. Prior to Obamacare, activists were proposing ETHA, the Early Treatment for HIV Act, which was introduced in Congress in 2007 by Nancy Pelosi with 26 Republican co-sponsors. ETHA, which facilitated an expansion of Medicaid coverage to HIV patients, was dropped because supporters maintained that Obamacare would make it unnecessary. However, Obamacare has many short comings, among them failure to expand Medicaid to cover adequately HIV in all states. Still, with government guaranteed universal coverage for HIV more patients would be in care, and drug costs would be in the hands of the government which has far greater powers to negotiate prices than do AIDS activists. So why aren't the pricing activists calling for a new ETHA to insure universal HIV coverage? —again, the non-answer answer is politics.

Another area of activism deserving more thought and energy is the stigma surrounding homosexuality that infringes on human rights and impedes access to healthcare. Especially among African Americans, stigma is a huge impediment to HIV testing and treatment. If the US government nationalized the AIDS drug companies, Larry Kramer's wet dream come true, and charged only the cost of manufacturing the drugs, the key impact would be to abort development of new and better HIV drugs. It would insure that we will never get an effective HIV vaccine or a cure, and never wipe out the disease. However, educational, moral, and social reforms to curb the stigma on homosexuality that is the source of the stigma on HIV disease could get more people into treatment expediting the end of AIDS. Curbing stigma would also cut high LGBT suicide rates, the deaths from despair, among our young, and it would be a big step toward equal rights for all. Such reforms would improve the lives of all LGBT people, and make America a better place, and Americans a better people. Why not prioritize that goal?

Let me conclude my screed contra Kramer, the grand master of screeds and diatribes with a mixed bag eulogy. Larry Kramer initiated a movement that has done more than anything else to focus the attention of America on its AIDS dilemma, and especially to mobilize the heavily afflicted and deeply oppressed LGBT community. His relentless urgency and totally out of the closet honesty about all the wrongs he sees has awakened many in our community and in our morally somnolent society.

Kramer is also the father of much expense of spirit in the shameful waste of his onslaughts on his one eyed cyclops, the pharmaceutical bogeymen. Why is it a such a waste? Because the most effective restraints on drug pricing are resistance of government payers to high prices along with measures to lower drug development costs. The proof of the former is in the lower drug prices of Europe and Canada. If Kramer and other liberals really want to impede exploitative pharmaceutical pricing, a worthy goal, they should work to grant government programs like Medicare and Medicaid greater ability to negotiate prices. VA is given stronger negotiation powers, and its drug costs are lower. Governments in other developed countries have more effective negotiating systems resulting in overall drug costs much lower than ours. Government negotiation is not regulation; it's introducing market principles to government purchases. The government negotiates the prices of most purchases; pharmaceuticals are the big exception.

In the 1990s I defended healthy profits and regulatory rollback as incentives to AIDS drug development in dozens of articles in papers all the way from *B.A.R.* to the *Wall Street Journal*. Kramer's New Yorkers dismissed my arguments on *ad hominin* grounds insisting that I must have been paid by drug companies. They demonized me as some sort of far right outlier—their label for LGBTs who refuse to be yellow dog Democrats. The accusation of being paid by drug companies to defend their prices was flat out false. Ironically, the people who benefit most from drug company largess are the activists that attack their pricing. The companies know it's far safer and more effective to pay silence money to temper their critics than to pay anyone to defend them. As Kramer himself put it:

> *How does Gilead get away with this? We are all helping them do it. They pour millions into organizations like this one to keep us quiet.*

Kramer is no hypocrite, blasting the companies until they back up a truckload of silence money to his doorstep. However, activists who mount similar criticisms have been rewarded just for toning down.*22* Those who attack profits are praised as idealists, sometimes even by the companies themselves; and they are ever the favorite beneficiaries of kneejerk liberal mega-rich foundations. Those who defend the need for profits to incentivize research are branded sell outs. It takes courage to defend R & D incentives. Any demagogue can inveigh against drug profits with impunity and more likely to his or her benefit. Welcome to the topsy-turvy world of AIDS activism!

Sometimes, no often, the good we accomplish is not the good we intend. Yet by just by taking action we propel our cause forward in unexpected ways. Larry Kramer has done nothing to address constructively the problem of high drug prices. He failed because he was attacking a bogeyman rather than an existential problem afflicting flesh and blood HIV patients. However, just by drawing attention to the epidemic itself, to the suffering and dying and the desperate need for action, by rallying people who otherwise might have remained passive, Kramer cleared a path for others to address the urgent questions on HIV in America. Larry was courageous, dauntless, and he inspired courage in others who might have remained passive. Rarely a reliable guide on what needed to be done or how to do it, his guiding truth was simply that something needed to be done. A peculiarly flawed hero, whom few followed exactly, Larry Kramer inspired many, including myself, to find and follow their own lights.

****

Have the drug companies price gouged on HIV drugs since the protease inhibitors were approved in 1996? You can make a clear case for price increases higher than the CPI, if you look only at their official or "average wholesale price," the AWP. More relevant is what the government and private insurers actually pay, and most important how many AIDS patients cannot get drugs because the costs to them are prohibitive?

Determining what the largest buyers, such as ADAP, Medicare, and Medicaid, actually pay is difficult because of confidentiality agreements and the complex system of rebates among the different tiers of buyers. Moreover, a major portion of AIDS drugs are purchased through the little known but vast and extremely lucrative 340B program. 340B works this way: The buyers, Federally Qualified Healthcare Centers (FQHC) serving low income patients, purchase the drugs at low 340B prices and then get reimbursed by private insurers, Medicare, Medicaid, ADAP etc. at much higher rates. Their profit, it's termed *program money*, is supposed to be used for additional services patients need. Accountability and enforcement, however, are almost non-existent. Part of that money goes to high salaries for the non-profits' executives or to purchase real estate and equipment. Some goes to lobbying and to support their executives' political causes de jour, typically through voter registration and so-called voter education. Some large AIDS non-profits have used 340B profits to fund lawsuits, and state ballot propositions, such as rent control, that are far afield from their patients' medical needs.

The actual price the companies can charge the FQHCs is much lower than what Medicaid, Medicare, or other insurers pay, which in turn is considerably lower than the AWP. Rebates can reduce the actual price further, but it is impossible to tell how much because rebates are covered by confidentiality agreements, i.e., they're secret. Drug costs are a little like airline fares. In the same aircraft flying to London in business class some passengers may be paying a full fare of $6000.00, others half that, and still others are using miles and pay next to nothing. But no one knows what each passenger pays other than the airline and the passenger herself.

The critical question remains, how many patients do not get drugs because of high cost? Outside of HIV it's a common problem. Too many patients cannot afford medication without draining down their savings and consuming all their disposable income. Paying for cancer drugs is a dire and frequent dilemma driving to many into bankruptcy. A simple solution could be twofold: catastrophic coverage for all Americans, and patient buy-in programs for Medicare or possibly Medicaid.

HIV drug costs are almost always short term issues that seldom pose serious long term barriers to accessing treatment. The HIV community would like legislators and the public to believe otherwise, but few hard facts support their professed concerns. That does not mean that all HIV patient needs are met, far from it. But unmet needs lie elsewhere in areas like testing, transference to and retention in care, difficulty accessing care especially in rural areas and the South and for minorities, deficient quality of care, and the high level of poverty among many HIV patients and in their communities. These patients often have difficulty accessing nearly everything they need, quality food, housing, transportation, education, legal services etc. All their problems are aggravated by stigma. Seldom are their problems directly aggravated by high drug prices.

APPENDIX III
Politicians' Sins of Omission

Before 1980 sins of commission against gay people were so rampant and severe that we paid scant attention to sins of omission. Flagrant discrimination was pervasive in the armed forces and throughout government and American society. In the State Department alone, more than 1000 employees were dismissed after 1945 for alleged or suspected homosexuality and many more were barred from joining through overt hiring discrimination. Under perdurable siege, we concentrated on dodging the slings and arrows of outrageous homophobia.

However, in the 1980s the AIDS epidemic precipitated a tectonic shift on our attitudes toward ourselves and in society's attitudes about gay people and our rights. President Reagan failed to utter the word AIDS while hundreds of thousands of his fellow citizens were caught in a terrifying AIDS epidemic. During his presidency AIDS killed 61,816, more than the 58,220 that died in the entire Vietnam war. Throughout his Presidency, Senator Jesse Helms and other demagogues fueled homophobia and AIDS phobia. Their worst sins of omission and commission ultimately backfired against the Republicans. They not only stirred sympathy for people with AIDS, it made the Democrats look virtuous at no political cost whatever by just by not being Republicans. Purblind Republicans handed the Democrats another massive voting block on a silver platter.

With the help of gay leaders like Jim Foster and David Mixner, the Democrats were quick to recognize the potential of the gay vote in places like California. It was there that the gay electorate first demonstrated the power of its numbers and money. Politicos in Harvey Milk's home town San Francisco, beginning with Mayor George Moscone, Diane Feinstein, and Nancy Pelosi established ground breaking paradigms for working openly with gay people that eventually gained support in the national Democratic Party.

All the Republicans weren't, however, entirely clueless. Most realized it would be counterproductive, and distasteful, to unleash full scale homophobia. Ronald Reagan as governor had helped us defeat the infamous Briggs amendment which would have stigmatized gays as potential sex offenders and barred us from teaching in the public schools. High level Republicans, like Orrin Hatch, Newt Gingrich, Pete Wilson, Jim Jeffords, Gordon Smith, Alan Simpson, and First Ladies Nancy Reagan and Barbara and Laura Bush, and Vice President Cheney acted to counter the abuses of the fanatics and demagogues. But their efforts weren't enough to temper let alone silence Hollywood backed anti-Republican crusades orchestrated by the Human Rights Campaign. Today the cost to the LGBT community for GOP tolerance of homophobia is on the rise again with the rising prominence of Mike and Karen Pence.

The highly effective and sustained Democratic outreach to gays continues to hurt the Republicans public image, and has contributed to losses at the polls as more and more LGBT people who had been Republicans yield to group pressure and identify with the Democrats. LGBTs' disproportionate preference for Democrats is a major reason California has become almost a one party state. It's becoming a big plus for Democrats in Florida and Texas, and is detrimental to Republicans in several other swing states, including Pennsylvania, Wisconsin, Colorado, Nevada, New Hampshire, and Ohio. It helps solidify Democrat strongholds in the Northeast, the Pacific Northwest, and Illinois.

LGBTs hale from all sections of the population, all classes, ethnicities, and religions. One would no more expect us to be inclined disproportionately to one party over the other, than expect left handed people to lean heavily toward one party. However, if one party embraced the left handed while the other party ostracized them as inveterate sinners, slandered them as a danger to children, and tried to deny them the right to marry, the southpaw vote would become a solid constituency for the party that valued their humanity and respected them as individuals. Therewith, LGBTs became a solid Democrat constituency.

AIDS was, and is still, an existential threat and crisis for LGBT people. The US still has nearly 40,000 new HIV infections per year, of these 26,000 are LGBT. Support for the AIDS cause, or apparent failure to support it, is not easily forgotten either way. Nevertheless, the actual difference between the parties' performance is not nearly as great as the perception of difference. The Democrats were far more supportive on HIV related civil rights questions and definitely better on some important AIDS prevention issues like clean needles, sex education, condoms access, and above all fighting stigma. Yet the parties have been more or less equally supportive of the Ryan White Care Act and other services for those with HIV. As we have seen, Republicans were better at removing regulatory obstacles to HIV testing, treatment, and care and far better on challenging FDA delays in drug development and approval. Indeed, President George W. Bush became the world leader in the initiatives to bring new AIDS treatments to the entire planet, and President Trump has shown more initiative on drug costs than any of his predecessors.

In politics perception often trumps reality, and sometimes perception is the only reality that counts. The good that the Democrats did was widely publicized in the national media and throughout the LGBT community. The bad that they did in supporting FDA was more difficult to assess, and harder to pin on them. FDA's patient shills, diehard Democrats all, worked ceaselessly to shield the Democrats and FDA itself from blame for delays in treatment development and access. Delays were always the fault of drug company greed or researcher ineptitude. We were advised we must wait for the science when we were really waiting only for pedantic regulators.

Republicans, have always underestimated the size and strength of the LGBT vote, and they remain oblivious to the still larger and ever increasing LGBT shadow vote, relatives and friends of LGBTs, or just conscientious citizens who want everyone's rights respected. They persist in denial of the wide and growing resonance of gay rights issues outside the LGBT community. They ignore the hand writing on the wall warning them of dramatic shifts in attitudes toward LGBTs among younger voters, especially millennials.

To the Republicans detriment, in the 1990s they did not want to be seen as pushing regulatory reforms for the benefit of AIDS patients, even though in many cases that was their prime motive. Republicans had brothers, children, other relatives, and friends who were gay or HIV infected as often as Democrats. As individuals they cared or didn't care about AIDS patients as often as Democrats. However, Republicans believed they had to be much more cautious than Democrats with letting constituents know they cared and, especially, why they cared. Always at their ear were professional homophobes whispering fear.

In America there is money to be made peddling anti-LGBT suspicion, bias, and prejudice, big money. The Family Research Council, a group founded at the height of the AIDS epidemic in 1992 and dedicated to opposing LGBT rights, reported revenue of $12,065,84 in 2016. Focus on the Family, FRC's parent organization, reported $95,209,896 in revenue in 2011. These groups anti-LGBT rights activities are conducted under the guise of "protecting the family" and defending "traditional values." Their facile presumption is that LGBTs, by being different from conventional families, are a threat or challenge to those families. Those who understand us know we are an alternative lifestyle and an alternative is not perforce a threat or even a challenge. Protestantism is an alternative to Catholicism, and Judaism and Mormonism are alternatives to both, but they are not necessarily threats or challenges to each other. Regardless, in America Protestants and Catholics must learn to tolerate one another, along with Jews, Mormons, Muslims, Buddhists, Hindus, New Agers, and the ever growing mass of secularists. America is no place for intolerance, racial, religious, gender or otherwise.

The writers of the US Constitution decided that in America alternative religious forms would be treated as alternatives, not as heresies. They took no position on alternative family forms, but the paradigm they set with religion was there from the beginning, and reinforced when the 14th Amendment dictated equal protection of the laws. Still, money is to be made from peddling prejudice, and it is always very hard to stop certain people from making money any which way they can.

The anti-gay organizations put the GOP in a bind. To placate them, Republicans needed to appear critical of gays, oblivious to our rights, and indifferent to our injuries. That often put the public *personae* of individual politicians at odds with their true attitudes. In my thirty years of dealing with elected officials and their staffs at the federal level, I've found that party affiliation does not usually affect private attitudes toward gays, though there were exceptions. The bigger differences were in the positions representatives of the party projected publicly. To their credit, Democrats tried to act like champions of LGBT rights and of AIDS patients, always taking care to avoid calling for changes, like gay marriage, before their voters were ready. The Republicans avoided open associations with LGBTs, our problems or causes. Thus, sins of omission became the Republican *modus operandi* with LGBT rights and AIDS.

From 1988 forward the GOP's general stance of ignoring its own achievements on AIDS and for gays (the latter are admittedly small), along with its numerous sins of commission and omission, brought a gradual erosion of support from gay people. When support for one party in a voter population achieves a certain critical mass, usually in excess of 65%, that party gains a big advantage among those who identify with the group. Peer pressure from other gay people pushed those who came out as gay toward the Democrats. It likewise pushed sympathetic members of their family and circle of friends to the Democrats creating the seldom identified bit potentially large pro-gay shadow voting bloc.

The result is a growing handicap for the GOP whose size and significance it has yet to recognize, let alone address. Every Republican President and major party leader, with the commendable exception of Vice President Cheney, has treated the problem as an untouchable third rail. So far it's worse under Trump than under Bush 43—mainly due to their VPs' opposite attitudes and actions in regard to LGBTs and our rights. As a result, LGBTs have become components, and casualties, in the plague of identity politics and the crippling polarization of the two major parties and of political life in America today.

Did Republican sins of omission worsen the AIDS epidemic? Yes, because they helped sustain and extend the stigma of being gay. That stigma has been a major obstacle to essential HIV testing and to treating the disease effectively. On the other hand, the Democrat commitment to dilatory drug approval policies posed a grave threat to the entire AIDS population in the 1990s. Activism by our community, quietly supported by key Republicans in Congress, prevented major delays in access to the life-saving cocktails when they were finally ready to be deployed. But, by keeping their support quiet, the Republicans never got credit, and some might say they didn't deserve it.

APPENDIX IV
High Ranking
Purveyors of Stigma

If a man also lie with mankind as he lieth with a woman, both of them have committed an abomination: they shall surely be put to death; their blood shall be upon them.

Leviticus 20:13

Stigma did not create AIDS. Yet the stigma of association with homosexuality prepared the way and speeded its ravaging course through America and the world. First stigma occluded understanding of the disease: it's a gay cancer, it's retribution from God, they brought it on themselves, so who cares? Then stigma delayed government action, research, and assistance for the sick and dying. Stigma made people afraid to get tested for HIV and reluctant to seek treatment. AIDS Stigma spread like a virus making people ashamed, isolating and alienating them from friends and family. Stigma cost people jobs, professional standing, housing, a seat on an airplane or in a dentist's chair. Stigma made many afraid to live, and want to die. But then it began to make some brave people very angry and AIDS activism was born. The activists realized that to fight AIDS we must fight stigma.*27*

AIDS activism did more to combat the stigma against homosexuality and AIDS than any other social force. AIDS activism, like the civil rights movement, became a great moral crusade, spreading truth, defending the innocent, restoring dignity to the violated, giving hope to the desperate, and reviving faith in the disillusioned. AIDS activism gave LGBT people courage, dignity, and power they had never held before. It inspired many to stand up and proudly proclaim who they are and who they love. Twenty-six of the world's most advanced countries now recognize gay marriage, and in 2020 a gay man openly married to another man was a prominent candidate for President of the United States.

Gay advances be damned, early in 2019 Karen Pence, wife of the current Vice President of the United States, resumed her teaching post at a school that systematically discriminates against LGBTs grounding their policies specifically on the afore cited cruel and barbaric verse from Leviticus. Why of all the 31,102 verses in the Bible, did the Pence's Immanuel School cherry pick that one? Despite Islamic excesses, not even the Quran demands that homosexuals be put to death. Did Immanuel or the Pences ever ask what text Jesus would have chosen to guide their policies toward gay people? Did they ever ask how their favored text squares with the over-riding ethical principle Jesus proclaimed in the Golden Rule? Evidently not.

The hypocrisy of Karen Pences' affiliation with Immanuel School becomes blatant in light of the little known fact that she is a divorcee. Karen married her first husband John Whitaker in 1978, divorced him later and drifted away from the Catholic Church she was raised in but whose strictures on divorce may have become disagreeable to her. Details on her previous marriage and divorce along with this part of her life are skimpy and hard to obtain.*28* 1985 brought second nuptials as she married Mike Pence, likewise raised in a strong Catholic family. After entering politics in 1988, the Pences started to attend the Grace Evangelical Church and began to style themselves born again Christians. Politically, church attendance was *de rigor* for a Republican in Bible belt Indiana.

Many Evangelicals, including those who run Immanuel School, assert that every verse in the Bible is literally the word of God that remains forever binding upon all mankind. Their view is not what Jesus taught by his words and example. He taught that the "law and the prophets" must be applied under the guidance of a higher general principle, the ethic of a God of love, "do unto others." He denounces the scribes and Pharisees as hypocrites for in effect failing to see the forest for the trees in interpreting such texts in the Old Testament.

So what does Jesus himself say in the New Testament about divorce and remarriage? As the Pences' former church, the Catholic Church, correctly teaches, Jesus Christ, no mere prophet but the veritable Son of God in Christian dogma, directly forbids divorce and remarriage— remember Henry VIII's marital troubles which led to the formation of the

Anglican Church! Jesus in fact specifically condemns men, like Mike Pence, who marry a divorced woman. For example, in Matthew 5:32 he states unequivocally: *"whosoever marries a divorced woman commits adultery."* Going back to a neighboring verse to Leviticus 20:13, Leviticus 20:10, we find that adulterers and homosexuals are condemned in the same words to exactly the same draconic fate: *"And the man that committeth adultery with another man's wife . . . the adulterer and the adulteress shall surely be put to death."*

How comes it that Immanuel School and the pious Pences confidently declare that their discrimination against LGBTs is commanded by God in Leviticus 20:13, (giving them no choice but to support discrimination, one supposes) yet they ignore Leviticus 20:10, only three verses before it, which condemns them to the same dark fate they consign to gay men? Their cherry picking of verses in service of personal biases, or bigotry, disrespects truth, the scriptures, and the Deity Who is presumed to communicate through the scriptures. It's the kind of blatant hypocrisy Jesus denounced in the pious frauds of his day. It's manifestly illogical, except in terms of the mercenary logic of the collection plate which regularly creates exceptions to the "word of God" and relaxes moral standards for the convenience of the heterosexual majority while tightening them for the LGBT minority. The Pences may not be the brightest bulbs in the Republican storeroom, but they're smart enough to catch the contradictions here.

The Pences' professed "religion" disregards the express words of Jesus declaring them adulterers living in sin, while it ignores the absence of any mention, let alone condemnation, of homosexuality by Jesus Himself. Ignoring as well prudential warnings to those who live in glass houses, the Pences confidently presume Leviticus 20:13 justifies "religious exemptions" to civil rights laws, laws whose ultimate ethical foundation is Jesus's Golden Rule. Upon the sole, isolated authority of that barbarous verse, the Pences pursue political expediency to embrace the full menu of homophobia. In the past they have even pushed gay "conversion therapy," an atrocity from the inquisition which is now illegal in 10 states, Brazil, Ecuador, and may soon be in Canada and Germany.

Jesus said, *"for with what judgment you judge, you will be judged; and with the measure you use, it will be measured back to you,"* Matthew 7:2. Applying this standard to the Pences, we must recognize Jesus's unmistakable words in the gospels of St. Matthew and St. Luke, mean Mike and Karen Pence are living in adultery along with the Trumps and millions of other American couples. However, rather than forbearing from casting stones as Jesus wisely commanded of all sinners (John 7:8), they have built Mike Pence's political career on casting stones, but not at adulterers, only at gays!

Indeed, Mike and Karen Pence have made their "religious" opposition to LGBT rights their political calling cards. Behind their façade of piety, so glibly accepted by the media, the Pences are modern Pharisees, hypocritical opportunists who cherry pick their moral stands for political gain, not religious conviction. For political gain, the Pences make a mockery of the spirit Jesus Christ's ethical teachings. Their heartless political opportunism is a bigger violation than any of Donald Trump's or Bill Clinton's specific sexual indiscretions because it seriously damages an entire section of the population.

So far it's working for them. Heirs to the niche left empty by Jesse Helms, they are America's best known and most successful hawkers of homophobia. By operating behind the scenes to fill sensitive positions in the Trump Administration with FOLKs, "friends of lovely Karen," they are slowly and quietly, but severely restricting LGBT rights while tainting Donald Trump with their signature homophobia. Though his transgressions may be many, the Donald has not hitherto been guilty of that one.

The Pences reflect and exploit an outrageous and shameful double standard that has become prevalent in respect to homosexuality versus heterosexual adultery and divorce. While Biblical codes on sexual conduct are relaxed or suspended for the convenience of straights, like Mike and Karen Pence, they are tightened for gays. For the Pences, and their heterosexual elect, adultery becomes a peccadillo and evidently divorce and remarriage are not sins at all. But to love someone of the same sex, *that* becomes the new sin against the Holy Ghost.

Decades ago flexible Protestants began a slow process of derogating clear scriptural injunctions against divorce in order to hold remarried divorcees blameless. Remember how Nelson Rockefeller's 1963 divorce and remarriage undermined his Presidential ambitions. Then divorce and re-marriage carried a powerful stigma as a threat to the family that was in some ways comparable to the stigma against LGBTs that the Pences promote today—except that divorce is a far more common and serious threat to family stability than homosexuality.

In recent decades, many Protestant churches, ever quick to grasp the economic effects of moral stands, choreographed some inventive theological acrobatics to fashion "morality" to the tastes of their majority heterosexual parishioners.*29* How then to redirect that rich, historic store of American Puritan moral censure of adultery memorialized in Nathaniel Hawthorne's *The Scarlet Letter.* The Lord of Convenience, Satan's comrade devil, smooth, sly Belial, whispered, "shift the focus of moral outrage!*30* Make homosexuality, not divorce and adultery, the great threat to the American family!" Mike Pence asked, "you mean give Karen and me a sin-pass, but sock it to the gays?" "Yeah," said Belial, "get the gays, that will get you votes!"

Thus did expediency make hypocrites of the generality and scapegoats of the few. And so it came to pass that the putatively pious Pences, a divorcee and her fellow adulterer (according to Jesus) spouse, became the chief torch bearers of anti-LGBT bias and stigma in contemporary American politics.

(Mike and VP Karen Pence)

So called social conservatives, led by the Pences, everywhere promote anti-LGBT stigma in the name of religion, and get a pass by claiming that their bigotry is rooted in pious devotion. A somnolent media rarely questions this. Due mainly to the Pences' "moral" influence within the Trump Administration, the "right" to stigmatize LGBT people, spread lies and hatred against us, and fill LGBT children with guilt and shame is defended as a sacred expression of "religious freedom" just as slavery, segregation, Apartheid, and anti-Semitism were all once defended in the name of obedience to God and the Bible. The largest US Protestant denomination, the Southern Baptist Church used the curse of Cain to justify slavery. Not till 1995 did this Church apologize for its shameful record of defending slavery, segregation, and racism. What motivates people to spread bigotry and rationalize discrimination in the name of the Deity? — the hatred that moves them surely comes from their own hearts, not God's.

While Americans must defend freedom of religion, we cannot avoid the complicated task of distinguishing between authentic religious commitments and social biases or political opportunism cloaked as religion. We reserve the right to be selective in the religious practices we allow, as the Mormons learned when Utah sought statehood. Our defining American narratives of the struggle for freedom and individual rights against slavery and discrimination teach us that we must not allow prejudice posing as an exercise of religious freedom to justify violating the basic human rights of citizens who are different from us.

Among the many costs of continued stigmatizing of LGBTs is a suicide rate for our young people under thirty of 4+ times the rate in general population. That equates to more than 1000 excess lives lost to bias and stigma each year; 1000 uniquely valuable human beings destroyed for the Pences' "right" to posture over what they pretend to be their "religion" in order to secure votes from the ignorant and bigoted. When will we recognize that human lives, rights, and decency must trump prejudice camouflaged under anachronistic religious dogmas? Must we also sanction the Aztec religion's rite of physical human sacrifice atop a pyramid by the same principle that we sanction the Pence's "right" to sacrifice LGBT lives through spreading the blight of stigma? When will we realize that a good God cannot demand unjust discrimination and cruel bigotry? Only evil people want that.

Those who oppose stigmatizing LGBTs are on solid ground ethically. Their basis for opposing stigma is not an odd verse cherry picked from an otherwise disregarded section of the Old Testament. It is the very core of Jesus's message and of the Judeo-Christian ethic: *"And as you would that men do to you, do ye also to them likewise."* (Luke 6:31) Who wants to suffer discrimination, who likes to be stigmatized? No one!

The Trump Administration boasts a plan "to end AIDS" that increases HIV testing and availability of pre-exposure prophylaxis, or PrEP. At the same time President Trump allows Mike Pence to give sensitive appointments in health and education to bigots who promote stigma and believe LGBTs should be treated in the draconic spirit of Leviticus 20:13. In the 2016 Republican Convention Trump promised, "As your President, I will do everything in my power to protect our L.G.B.T.Q. citizens from the violence and oppression of a hateful foreign ideology." As President he has protected LGBTs from Sharia, only to subject us to the Pences' hate based native born bigotry. Trump pretends to give to LGBTs with one hand while through Pence he takes back with the other.

A few, too few, are asking, how can you end AIDS by promoting stigma? You can't. Promoting stigma impedes HIV testing, treatment, and safe sex practices, things we need to do to stop the spread of the virus. Promoting stigma profoundly violates the stigmatized. It incites many to despise, fear, and discriminate against LGBTs, and causes some of us to loathe, fear, and even seek to kill ourselves. If Mr. Trump is serious about ending AIDS and protecting LGBTs, he needs to get serious about combatting stigma. That will require either a "road to Damascus" experience for Mr. Pence or, more likely and more credible, replacing him with a Vice President who has the tact and good sense not to endorse LGBT policies based on a scripture calling for gays to be put to death.

When he first ran in 2016 Trump fashioned himself a champion of gays. If he keeps an unrepentant Mike Pence as his Vice President, Donald Trump May well leave office as the most anti-LGBT President so far. Worse still, keeping Pence will position this opportunistic bigot to become Trump's successor. A Pence who has damaged and deeply alienated 6 percent of the electorate by peddling prejudices antithetical to the beliefs of the great majority of voters under 50 will likely loose. A Pence defeat will morally empower the Resistance Democrats who will attempt to reverse Mr. Trumps measures to make America better. Again controlling the justice department, they will be free to pursue their dreams of extracting long desired pounds of flesh from Mr. Trump's ample body and go on to his hapless family.

A dear friend long passed into the dark night of HIV was profoundly troubled by church people spreading hate and stigma in the name of a God Whom they claim is love. "A deity who stigmatizes the innocent and teaches people to hate and discriminate against their neighbors cannot be loving or good," he said. "Those who follow a deity who condemns gay people for a trait they are born with and teaches followers to despise, persecute, and stigmatize us, serve God's Adversary and blaspheme the true God. They are of the party of the devil without acknowledging it. Our constitution guarantees people the right to worship whatever God they see fit. But what if they make God evil by attributing to Him hate and lies in the place of love and truth? Do they have the right to inflict evil on others in their evil God's name?"

I replied, "They have the right to say that God is like themselves, but not the right to inflict evil on others in God's name. Under the constitution human rights trump religious doctrines."

He answered, "And we have the right and duty to speak the truth about ourselves and our God of love to those who hate us. Only truth can cleanse hearts poisoned by hate filled lies so that love can take root and finally bloom."

ENDNOTES

1. Randy Shilts, *And the Band Played On*, (New York St. Martin's Press, 1987); Sean Straub, *Body Counts*, (New York, Scribners, 2014.)
2. David Kessler & Karen Felden, "Faster Evaluation of Vital Drugs," (March 1995, *Scientific American,*) pp-48-54.
3. Use of the geometric mean rather than the arithmetic mean always lowers the estimate, but all of these numbers are just estimates, even the past data. Statistics compiled by Andrew J. H. Vogt, Professor of Mathematics, Georgetown University.
4. I use the figure 170,000, a lower figure than would have been the case if the projection followed the same rate as the 1996-1999 projection. I assume the rollout would have been faster in the later period.
5. Trevor Project statistics, *Facts About Suicide*, see website; *Trevor Project National Survey on LGBTQ Youth Mental Health, 2019.*
6. James Driscoll, *Identity in Shakespearean Drama*, (New Brunswick, N. J., Associated University Presses, 1983); The *Unfolding God of Jung and Milton*, (Lexington, Ky., Univ. of Kentucky Press, 1993).
7. For a discussion of opposition to Compound Q see: "FDA Probes Underground Testing of AIDS Drug." *LA Times* June 28, 1989. Dr. Marcus Conant remarked: "*This is a logical outgrowth of what we have seen during the epidemic,*" said Dr. Marcus Conant of San Francisco, a prominent AIDS doctor who declined an invitation to participate in the trial. "*These patients are young and well-educated and are not going to sit around while institutions like the FDA fail to save them.*"
8. See: *Statement of Anthony S. Fauci, M.D., on the Death of Martin Delaney,* National Institute of Allergy and Infectious Diseases, Jan 22, 2009. *Anthony S. Fauci, M.D., director of the National Institute of Allergy and Infectious Diseases (NIAID) of the National Institutes of Health (NIH), said, "The NIAID community is deeply saddened by the death of Martin Delaney, a true hero in the fight against HIV. Marty worked tirelessly as an advocate for HIV-infected people, and made enormous contributions to framing and advancing the HIV/AIDS research effort at NIAID and elsewhere. His life is a testament to the power of committed advocacy and activism to advance public health.*"
9. David Groff, *Slate,* Sept 20, 2017.
10. Jonathan Kwitney, *Acceptable Risks*, (New York, Simon & Schuster, 1992).
11. See Paul Sergios account of his adventures in the AIDS drug underground in *One Boy at War*, (New York, Knopf, 1993)

12. Lisa Krieger, "Notes from The Underground," *San Francisco Examiner*, Sept 15, 1991.

13. *The Advocate*, "War over Compound Q," 7/31/90, p.32

14. In his official NIAID statement on the death of Delaney, Fauci confessed: *"I worked closely with Marty for nearly a quarter century and will greatly miss his astute insights and advice. Many others at NIAID involved in the HIV/AIDS research effort also have benefited from his well-informed wisdom and counsel.".* . . Mr. Delaney was a member of the NIAID AIDS Research Advisory Committee from 1991 to 1995, served on NIAID's National Advisory Allergy and Infectious Disease Council from 1995 to 1998, and also served in many other advisory roles for the Institute.

15. Kwitney, pp, 391-3

16. Kwitney, pp 423-7.

17. Federal positions began to open up for LGBTs under Bill Clinton who in May 1998 issued and executive order 13087 protecting them from discrimination in Federal employment. It supplanted the 1953 order 10450, which resulted in more than 5000 Federal employees being fired for suspicion of homosexuality.

18. Straub, *Body Counts*, 261-2.

19. See Randy Shilts, *Conduct Unbecoming*, (New York, St. Martin's Press, 1993).

20. Ron Baker, "Accelerated Approval for New AIDS Drugs Faces an Uncertain Future," *Beta*, September 1994.

21. For TAG's own account of their actions in this period see: Mark Harrington, "On a Darkling Plain –The years of Despair." *The Body*, Oct 21, 2012. Harrington recounts the troubles with AIDS drug testing and approval, yet conveniently stops before the cocktails turned AIDS into a manageable condition in 1996.

22. Elon Musk, from website: *https://www. uschamber.com/above-the-fold/elon-musk- knows-more-about-regulation-the-regulators*)

23. See Sarah Boseley, "Mbeki AIDS Policy Led to 330,000 Deaths," *The Guardian*, Nov 26, 2008.

24. See Zoe Corbin, "AIDS Researcher Cleared of Misconduct," *Nature*, June 22, 2010.

25. Anne Paxton, "Rapid HIV test whips up waiver debate," *Cap Today*, Feb.,2003.http://www.captodayonline.com/Archives/feature_stories/rapid_h iv_test_feature.html

26. Elinor Burkett in her acerbic survey of AIDS activism, *The Gravest Show on Earth*, (New York, Houghton Mifflin Harcourt, 1995) provides a typical example of journalistic over-simplification on drug pricing and the role of the pharmas when she quotes approvingly a Dr. Charles van der Horst's crude analysis of FDA's community critics:
"What we've got is an unholy alliance of Republicans and libertarians, the Wall Street Journal, the pharmaceutical companies and activists" Many *people with AIDS go further,* [Burkett continues in her own voice—JD]

accusing TAG of selling out to the pharmaceutical companies, which after all have shown extraordinary generosity to the group.

Burkett's book is written with intelligence, but that intelligence did not extend so far as to grasp what nearly every perceptive activist knew, that the ready, easiest, and most profitable way to sell out to the drug companies was to sell out first to FDA. Had she checked out political contributions from the pharmaceutical companies she might have spotted the clue she needed: at that time the two biggest beneficiaries in Congress were FDA's two most powerful allies and champions, Henry Waxman and Ted Kennedy. Following that money could have told her how things work in the real world of the regulators, the regulated, and patient advocates.

27. Part of this appendix was adapted by my opinion piece, *The Most Insidious Virus: Stigma*, in the Nov. 7, 2019 *Washington Blade.*

28. Details on Karen Pence's divorce are hard to come by and amazingly sparse considering that she could well be the next first lady on the United States. There are three books on Pence: Tom Lo Bianco, *Piety and Power*, (New York, Dey Street Books, 2019); T*he Faith of Mike Pence*, Lesley Montgomery, (Kensington, Pa., Whitaker House, 2019; Michael D'Antonio and Michael Eisner, *The Shadow President,* (Thomas Dunn Books, New York, 2018). None deal in any detail with Karen and her first marriage, surprising considering that she is currently the most influential person in Mike Pence's life.

29. See John Milton, *The Doctrine and Discipline of Divorce*, (Wolcott, New York, Scholar's Choice, 2015—first published in 1643.) for the classic Protestant argument for divorce. Modern scholars have pointed out that the same line of reasoning Milton uses to allow divorce, essentially the argument that divorce is necessary to insure the happiness of those caught in a loveless marriage, also can work to justify homosexual marriage.

30. Belial is the devil associated with lust, sensuality, moral sloth and convenient adaptation to evil in Milton's *Paradise Lost.*

Epilogue: FDA and COVID-19*

Were historian Barbara Tuchman, author of *The March of Folly*, still alive today, she would not want for newer materials. There would be the stories of disastrous US policies on Iran, the Soviet misadventures in Afghanistan that brought the fall of the centuries old Russian empire, the US Iraq War launched to seize non-existent weapons of mass destruction, a war every bit as misguided as Vietnam. Then she could turn to the West's trade policies toward China that decimated our working classes while elevating China to a totalitarian superpower able and eager to challenge the Western democracies for World domination. If these weren't enough, a brand new opportunity for mega-folly appeared earlier this year, the Covid 19 pandemic and the paralyzing panic it created wherein we are still caught as of this writing.

A key feature these ruinous historic follies share is irrational over-reaction to real and imagined threats. Another is that once the leaders set down the path of error, they never look back until too late. Thus, Donald Trump and his healthcare generals, NIAID's Dr. Fauci and FDA's Dr. Hahn, overseen by his imperturbable yes-man Vice President Mike Pence, became todays successors in folly to Lyndon Johnson, Dean Rusk, and General Westmoreland in Vietnam as well as to George W. Bush and Donald Rumsfeld in Iraq. Yet another key factor is deficient oversight on powerful, self-serving bureaucracies, in Trump's case FDA, CDC, and NIH-NIAID. Such is the view emerging among critics alarmed by the disruptive social and economic measures taken to counter a virus that poses only a minor threat to most of the population. Whether theirs will prove to be another conspiracy theory generated in our national climate of hyper partisanship, or a sober analysis is yet to be determined.

From the onset, panic was sparked by wildly exaggerated "scientific" speculations on Covid 19 mortality and aggravated by failure to account for differences in mortality by age and co-morbidities. For children and adults under sixty without co-morbidities, Covid 19 is significantly less deadly than an ordinary seasonal flu; for those of advanced age, especially patients with morbid obesity, diabetes, heart conditions, or cancer, mortality is far higher. CDC did not act quickly to warn and protect the most vulnerable. Their bureaucratic ineptitude resulted in exceptionally high mortality rates where the US epidemic first hit in the Northeast. Next FDA and CDC were too slow to approve and implement essential testing. Panic and confusion intensified due to our lack of a unified national response. Without federal standards for lockdowns and preventive measures, we were left with fifty divergent state responses fashioned more to the vagaries of local politics than to any reliable scientific assessment of medical needs. Finally, FDA and its longtime ally NIAID's Dr. Fauci fought tooth and nail the repurposing of cheap existing drugs, like the hydroxychloroquine (HCQ) combinations, that might compete with funding for what these agencies really wanted: to develop, test, and license novel high tech vaccines. Their vaccines will need to be administered universally to a resistant population among whom a third say they would refuse to take them. The vaccines seem promising, but why rely on them exclusively, and why reject and refuse to properly test other readily available treatments while the virus continues to kill tens of thousands?

Dr. Fauci and FDA assert that their trials show HCQ combinations to be useless against Covid 19 infection. Notwithstanding, researchers like Doctors Harvey Risch, Scott Atlas, and Bruce Dale counterclaim that HCQ can bring a 70+% decrease in deaths lowering mortality to the levels of a seasonal flu. The trials they cite specify: HCQ + azithromycin + zinc administered in the *first stage* of the disease.*1* The trials FDA references were limited to patients who had advanced to the *second stage*; moreover, they were not the specified combination and dosages. For example, zinc was left out and/or the dosages were changed. Such trials did not prove HCQ failed to work, they proved only that it did not work when the specified regimen was altered. Rather than following specifications for the trials that had demonstrated efficacy, the FDA's trials were *designed to fail*—a decades old subterfuge FDA relies on to debunk vitamin claims and support the agency's never say die efforts to regulate vitamin and other supplements—this is an old, old story.

As if their bogus efforts to disprove the efficacy of HCQ based treatments were not enough, FDA gratuitously raised red flags about the safety of HCQ, an old drug that has been used safely for decades and in much higher dosages by hundreds of millions of patients as a preventative for malaria and a treatment for rheumatoid arthritis and lupus. Mainstream media, whose education in pharmacology appears limited to speed reading FDA press releases, hysterically denounced the re-purposed HCQ treatments as perilous frauds, and liberal governors rushed to ban them. Their claim was backed only by a benighted assumption that FDA is always trustworthy. FDA is a government agency, but it is also a cornerstone of our *pharmaceutical testing, licensing, and marketing establishment* with its many hidden agendas, chief among them attaining power, fame, and profits for their principals.

The challenges to the US testing, licensing and marketing establishment's opposition to re-purposed drugs raise urgent questions. Particularly: are the re-purposed drugs reducing mortality, as is claimed, in India, Israel, Australia, Korea, and Turkey where they are widely used? Could early treatment and prophylaxis with HCQ have saved lives in the US and EU where regulators impeded their use? Could this strategy have eased the destructive lockdowns that have severely damaged our economy and rent the fabric of society? What can we do to prevent regulatory over-reach in future pandemics, and in all healthcare? How do we establish effective independent oversight on FDA, CDC, NIH, NIAID, and CMS? But these questions are dismissed by mainstream media who assume scientists working for government bureaucracies like FDA possess godlike wisdom and the right to define science itself. They fail to grasp that government scientists are bureaucrats first, and scientists second. In every decision their primal consideration is the provenance of their paychecks.

FDA and Fauci's shills in the media naively assume that FDA's official opinions on Covid 19 are settled science. The history of science shows that in the real world the science is seldom settled at the beginning of a new problem or situation. Settled science comes later after more evidence is gathered empirically and analyzed. Final results very often conflict with the early opinions of establishment scientists like Doctors Fauci and Hahn.

The history of science and medicine is replete with ideas opposed initially by the official establishment but that prevail eventually. The opposition does not usually change its mind, it just dies off and is replaced by others who learn the new ways. FDA's insistence that scientific truth comes only by its approved methods reduces science to institutional politics. You might as well rely on the Inquisition or the Communist Party to validate your science as rely on FDA.

Yale Medical School Professor of Epidemiology Harvey Risch is a scientist who refuses to make FDA-NIH testing and approval the final arbiter of scientific truth. Risch cites the 1987-9 delays with the AIDS drug Bactrim as an example of the fatal rigidity of the NIH-FDA testing and licensing establishment. Dr. Fauci refused patient requests to issue guidelines for using Bactrim for pneumocystis carinii pneumonia (PCP), a deadly AIDS opportunistic illness, and he declined to run NIAID trials to test it. Bactrim, like HCQ was an old, cheap, off patent drug, something the US testing, licensing, and marketing establishment cannot profit from. Hence, the patients and their doctors were forced to run their own trials taking two years during which 17,000 died of PCP. Risch contends the situation with FDA and Fauci's opposition to HCL is comparable. *2*

What is the prime lesson of the HCQ controversy? I believe it is this: Regardless of how well HCQ ultimately may prove to work for Covid 19, FDA crossed the line by making bogus claims about HCQ in order to insure reliance on and funding for their massive FDA and NIAID vaccine testing and licensing efforts. Their misinformation influenced broader public issues, like shutdown policies, with far reaching implications for all Americans. In a democracy, such momentous issues should be openly debated and then decided by the people's elected representatives, not gas lighted by unelected career bureaucrats.

Like nearly every writer who tackles controversial subjects, I have a point of view. Long experience has taught me that powerful "independent" Federal bureaucracies, e.g. FDA, FBI, CIA, DEA, IRS, CDC, NIH, NIAID, and CMS, often act as sovereign entities outside the authority of the national governments, against the needs of the people, and in defiance of Judeo-Christian ethics. Indeed, they casually put their own institutional interests above the interests of society and humanity.

President Eisenhower's farewell address made the world aware of the dangers of loose cannon bureaucracies by warning about the Military-Industrial Complex. In subsequent decades we launched ruinous wars, like those in Vietnam and Iraq, for which the M-IC stealthily lobbied. The problem is endemic to all large bureaucracies. We know the massive cover ups of systematic criminality by totalitarian regimes like Nazi Germany, Soviet Russia, and Red China. Indeed, Adolf Eichmann's "I only followed the rules" is the paradigm of the modern bureaucratic mentality and morality. As Nazi Germany illustrates, democracies must be ever vigilant against the totalitarian impulses that their bureaucracies harbor and enable.

To maintain an optimistic front, President Trump minimized the threat of Covid 19 from the onset. Realism, however, seems needed until a vaccine and/or authorized re-purposed treatments permit society and the economy to return to normal. The enormous economic cost of our chaotic over-reaction to Covid 19 will likely damage Western societies for years to come. Indeed, measures to combat the virus are likely to increase the total US Federal debt burden by at least 50% with similar increases in other democracies already heavily burdened with debt. The ability to maintain essential safety nets, especially for healthcare, is being undermined across the globe.

Trump's political opponents are correct to accuse him of mismanaging the Covid 19 crisis. Unfortunately, their solution has been bureaucratic mismanagement on a much grander scale. They've sought broader lockdowns, including school closures, and more intrusive regulation of research and drug access by FDA, which can only further aggravate the crisis. Such opposition may be well intended, even if poorly informed. The Federal bureaucrats, however, knowingly used the crisis to expand their power, cost to society be damned. To protect our democracy, we need more effective oversight on our increasingly powerful independent bureaucracies, whether they be DOD, IRS, State, FDA, CIA, NIH, or mega-corporations like Google, Microsoft, Facebook, or

Amazon. Remember: Power corrupts, and absolute (or monopoly) power corrupts absolutely.

Much has been written comparing the Covid 19 epidemic with the 1918-19 flu that ravaged the world and killed an estimated 675,000 Americans, about the same number as died with AIDS. Comparisons may be odious, they can also be instructive. Government did little to curb the earlier flu whose death toll was far higher than the Covid 19 toll has been. However, the non-interference limited the overall damage to the economy along with the social and political harm.

Comparisons of Covid 19 with the AIDS epidemic are infrequent, but they can be more instructive because medical technologies and institutions during the AIDS epidemic more closely resembled those of today. In 1918 we neither had antibiotics nor knew what a virus was. CDC was yet to be established, and the role and power of FDA was, mercifully, more limited. During the AIDS epidemic, CDC and FDA were crucial factors, as they are now. So the mistakes FDA made in AIDS can be instructive today—*if* we are willing to learn from them.

As I've shown, FDA's greatest mistake on AIDS—their attempt to delay approval of the protease cocktails at least three years to more thoroughly test their efficacy-- was forestalled by protesting AIDS activists and their doctors. Had FDA prevailed, AIDS would have taken 86,000 additional American lives during those years, and tens of thousands more afterwards. Neither Congress nor any administration ever called FDA into account for a near disaster rooted in its ossified culture of delay. Neither were any investigations done on the delays in approving Bactrim and other early drugs useful for HIV, nor on the criminal collusion of FDA with an illegal underground producing dangerous, knockoff ddC in order to relieve pressure on the agency to expedite approval of that drug.

In the Covid 19 epidemic, our failure to learn from past FDA mistakes presaged the US lagging the developed world in deploying Covid 19 testing. South Korea and Taiwan halted the spread of the virus early by testing early, while US testing was mired in a regulatory swamp. The specifics are murky, fodder for historians, but we know where the delays occurred---deep within the bureaucratic morass of FDA and CDC.*3* At the epidemic's inception, FDA and CDC spurned the available WHO and

German tests, just as they spurned HCQ and other repurposed treatments in order to develop vaccines. Likewise, they rejected available tests in order to develop their own in house tests, all the while forbidding private US laboratories to make tests independently. If that weren't enough, the first FDA-CDC tests failed due to defective reagents. Consequently, the US response was delayed for precious weeks while the Covid 19 virus swept across the nation.

Fundamental reform of FDA's culture and regulatory philosophy is long overdue.*4* That should have been a prime lesson of the AIDS epidemic, but the lesson was ignored for political reasons. At the beginning of his term President Trump, a man who appreciates how regulation can impede innovation and deny patients the right to try new treatments, contemplated appointing a committed reformer as FDA Commissioner. He considered James O'Neil, a colleague of Peter Thiel, and other prospects who wanted to re-invent FDA to make it innovation friendly. However, pressure from the FDA bureaucracy, backed by Big Pharma lobbyists, prevailed. Michael Gottlieb, Trump's first Commissioner made surface improvements yet left unchanged the atrophied FDA culture and obsolete practices.

Trump knew FDA, CDC, and NIH were deep swamp territory. Losing his nerve, he turned their swamp over to his in house swamp creature, VP Mike Pence and Pence's lobbyist cronies. Trump hoped he could just forget the healthcare swamp and focus on the economy. Yet, having failed initially to reform FDA, in crucial moments in the Covid 19 crisis he failed to exercise sufficient oversight on FDA, CDC, and Fauci's shop. FDA and Fauci soon became the proverbial loose cannons on Trump's drifting healthcare ship.

One hopes that FDA's mistakes with Covid 19 will give President Trump, if re-elected, impetus and ammunition for reforms to drag the agency along with CDC, NIH, CMS, and NIAID into the 21st century. So far Trump has shown scant recognition that the vast expanse of "deep state swamp" occupied by FDA, NIAID, NIH, CDC, and the hated pharmaceutical industry, has become as dangerous as Eisenhower's Military Industrial Complex.

There is no indication that we as a nation have yet learned anything to help us avoid repeating Covid 19 mistakes. To survive modern epidemics, we must streamline 21st century drug testing and licensing regulation. FDA's culture, and its regulatory philosophy, based on its long outdated thalidomide inflatus and its sacrosanct double blinded placebo testing, requires a paradigm shift. We need an FDA whose motto is not Prevent Thalidomides, but Promote Innovation.

Our leaders should be asking do we need our current FDA at all? Government protection of public health is essential, but that might be better served by different institutions with new policies and people. We need to re-think and begin to re-invent FDA once the Covid 19 pandemic is under control. Re-invention should start with speeding testing and approval of all treatments, especially cheap, immediately available repurposed treatments, like HCQ combinations. Finally, re-thinking must include frank recognition and honest analysis of FDA's "loose cannon" conduct during the AIDS epidemic.

FDA's mistakes and abuses of power with AIDS were in part a moral failure rooted in America's reluctance to grant full equality to LGBT people. FDA got away with delaying early AIDS drugs and with scheming to delay the life-saving cocktails chiefly because the victims, gay AIDS patients, were despised outcasts whose humanity is routinely devalued. FDA was never held responsible, just as Vice President Pence and his wife have never been called to account for their close affiliation with a school that justifies gross discrimination against LGBT people by citing an ancient text asserting that God wants all of us to be put to death! Thus, in part at least, the high price America will pay for FDA mistakes with Covid 19 is payback for its continued sins in marginalizing LGBT people and devaluing our humanity.

1. See, Harvey Risch, "Early Outpatient Treatment of High Risk Covid 1 Patients that Should Be Ramped-up Immediately," *American Journal of Epidemiology*, 27 May 2020; Bruce Dale, "Hydroxychloroquine Can Prevent Many COVID-19 Related Deaths, *Medium*, June 3; Rick Hayes, "Why Would the FDA Ban a Drug that Safely Saves the Lives of Patients?" American Thinker, Sept 1, 2020; Roni

Rabin, "Steroids Can Be Lifesaving for Covid-19 Patients, Scientists Report," NYT Sept 2, 2020.

2. See "Mark Levin interviews Harvey Risch," *BIT Chute*, August 24, 2020.

3. "How Delays in Testing Set Back US Covid 19 Response," *New York Times*, March 10, 2020.

4. Some recent calls for FDA reform are Robert Zubrin, "The FDA is Stifling Innovation," *National Review* Sept 2, 2020; Mary Ruwart, *Death By Regulation*, Sunstar Press, April 2018; Brian Blasé, "FDA Desperately Needs an Overhaul," *Washington Examiner*, May 9, 2020; David Clement, Anthony Belliotti, *Washington Examiner*, June 18, 2020; Adam Barsouk, Covid 19 Reveals Urgent Need for FDA Reform, *Washington Examiner,* March 17, 2020.

*Written in September 2020 for the paperback edition.

Index

The Author, recent photo.

www.ingramcontent.com/pod-product-compliance
Lightning Source LLC
Chambersburg PA
CBHW061002280326
41935CB00009B/803